BIRTH WEIGHT AND ECONOMIC GROWTH

W. PETER WARD

BIRTH WEIGHT AND ECONOMIC GROWTH

Women's Living Standards in the Industrializing West

The University of Chicago Press
Chicago and London

W. Peter Ward is professor of history at the University of British Columbia

The University of Chicago Press, Chicago 60637
The University of Chicago Press, Ltd., London
© 1993 by The University of Chicago
All rights reserved. Published 1993
Printed in the United States of America
02 01 00 99 98 97 96 95 94 93 1 2 3 4 5
ISBN: 0-226-87322-6 (cloth)

Library of Congress Cataloging-in-Publication Data

Ward, W. Peter.
    Birth weight and economic growth : women's living standards in the
industrializing West / W. Peter Ward.
       p.   cm.
    Includes bibliographical references and index.
    1. Women—Europe—Economic conditions—Case studies.   2. Women—
North America—Economic conditions—Case studies.   3. Birth weight—
Economic aspects—Europe—Case studies.   4. Birth weight—Economic
aspects—North America—Case studies.   5. Cost and standard of
living—Europe—Case studies.   6. Cost and standard of living—North
America—Case studies.   I. Title.
HQ1381.W37   1993
305.42'094—dc20   93-3046
                                                            CIP

for

KATIE and ANNA

with my love

CONTENTS

FIGURES

TABLES

ACKNOWLEDGMENTS

Like all practitioners of my craft I've relied on many others for assistance and support. But I stand in deeper debt than most, for during the course of this inquiry I've depended heavily on—and learned greatly from—an unusually large number of historians, economists, demographers, statisticians, archivists, and librarians, as well as medical researchers and practitioners. I must admit that from the start I had much to learn, and it's been my good fortune that many others have been so free with their knowledge, their time, and their encouragement. I've discovered to my great pleasure how broad, open, and generous the world of learning can be. My obligations are so numerous that they cannot all be acknowledged here. But I hope that, in compensation, I will often have the opportunity to assist others as so many have helped me.

My chief debt is to my wife, Patricia Ward, who for many years has shared with me her professional and personal interest in pregnancy, childbirth, and the care of newborn children. Through her influence these matters have assumed a large place in my curiosity about the past as well. She collaborated with me in the early stages of this study and maintained an active interest in the project throughout its development. I'm much beholden to her for advice, help, and encouragement, to say nothing of countless acts of kindness and generosity, great and small.

I'm also exceedingly grateful to my statistical consultant, Virginia Green, who has been my patient teacher and adviser from the beginning of the project. I could not have written this book without her help. She allayed my early skepticism about quantitative history, helped me find my footing in statistical analysis, and taught me how to read the record of the past with fresh eyes. If deficiencies there be in the tables and figures which follow, the problem lies not with her instruction but with a less-than-apt pupil.

In addition I've been blessed with colleagues and good friends who have offered advice and support as I proceeded on my way. Donald Paterson has given me sound counsel, statistical and historical, for many years. More than that, he has opened a window for me on the world of econometric history and enlarged my field of vision in the process. John Norris has long shared with me his great knowledge of, and enthusiasm for, the history of medicine; he has also read the full manuscript with care, living up to his reputation as an energetic and highly constructive critic. Very early on, J. M. Tanner, of the Institute of Child Health at the University of London, encouraged my pursuit of this subject and since then has given generously of his advice. He, too, has commented on the entire manuscript, and I've profited from his suggestions. I'm indebted as well to José Villar, Area Manager for Latin America in the World Health Organization, Geneva, for sharing his research team's important findings on newborn size in underdeveloped societies, and for comments which have spared me from serious pitfalls.

I've also benefited from the kindness of others who have shared their knowledge of the history of the cities considered in this book. Rosalind Mitchison and Christopher Smout were generous advisers and hosts when I visited Scotland, and their critical reading of the Edinburgh chapter was a great help. Michael Mitterauer and Josef Ehmer, of the Insitut für Wirtschafts- und Sozialgeschichte in the University of Vienna, offered advice during the course of the research and cast a constructive eye over the draft chapter on Vienna. Mary Daly and Cormac Ó Gráda guided me over the shoals of research in Irish history while I was in Dublin, and later suggested improvements to the Dublin chapter. Stephan Thernstrom gave me a helpful introduction to the literature on Boston's history. At one time or another John Komlos, Eric Nellis, Angela Redish, Jean-Claude Robert, Richard Steckel, and Richard Unger have also read draft papers or chapters and have given me the benefit of their counsel. Frank Flynn helped me untangle some initial statistical problems. At an early stage of the project James King, then Head of Obstetrics at Grace Hospital in Vancouver, discussed the subject of newborn weight with me from a clinician's point of view. The weekly seminar of the Department of Health Care and Epidemiology at the University of British Columbia also offered me sound advice, for which I'm most appreciative.

I relied very heavily on research assistants to compile the large data bases created for this study. I'm particularly grateful to Tina Loo and Elizabeth Mancke, who did the great bulk of the work and who shared with me the insights they gleaned from their close readings of the documents. Paul Molnar, Jane Tiers, and Nathalie Bédard pioneered this work in the twilight days of punch card data processing technology, while Glenda Matthews, Michael

Quinn, and Chris Wiesinger helped gather the ancillary demographic and economic statistical information needed to place the birth size data in context.

I'm also pleased to acknowledge the assistance of George A. Venters, of the Lothian Health Board in Edinburgh, who gave me permission to consult the patient records of the Royal Maternity; and George Henry, then Master of the Rotunda in Dublin, who not only gave me access to the hospital's case records but also provided the office space where they were consulted.

Funding for this study has come principally from a succession of grants awarded by the Hannah Institute for the History of Medicine, a division of Associated Medical Services in Toronto, and the Social Sciences and Humanities Research Council of Canada, with additional support from the Humanities and Social Sciences small grants program at the University of British Columbia.

This book is dedicated to my daughters, Kathryn and Anna Ward. Though they may not know it, they too have shaped this book in subtle but important ways. I'm grateful beyond words for their interest, for their encouragement, and most of all for their love.

INTRODUCTION

This book examines the history of newborn weight in western Europe and North America between 1850 and 1930 through a series of case studies. It traces the changing course of fetal size in Boston, Dublin, Edinburgh, Montreal, and Vienna during these years, and explores its relationship to social and economic conditions in each of these cities. In doing so it offers a novel vantage point on human welfare in the past; it also provides a means of comparing levels of well-being within a community during extended periods, as well as between different communities at various points in time.

In a more general sense, this inquiry is set in four distinct but interrelated contexts: the history of human growth, living standards and nutrition, inequality and poverty, and women's economic status. A multitude of inquiries over the past two centuries have revealed that human physical development varies considerably from one population to another, and also within a single population over time.[1] These differences are evident in the growth patterns of children as well as in the ultimate size attained by adults. While many factors are known to influence physical growth, variation in stature both within and between groups seems to reflect differences in living standards from time to time and place to place. The principal focus of most inquiry into forms of physical growth has been the development of length or height from infancy onward, perhaps because it has always been comparatively easy to measure.

In contrast, fetal development—usually expressed in terms of birth weight—has garnered rather less attention. Moreover, until the mid-twentieth century, most of that which it did attract came from obstetricians more interested in the health of pregnant women than in the development of their unborn children. One result of this circumstance has been that weight at birth was long thought to vary much less than the size of children and adults, the implication being that differences in living standards had little influence on the unborn but instead left their mark upon postnatal development. The recognition that environmental factors also affected *in utero* growth has only been widely acknowledged in the fairly recent past and then, by and large, on the basis of comparisons drawn between contemporary developed and developing societies.

Although the systematic study of weight at birth reaches back to the later eighteenth century, current understanding of the factors which influence fetal growth is based largely on investigations undertaken during the past thirty years. The great majority of these studies have been done in western Europe and North America—societies in which general living standards have been higher than at any other time in human history. For this reason, most of what we now know about newborn weight has been learned from historically atypical populations, although this fund of knowledge is gradually being deepened by research in the underdeveloped world. In addition, although the routine weighing of newborn children commenced in some European maternity hospitals during the early nineteenth century, virtually no interest has ever been shown in long-term trends in weight at birth, and few studies of fetal growth—past or present—have paid much attention to patterns of change over time. Similarly, few attempts have been made to explore the relationships between social structures or patterns of economic development and birth weight.

This book thus offers a new approach to a very old problem in the history of human growth. It examines long-term trends in fetal weight in Europe and North America during extended periods between the mid-nineteenth century and the great depression of the 1930s, drawing upon the voluminous records left by maternity hospitals. The evidence is sufficiently full to assess the influence of living standards on newborn size, and to explore the relationship between measures of economic development and trends in weight at birth. The contemporary relevance of this information should also be acknowledged, for some developing societies are now passing through stages of economic and social development in many ways comparable to those experienced in western Europe and North America during the years considered here. In this instance the past may help us better understand how the social benefits of economic growth are distributed, particularly to the poor, during periods of extensive growth and change.

The second setting of this book is that of the history of living standards, nutrition in particular. The standard of living in earlier times has preoccupied successive generations of historians, economists, sociologists, and social investigators for much of the past two centuries. Their initial concerns lay with the influence of industrialization on the economic welfare of industrial work-ers, but over time the reach of their inquiry broadened to include most forms of economic development, many facets of the human condition, and all seg-ments of society. Early interest in proletarian well-being gradually gave way to a more generalized curiosity about levels of prosperity, health, and comfort among all social groups.

Despite this longstanding interest, however, ongoing debates about the ben-efits and detriments of economic growth have gone largely unresolved.[2] Most attempts to evaluate historical living standards have been hampered by inade-quate sources. No single measure—be it an index of wages, prices, or mortal-ity—can measure living standards adequately, and the records of most com-munities do not yield that telling cluster of indices which might produce more reliable estimates. The problem is compounded by imperfections commonly found in historical statistics: often they were unsystematically gathered, or are fragmentary or specific to a single locale. As a result they often fail to estab-lish firm foundations for generalizations about conditions of life in the past. Much of the controversy over living standards in earlier times has derived from such ambiguities, and given the intractable nature of these difficulties the best hope of learning more about these matters now lies in previously unex-plored sources—in this case the record of size at birth.

The problem of understanding nutrition in history is particularly difficult. As one of life's more mundane experiences, eating has seldom prompted more than passing note, and when it has, the occasion has usually been a moment of feast or famine. Thus the food habits of our ancestors are poorly docu-mented in the written record, and for this reason those who study nutrition in the past have long faced serious obstacles. In matters concerning the history of diet, our knowledge of the exceptional is far richer than is that of the com-monplace. We understand a good deal about both excess and dearth in former times, but we still know relatively little about those habits which formed the nutritional foundations of past populations. As with so many features of everyday life in history, what was once customary and familiar has now become obscure.

In the absence of an extensive record of individual food consumption pat-terns, historians have approached the study of nutrition in several ways. Some have assessed the relative abundance of food supplies in a particular commu-nity over a period of time, either by examining changing patterns in the pro-duction of specific foods or, less commonly, by estimating the availability of basic staples per capita.[3] The result, in most cases, is an estimate of the access which an entire population had to the primary elements of nutrition.

Other investigators have viewed the problem from the standpoint of con-sumption instead of supply. One approach has been to examine additional fac-tors which have affected intake, including the cost of food in relationship to family incomes and budgets, shifts in dietary tastes and habits, and patterns in the diffusion of various foods. Another has been to analyze institutional diets, especially those provided for prisoners, hospital patients, poorhouse inmates, and military personnel. The small-scale dietary surveys which pioneer social investigators undertook during the late nineteenth and early twentieth centuries generally described the characteristic elements of working-class diets; they also established a basis for subsequent analysis of their nutritional value. Some attempts have also been made to estimate the quantities of common foods annually consumed per capita on a national scale, at least in England and Germany. The study of cookbooks and cooking practices, yet another approach to understanding what people ate, has also proved illuminating. But whether they are concerned with supply or consumption, these various approaches to the study of nourishment in history share one common feature: all are concerned with nutritional inputs. They do not assess results.[4]

Thomas McKeown adopted another approach to the history of nutrition in his attempt to explain the great increase in the world population over the past three centuries. McKeown held that the key to an explanation lay in understanding the mortality decline in advanced societies during the period or, more precisely, the reduction in deaths caused by infectious diseases.[5] By process of elimination he discarded a series of possible causes: advances in immunization and medical therapy, the declining virulence of killing diseases, and improvements in the quality of the environment (which, he argued, likely had no effect before the second half of the nineteenth century). "The most acceptable explanation of the large reduction of mortality and growth of population which preceded advances in hygiene," McKeown concluded, having seemingly accounted for all other possibilities, "is an improvement in nutrition due to greater food supplies." In support of this contention he cited evidence of the great increase in the amounts of food available during these years, combined with recent medical knowledge of the close relationship between malnutrition and infectious disease.[6] In other words, McKeown explored the issue of nutrition from the standpoint of its consequences rather than its principal elements. In his view, declining mortality was a result—perhaps even an index—of rising standards of nutrition.

McKeown's hypothesis rested on the logic of a reductive argument as well as information about food supplies provided by other historians. It has come in for a good deal of criticism, a fact which should scarcely surprise us considering the broad brush strokes with which it was painted. Subsequent research has sustained some parts of his thesis while at the same time exposing its limitations.[7] Perhaps the most serious weakness of his argument is that it is based neither on direct evidence of food consumption patterns nor on any measure of general nutritional status.

These same problems beset the work of the demographer Massimo Livi-

Bacci, one of McKeown's most recent and most telling critics. In his reexamination of the origins of the modern mortality decline, Livi-Bacci rejects the nutritional hypothesis in favor of one which underscores the leading role of infectious and epidemic diseases.[8] But many of his grounds for challenging McKeown's nutritional theories rest on the traditional sorts of evidence offered by most historians of diet, including estimates of available food supplies and observations of customary diets.

Until recently, in fact, all attempts to explore the history of nutrition have foundered on the problem of how it might be measured. No estimate of available food supplies or common consumption patterns, whatever its precision, can provide reliable information on how well nourished a population might have been. During the past decade, however, anthropometric history—the study of human dimensions in earlier times—has yielded a new body of evidence on the question. It provides new ways to assess the living standards and estimate the nutritional standing of earlier populations, and to examine changing patterns of well-being over time. An individual's height and weight, in particular, are deeply influenced by his or her nutritional condition, and when these physical characteristics are carefully analyzed for large populations over long spans of time they may be used to create a nutritional index for their respective communities.

One such attempt, the recent investigation of stature in past populations, has produced impressive results. Most of the analysis has focused upon height in late adolescence and young adulthood, the bulk of the data coming from military recruitment records.[9] By the very nature of their sources, most height studies have explored the stature and nutritional condition of young, healthy males of low or middling socioeconomic status. But important though they are, these inquiries have two significant limitations. First and most obvious is their sex bias: they deal almost exclusively with boys and young men. Second, because they usually examine the heights of fully grown populations or those at the end of their growing years, they reflect only the cumulative effects of factors affecting growth, the net benefit of influences acting over the entire growth span from conception to adulthood. Thus they can identify long-term trends in height and nutrition, but they reveal little about short-term fluctuations which might be associated with cyclical social and economic influences.

The study of birth weight in history can remedy these deficiencies. As a recent World Health Organization report has noted, weight at birth "is strongly conditioned by the health and nutritional status of the mother"[10] and therefore it is linked to circumstances specific to women. In addition, because birth weight is sensitive to environmental factors acting during the nine months of gestation (especially the final three months) as well as the long-range effects of changes in living conditions, it reflects both short- and long-term trends. The analysis of newborn weight thus complements studies on growth patterns and achieved height in the past. Both approaches explore the relationship between physical size on one hand, and nutritional standards and economic growth on the other, though they come to the problem from quite different perspectives.

Thirdly, this book brings a new body of evidence to bear on the history of economic and social inequality. The nature, extent, and causes of inequality in the past have been longstanding concerns among historians. Historical writing about most western societies has been distinguished by numerous attempts to identify, measure, and explain differentials in the distribution of wealth and income, in the experience of health and mortality, and in access to social benefits.[11] The effects of industrialization, in particular, upon these forms of inequality have long been a major concern, as the ongoing standard of living debate reveals. But while we now know the broad contours on the outline map drawn of these questions, some familiar terrain still remains hotly contested while much more has yet to be explored. Among the most important of these ill-mapped areas is the subject of gender and inequality in the economies and societies of other times. The study of newborn size in history allows us to address these issues.

Finally, this work is a contribution to the economic history of women during the nineteenth and twentieth centuries. Despite the sharp rise of interest in women's history during the past decade or so, surprisingly little work has been done on the economic lives of women in earlier times. The historical literature of most western societies now includes a small body of studies on the economic status of women, most of it confined to a limited range of themes: the place of women in the wage labor force, the changing nature of women's work, and the continuing gap between the wages of laboring women and men.[12] The question of women's living standards has been largely ignored. In fact, historical living standards have seldom been thought to possess a sexual dimension, and perhaps for this reason little consideration has been given to the question before now.

But feminist historians have shown us that women's experiences have often differed—sometimes profoundly—from those of their husbands, fathers, and brothers. The categories which have long guided historical analysis, social class for example, have not always proved capacious enough to include the condition of women. The voluminous literature on the history of living standards and wealth distribution is a case in point, for it almost invariably overlooks the possibility that the female experience of inequality was distinctive in important respects from that of men. At this point we can no longer assume that women inevitably or invariably fared as men did during the great transformation which swept the Western World during the nineteenth and twentieth centuries, as the findings of this study generally indicate.

They also reveal how little we yet know about the economic status of women in the past. What effects had economic change upon women's work and incomes, and therefore their well-being? To what extent did women share in the benefits and liabilities which accrued from economic growth and decline? How and why did these patterns vary among women from time to time, place to place, and social group to group? What was the relative economic status of women and men, and how and why did it vary over time, within and between the many societies of Europe and North America? This book raises these questions and it offers fresh evidence about them. But it answers none of them conclusively. Still, they remain central to our understanding of the circumstances of women in history and they should head the agenda of future research on women's economic past.

The cities examined in this study were chosen for two principal reasons, one wholly practical, the other theoretical. In the first instance, they were places where philanthropy and the practice of obstetric medicine had combined to found maternity hospitals, where patient records had been kept carefully and routinely over long spans of time, and where these records had survived the depredations of passing years. Invariably these were cities where important medical schools were located, where leading physicians worked and taught, and where the practice of scientific obstetrics had urged the systematic recording of facts about the delivery of newborn children. These five cities were also selected because, while all of them possessed important common features, their histories of growth and development were sufficiently distinctive that they could usefully be compared with one another. They ranged widely in size, growth rate, and social and economic structures, their very diversity providing an opportunity to examine the relationship between human biology and its environmental setting in the everyday miracle of human birth. In particular, they offer us an opportunity to compare conditions of life in the Old World and the New at a time when industrialization, population growth, and unprecedented migration were transforming both Europe and America.

This books falls into three parts. The first chapter examines the theoretical and historical settings of the study. It surveys contemporary medical understanding about the primary influences upon fetal development, and it explains the intellectual and institutional context in which the sources of the information used in this study were first gathered. In chapters 2 through 6 the economic and demographic history of each city during the period under consideration is surveyed and the characteristics of their hospital's patients are discussed. Following this, the birth weight data are analyzed and the relationship to their social, economic, and institutional settings is explored. In the final chapter the birth weight findings for each city are compared, and conclusions are drawn, about the relationships among birth weight, social and economic change, and women's living standards.

Two brief methodological points should be made at the outset. Much of the statistical analysis which follows proceeds by multiple and linear regression analysis. In all instances the null hypothesis is rejected at a critical level of .05 unless otherwise noted. In addition, tests for higher order interactions among variables were routinely employed, but results are only reported when a statistically significant relationship was detected.

1

BIRTH WEIGHT PAST AND PRESENT

This study rests principally on the analysis of information from case records kept by maternity hospitals in western Europe and North America between the mid-nineteenth century and 1930. But the larger meaning of its findings can only be explored when they and their documentary sources are placed in two broader contexts. The first is provided by the voluminous modern scientific literature on fetal growth and birth weight. While the nature of human development *in utero* has absorbed growing scientific interest over the past two centuries, a vast explosion of research has occurred during the past thirty years. We now know much more about the course of fetal development than was known a generation ago, and this knowledge, in turn, deepens our understanding of the information gleaned from these long-forgotten clinical records.

The second context is historic. The old patient registers used in this inquiry were created by physicians who occupied their own distinctive world of scientific ideas and medical institutions. The creation of these records reflected a growing medical awareness from the late eighteenth century onward that systematically gathered information about the common features of human biology could create a larger understanding of both the normal and the pathological aspects of life. The hospital practice of routinely recording facts about each maternity patient and newborn child was first introduced by doctors gathering information for their own research purposes. It soon became an important tool of medical diagnosis. In both cases it reflected the spread of a scientific and statistical view of medicine and, more particularly, a concern for precision in measurement and analysis. Beyond the concerns of medical science, the history of medical advice and care during pregnancy also forms an important part of the setting of this study, as does the social history of the lying-in hospital. Thus this chapter examines the intellectual and institutional settings, historic and modern, of the meaning of weight at birth.

The significance of birth weight

The average time from conception to birth in humans is 265 days. But because the date of conception is usually unknown, gestational age is normally dated from the beginning of the last menstrual period before pregnancy, on average about 280 days (or forty weeks) before delivery. There is, however, a good deal of variation in the length of gestation and, for this reason, all children born between thirty-seven and forty-one completed weeks of pregnancy are usually considered full-term newborns.[1] Those delivered earlier are, by definition, premature.

Until the spread of ultrasound diagnosis of *in utero* growth during the 1980s, the most commonly used index of fetal maturation was newborn weight. Many other characteristics of the growing fetus mark the stages in its evolution from embryo to newborn—skeletal formation or the development of vital organs, for example—but weight has long been by far the easiest to determine, and it provides a reliable measure of the growth process. The normal rate of fetal weight gain varies considerably during the course of pregnancy, as figure 1.1 reveals.[2] It is very low during the embryonic stage, the first three months (or trimester) of gestation. Thereafter it rises steadily to an average of about 100 grams weekly by the end of the second trimester, and then to over 200 grams by the end of the third, before dropping off very sharply when infants are born beyond term.

The rate of weight gain during pregnancy, and therefore weight at birth, varies considerably from one newborn to the next. Marked differences in birth weight also are found across social, economic, ethic, racial, and national boundaries in the contemporary world. By and large, the most privileged social groups bear the heaviest babies while the most disadvantaged have the lightest. These differences, in turn, reflect the fact that fetal growth and weight at birth are influenced by a wide range of biological, social, and economic factors, not all of which are fully understood.

From the standpoint of neonatal mortality the optimum weight of a newborn child lies between 3500 and 3900 grams. Infants born outside this range have higher mortality levels than do those within it. The risks are especially great among those weighing considerably less than the optimum. Estimates suggest that the chance of death during the first week of life increases by 40 percent, and the risk of fetal death by 25 percent, for every 100-gram decrease below the optimum level of weight. Moreover, weight at birth is by far the

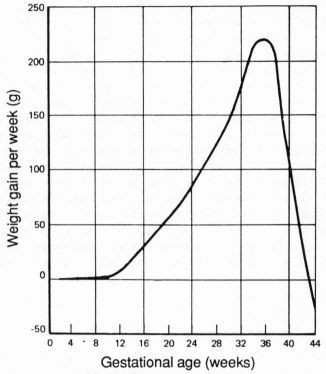

Fig. 1.1   Fetal weight gain per week

most important factor affecting the life chances of the newborn. One team of researchers has indicated that birth weight accounts for over 90 percent of variance in the risk of perinatal (late fetal and early postnatal) mortality.[3]

In 1976 the World Health Organization (WHO) adopted the current international standard for defining abnormally light infants. It is now general clinical and epidemiological practice to distinguish newborns weighing 2500 grams or more from those weighing less. The latter are designated low birth weight infants, those newborns at greater risk. In a clinical environment, at least in developed societies, this distinction identifies those babies to whom intensive medical care should be given.[4] To epidemiologists and health planners it offers a means of defining a major public health problem. The WHO has observed that "low birth weight is, universally and in all population groups, the single most important determinant of the chances of the newborn to survive and to experience healthy growth and development."[5] Therefore, the proportion of newborns weighing less than 2500 grams is a major concern among health professionals and social planners in any community.

For this reason the routine weighing of newborns is now common practice in clinical or institutional settings in most societies. Two measures of fetal development are generally used to identify community standards: mean weight at birth and the proportion of low birth weight infants. Unfortunately, when investigators report this information they seldom adhere to a common standard or format, complicating the task of comparing one community with another. But despite these complications it is possible to place most contemporary nations on a comparative birth weight scale. A WHO report in 1980 indicated that birth weight means ranged from just below 2500 grams in some parts of India to around 3500 grams in Norway, Sweden, and the Netherlands. Low birth weight rates ranged from as low as 3.6 percent in Sweden to 50 percent in Bangladesh. Broadly speaking, the developed countries enjoyed birth weight levels substantially higher than those in the developing world.[6] Not surprisingly, mean birth weight and the prevalence of low birth weight are now considered indices of social and economic development, alongside other measures in common use today such as mortality rates and per capita measures of wealth. In particular, "low birth weight can be regarded as an indicator of the health and nutritional status of the pregnant mother," according to the WHO.[7]

Factors influencing the course of fetal growth

The genetic influences upon birth weight derive from two sources: the mother's genetic constitution and her child's genetic character, a legacy which both parents bestow in equal measure on their offspring. But the extent of this influence is not wholly clear. One recent series of studies holds that genetic factors may account for as much as 72 percent of variation in newborn weight.[8] Most evidence, however, supports the view of geneticist D. F. Roberts, who concludes that "variation in the final manifestation of fetal growth, the size of the normal infant when it is launched on its own independent life at the moment of birth, is seen to be largely influenced, not by its own genes, but by the maternal environment and the maternal genotype."[9] Roberts places the genetic contribution to birth weight variation at 38 percent—20 percent derived from the maternal legacy and 18 percent from fetal genetic constitution. These figures agree broadly with other estimates indicating that fetal and maternal genetic influences account for about one-third of the variance in newborn weight.[10]

One fetal genetic factor associated with birth weight differences is the sex of the newborn. On average, male infants born in contemporary developed societies weigh about 150 grams more than females, although lesser differences between the two sexes are common in the underdeveloped world.[11]

Newborns suffering from genetic disorders also tend to be smaller than normal.[12] Two maternal genetically linked characteristics have also been identified as affecting neonatal weight: height and race (or ethnicity). The former case is clear. Maternal height has an independent effect on newborn weight: taller women tend to bear heavier babies than do shorter ones.[13] The evidence concerning ethnicity and race is rather more ambiguous. Certainly, widespread differences in mean birth weight have often been observed among various racial and ethnic groups,[14] and they have commonly been attributed, at least in part, to genetic causes. But it is by no means clear that these differences have a genetic basis, and are therefore intrinsic or unchangeable. In a review of the subject, Kline, Stein, and Susser take the view that the case for separate birth weight norms for blacks and whites in the United States is not strong enough to be convincing.[15] At this point it seems unlikely that the well-known discrepancies among the birth weight means of various racial and ethnic groups are caused by gene pool differences.

Maternal factors related to the history of a particular pregnancy form a second group of influences upon weight at birth. Gestational age (the duration of a pregnancy) has an important bearing on neonatal weight. Parity, or birth order, also affects newborn size. Firstborns are lighter than their subsequent brothers and sisters, by between 100 and 150 grams for either sex. Some studies also indicate a progressive increase in average weight up to the fifth child, after which a decline occurs, although the literature disagrees on this point. A woman's age, however, has only a slight effect at best upon the birth weight of her children. Birth order, not age, is the principle determinant of the rise in infant weights observed in multiparous births.[16] Multiple pregnancy also affects birth weight. Twins and triplets have strikingly different fetal growth histories than do singletons and are significantly lighter at birth as a result.[17] Finally, some evidence suggests that the spacing between births also influences neonatal weight, at least if the interval is very short. A recent study based on Swedish data reports a 30 percent increase in the risk of fetal growth retardation among newborns delivered within a year of an older sibling when compared with infants born after an interval of eighteen to fifty-nine months.[18]

Environmental influences also have an effect on weight at birth. Children born of mothers who live at high altitudes reveal lower-than-normal weight means, perhaps because of reduced oxygen supply to the placenta and fetus.[19] The association between climate and newborn size, however, is far less clear. There is some suggestion of a statistical relation between temperature and birth weight, mean weight declining as annual temperature means rise. In this instance, however, the relationship is almost certainly not causal. Rather, temperature is more likely a proxy for other seasonal factors, perhaps nutritional, perhaps medical, perhaps economic, which may exert an influence on fetal growth. At any rate, an association between average annual temperature and birth weight means has been observed, but it cannot be explained satisfactorily.[20]

The connection between a woman's medical circumstances and the growth of her child *in utero* is much more clear. A wide range of diseases has been linked with depressed birth weight levels, including chronic respiratory infections, tuberculosis, malaria, and congenital heart disease. (Diabetes, on the other hand, tends to enhance fetal growth, and therefore diabetic mothers sometimes bear unusually large children.) Diseases peculiar to pregnancy are also associated with lower birth weights. Among the most important is pre-eclampsia (hypertension and protein in urine) which, if unchecked, may lead to death. Others include hypertension and various disorders of the placenta.[21] Some of these diseases retard fetal growth while others dispose toward premature delivery. In either case the result is likely to be an abnormally light child. Not surprisingly, earlier pregnancy history is predictive of the birth weight of a subsequent child. A woman who has once delivered a growth-retarded infant has an increased probability of doing so again.[22] Fetal infection is yet another medical cause of lower birth weight. Congenital rubella and syphilis, as well as other serious diseases which the fetus contracts from its mother, are further sources of growth retardation during gestation.[23]

Cigarette smoking and alcohol consumption, two additional factors related to maternal health, also influence weight at birth. The adverse effect of smoking on fetal growth is now a well-established fact. Many studies reveal that women who smoke bear significantly lighter infants than those who do not.[24] One Canadian inquiry has gone so far as to quantify the effect precisely, noting that smoking reduced birth weight in its study population by 13 grams per cigarette smoked per day.[25] In addition, there are strong indications that a woman's indirect or passive exposure to cigarette smoke is detrimental to her fetus as well.[26] Moreover, these effects are broadly similar across the social spectrum. Although smoking has a direct connection with social class—the tendency to smoke increasing with declining social status—one British study indicates that birth weight disadvantages due to smoking seem to be broadly similar regardless of the smoker's social position.[27] Nutritional experiments indicate that the reduction of newborn weight caused by smoking may be offset, at least in part, by prenatal dietary supplements, but this hypothesis remains to be confirmed.[28]

Alcohol and drug consumption also have an effect on fetal growth. Heavy alcohol use can cause fetal alcohol syndrome, a condition distinguished by growth retardation, malformations, and mental dullness among newborns. The influence of lesser amounts of alcohol, however, are not as pronounced. Moderate drinking increases the risk of growth retardation but without the more serious consequences of fetal alcohol syndrome. Light or occasional drinking seems to have no adverse consequences at all for the fetus. But the quantitative boundaries between these distinctions are far from clear, and the possibility of widespread variation among women exists. Thus we cannot speak with much precision about the relation between the amount of alcohol consumed and the degree of retardation experienced.[29] The use of addictive drugs has a similar association with fetal addiction and lower weight at birth.[30]

A group of social and economic factors, some of them interrelated, form a separate category of influences upon newborn weight. Prominent among them is a woman's place in the social structure of her community—her class or status. The definition of class position varies from one society to the next. In Great Britain, for example, class is often defined in terms of the Registrar General's Social Classes, a system of categories based upon occupational groups. In countries such as the United States, where social boundaries historically have not been so sharply drawn, other classifications based upon occupation, income, or education serve similar ends. Regardless of the system employed, many studies done in developed societies during the past two decades reveal a relationship between a woman's social position and the birth weight of her infant.[31] Those of higher socioeconomic position bear heavier newborns than their less-privileged contemporaries. But social class is not a factor which can easily be isolated from other influences affecting weight at birth. A British study in the late 1960s, for example, revealed that lower-class mothers were significantly shorter than their upper-class counterparts, and this difference accounted for some of the discrepancy in their infants' birth weight averages.[32] Members of the upper ranks of most societies commonly enjoy other advantages as well, including superior levels of health and nutrition. Thus class position itself is not a causal influence upon birth weight; rather it is an index of relative social and economic advantage which, in turn, may exert such an influence.

Marital status is another social factor occasionally linked with birth weight outcomes, unmarried mothers bearing slightly lighter children than do married women.[33] In contemporary Scandinavian society, where consensual unions have come to supplement marriage as an important setting for procreation and child nurture, mothers living alone experience a higher incidence of abnormally low weight newborns than do those who cohabit.[34] In this case, too, the likely association is not with marital status per se but with the greater socioeconomic security experienced by women living in stable unions. Most birth weight inquiries, however, ignore the marital status factor, though whether this is because it has been omitted from research designs or because it has been included but found not to be significant is unclear.

The quality of medical care for expectant women also seems related to weight at birth. Two studies published in 1984 suggested that women who enjoyed adequate medical care during pregnancy (adequacy being determined by the number of prenatal care visits made to medical advisers) bore heavier children than those who did not, even when other factors affecting birth weight were controlled.[35] This relationship held equally in both the developed and the underdeveloped world. In this instance, presumably, the influential factors were the educational benefits which mothers-to-be derived from practitioners (none of which were demonstrated) and the more systematic medical oversight of fetal growth. It should be noted, however, that neither study employed precise measures of social class or status. Thus the prospect remains that much of the advantage enjoyed by women with superior medical care can be attributed to their social position, for, generally speaking, those of higher social standing have easier access to medical advice, and they are more likely to seek and take it.

The effect of work upon birth weight has been examined intermittently since the late nineteenth century. The first group of studies, done in Paris during the 1890s, indicated that infants delivered by women who did heavy physical work until the end of their pregnancies weighed less than did those whose mothers had enjoyed a period of rest before giving birth.[36] Several investigations during the first half of the twentieth century reached much the same conclusions.[37] Between 1945 and the late 1960s, however, similar inquiries produced contradictory findings: some indicated that work had a detrimental influence on fetal growth, others that it did not. Studies done since 1970 reveal that in developed societies working women now tend to have superior birth weight histories, delivering proportionately fewer abnormally light infants than the population at large. These differences over time in the influence of work on fetal growth are due to several factors, the most important being gradual changes in the nature of women's work, especially the decline of heavy labor and a general improvement in working conditions.[38] Nonetheless, the evidence remains clear that strenuous work still adversely influences birth weight in even the most privileged societies.[39] In less-developed communities the cyclical demands of hard work upon women employed in agriculture have contributed to marked seasonal fluctuations in weight at birth, while in urban places the physical demands of domestic and wage labor are related to variations in birth weight outcomes.[40]

One of the most striking features of weight at birth in the contemporary world is the social gradient of birth weight distributions. Even in Scandinavia, where social differences are among the smallest in the modern world (and probably among the smallest ever known in any advanced society), the newly born vary somewhat in size according to their parents' social and economic status.[41] These differences are rather more pronounced in Great Britain, the United States, and other countries whose social and health care policies have been less egalitarian than those of northern Europe. To date, few studies of long-term or secular change in birth weight have been conducted, and most of them are confined to the years after World War II, a period of unprecedented economic growth, rising prosperity, and declining economic inequality virtually everywhere in the developed world.[42] It thus seems reasonable to suppose that, in the far less egalitarian societies of western Europe and North America of an earlier era, the social gradient of weight at birth was at least as steep as, if not steeper than, it has recently been in these countries.

Finally, the influence of maternal nutrition on newborn weight must be considered. The relationship is complex and, at this point, not fully understood. As Metcoff observes,

> Clear-cut relationships between maternal nutrition during pregnancy and fetal growth are difficult to show especially in industrialized societies where obvious malnutrition is uncommon and diet variability among pregnant women is great. Fetal growth may be the best method to assess the consequences of maternal nutrition during pregnancy. However, to assess the nutritional effects on fetal growth, other influences such as socio-economic status, smoking, alcohol and other drugs, infections, and other complications of pregnancy, the influence of maternal size and race, the sex of the baby, and duration of gestation must be taken fully into account.[43]

In other words, newborn size is an important measure of a mother's nutritional status, but the precise contributions of diet to fetal growth remain difficult to assess.

Part of the explanation lies in the limits of present biochemical knowledge. Metcoff explains:

> Although dietary recommendations for pregnant women abound, neither the maternal macro- or micronutrient requirements nor the interrelationships between them needed at progressive stages of pregnancy to support optimal growth of the human fetus is known. Furthermore, the type and extent of placental processing or synthesis of nutrients being transported from mother to fetus are inadequately understood.[44]

Nevertheless, we now possess a growing body of information about the effects of maternal nutrition on fetal development.

At the outset the obvious point should be made that pregnancy imposes added nutritional requirements on the mother-to-be. Not only must she maintain her own body processes throughout the course of gestation but she must also support both the growing fetus and the extensive hormonal and metabolic changes associated with pregnancy, birth, and lactation.[45] These changes require increased energy and protein consumption, as well as the greater intake of many vitamins and minerals.[46] Because of their enhanced needs, pregnant women are (apart from young children) the group most vulnerable to malnutrition in less-developed societies today, and perhaps among the most vulnerable to mild malnutrition in the developed world as well.[47]

Health scientists, however, find the food values of diets difficult to measure, at least on a daily basis over long periods of time. For this reason, two more accessible indices have often been employed to determine the nutritional status of expectant mothers: prepregnancy weight and weight gain during pregnancy. Both of them reflect the abundance of maternal nutrient supplies available to the fetus and both are correlated with newborn weight. In particular, abnormally light mothers deliver smaller babies than do women of normal weight, as do women who gain low amounts of weight during gestation. (Women who gain less than eight or nine kilograms during a full-term pregnancy must break down some of their own body tissues if they are to bear a child in the normal weight range.) An underweight woman whose weight gain in pregnancy is inadequate runs a greatly increased risk of bearing a growth-retarded child.[48] Weight gain is also associated with the length of gestation. In cases of preterm delivery, both mothers and babies have not had enough time to gain the amount of weight put on during normal pregnancies.

As to diet itself, our understanding of the effect of food consumption on fetal development derives from three sources: studies of wartime famines, observational inquiries, and diet intervention trials. The effect of grave malnutrition on birth weight is clear. Several studies of famine conditions in Europe during World War II revealed sharp falls in mean birth weight during periods of severe dearth. The most dramatic reductions—between 400 and 600 grams—were recorded during the siege of Leningrad from August 1941 to January 1943.[49] A decrease of 300 grams occurred in western Holland during the shorter Dutch hunger of 1944–45.[50] Other reports of wartime birth weight reductions, while not as well documented, observed declines of similar magnitude in wartime Germany, Austria, and Italy in conditions of chronic undernutrition.[51] We should note, however, that these events occurred among previously well-nourished populations and that, once food shortages disappeared, the wartime birth weight deficits also vanished.

Many observational studies of the effect of everyday nutrition on weight at birth have been done over the past half-century and, as might be expected, their results have varied. Investigations undertaken before the 1970s yielded contradictory findings—some supporting the association of diet and fetal weight, others finding no significant relationship—but they often suffered from methodological weaknesses which confounded their reliability.[52] Since then, however, more persuasive findings have been reported. A relationship has been demonstrated between seasonal dietary patterns and changing birth weight levels among agricultural populations in several underdeveloped countries. In developed nations, as well, the nutritional value of pregnant women's diets has been shown to affect newborn weight.[53]

Diet intervention studies have also added to the fund of information about nutrition and fetal growth. But work has proceeded slowly in this area, not least because ethical considerations limit the range of experimental designs. Women cannot be deprived of food experimentally merely to explore the effects of malnutrition on their unborn children. For this reason experiments have been limited to providing nutritional supplements for groups of pregnant women in controlled settings. Those conducted in developed communities have provided urban women of low social and economic status with additional sources of calories and proteins. Some of them reveal an association between supplementation and a small increase in birth weight, particularly among women thought to be at risk of delivering growth-retarded children. One study also suggests that protein supplementation might even be harmful to the fetus if provided to women whose protein consumption already was adequate.[54]

Diet supplementation trials have also been held in less-developed countries, all of them among poor women and most of them in areas suffering from chronic undernutrition. The supplements reinforced local diets with additional energy and, in some cases, protein supplies. Most studies have found small but significant increases in the weights of infants borne by supplemented mothers.[55] One major project, in rural Guatemala, also revealed a substantial reduction in low birth weight among supplemented populations. It indicated that superior birth weight performance was associated with caloric rather than protein supplementation. It demonstrated that the duration of supplementation affected the birth weight increase. And it revealed that the supplements yielded their greatest results among the shortest and poorest women, those presumably in most need.[56]

Other constituents of diet may also affect fetal growth. Recent research indicates a relationship between low calcium intake and premature birth, at least among women at high risk of early delivery.[57] Pregnancy also greatly expands the need for folacin and iron, in large part because of the substantial increase in maternal blood supply. Folacin plays an important role in forming red and white blood cells and in supporting fetal-placental growth, while iron is an essential part of hemoglobin, the oxygen-carrying component of red blood cells. Iron-rich foods include red meats and fish as well as whole grain cereals, seeds, dried beans and fruits, and dark green leafy vegetables. Liver and dark green edible leaves are principal suppliers of folacin, small amounts of which are found in fresh fruits and vegetables as well. Deficiencies of both cause anemia and have been linked with complications of pregnancy, fetal abnormalities, and reduced birth weight. The precise consequences of such deficits for fetal development, however, are still a matter of controversy.[58]

The evidence thus reveals that diet during pregnancy influences weight at birth, but that the degree of influence varies considerably. Severe deprivation reduces birth weight substantially, moderate malnutrition much less so. Birth weight is affected by the caloric or energy value of diet, but not necessarily by its protein content. It may also be influenced by patterns of iron and folate consumption. Poorly nourished women profit from programs to improve their nutritional well-being and therefore bear heavier babies when their diet improves. By and large, adequately nourished women do not. In the eyes of one team of investigators, this fact suggests the existence of a nutritional threshold, a minimal level of nutrients for the adequate support of fetal growth as measured by weight at birth. Below it, the neonate likely will suffer growth retardation; above it, wide variation in intake and maternal weight gain may occur without affecting birth weight.[59]

Low birth weight

As noted above, low birth weight infants—those weighing less than 2500 grams at delivery—form a separate category of newborns and are exposed to heightened risks. Low birth weight is associated with two different conditions: preterm delivery and poor growth during gestation. Those born too soon have missed some part of the gestational cycle and are therefore immature. Those born too small are mature but have suffered from growth retardation. In some cases, infants are born both too soon and too small, and they are at highest risk. Early babies are commonly identified as preterm or premature; the mature but too small are variously known as small for gestational age, small for dates, or as suffering from intrauterine growth retardation (IUGR).

The 2500-gram benchmark is an approximate measure and therefore does not include all abnormally developed newborns. Some premature infants weigh more than this limit even though they are not fully developed. Newborns exhibiting IUGR are identified by comparison with reference to distributions of birth weights for specific stages of development or gestational age. The growth-retarded category is usually defined in one of two slightly different ways: either those infants whose weights fall below the tenth percentile or those whose weights are lower than two standard deviations below the mean, of all neonates of the same gestational age.[60] In either instance some IUGR babies also weigh more than the low birth weight maximum. Yet the use of the 2500-gram limit persists, in part because of its universality and simplicity, in part because it identifies a population at greater risk—whatever the cause of its disability.

The latest estimate of the global incidence of low birth weight, based on a WHO survey, concluded that 20.6 million low birth weight children were born in 1979, about 17 percent of all live births.[61] The rates varied widely, from 7 percent in North America to 31 percent in middle South Asia and, more generally, between 7 percent in the industrialized world and 18 percent in developing societies. Some 94 percent of low birth weight infants were born in the poorer nations. Thus, low birth weight has long been a critical health problem, as it remains today.

The causes of low birth weight vary considerably between developed and developing countries, as table 1.1 reveals. Prematurity is the principal cause of low birth weight in wealthy societies while growth retardation is the leading cause in poorer communities. Moreover, while the rate of premature birth in underdeveloped countries is double that of the developed world, that of IUGR is over six times as great. These differences seem due largely to socioeconomic characteristics associated with a community's level of development, nutritional factors in particular.[62]

The effects of nutritional deprivation on fetal growth differ with both the severity and the timing of the deprivation. According to Stein and Susser, "milder degrees of malnutrition result in depletion of soft tissues; the infant has a deficit in weight but not in skeletal growth. Severe malnutrition results in regarded skeletal growth as well, so that infant height and head size are reduced."[63] As to timing, when deprivation occurs in the first trimester or is chronic, growth retardation is proportional: weight, length, and head size are all affected. If it occurs in late pregnancy, weight alone will be reduced, for by this time skeletal growth has been largely achieved but the rate of weight gain has only reached its peak. Proportional or symmetric growth retardation is the most common form of IUGR in less-developed societies, where chronic undernutrition is often widespread. In the developed world, weight is more often affected than is skeletal structure, and no more than half of low birth weight newborns are symmetrically growth retarded.[64]

As to the implications of low birth weight for the further development of newborns, the prognosis for premature and IUGR infants differs somewhat. Premature infants are more likely to die than those who are growth retarded. On the other hand, the growth retarded seem more often to suffer from impaired neurological development later in life.[65] These differences, in turn, are reflected in developed and underdeveloped communities according to their differing sources of growth retardation, and have important implications for public health programs in rich and in poor nations alike.[66]

Table 1.1   Incidence of low birth weight in developed and developing nations

Source of LBW	Developing nations (%)	Developed nations (%)
IUGR	17.0	2.6
Prematurity	6.7	3.3
Total	23.6	5.9

Source: Villar and Belizàn, "The Relative Contribution of Prematurity and Fetal Growth Retardation to Low Birth Weight," 796. (This study draws on information from eleven developed nations and twenty-five developing areas.)

The history of measuring newborns

The accurate weighing of infants at birth began in the mid-eighteenth century. Until then the only published observations about the normal weights of newborns usually placed them between 12 and 15 pounds. In 1753, however, the German physician J. G. Roederer corrected these impressions when he declared that the average of twenty-seven full-term infants he had weighed lay between 6 and 7 pounds (2.72 and 3.18 kilograms).[67] During the rest of the century and the early part of the next, other reports confirmed Roederer's findings. Joseph Clarke, Master of the Dublin Lying-in Hospital (later the Rotunda), found a small sample of male children to weigh 7 pounds 5 ounces (3.32 kilograms) on average, while a small sample of females weighed 6 pounds 11 ounces (3.03 kilograms).[68] The Edinburgh physician James Hamilton noted weights of the same range in the obstetric casebook he kept in 1793 and 1794, though he never considered these facts important enough to publish in his *Select Cases in Midwifery,* which appeared in the following year.[69] A similar report, placing mean birth weight for over 7000 infants of both sexes at 2.94 kilograms, came from the Maternité de Port-Royale in Paris, where routine weighing was introduced soon after the turn of the nineteenth century.[70]

The motives behind these early investigations were diverse. Roederer was no doubt prompted by the medical scientist's desire for a more accurate understanding of human biology. Clarke was concerned about the higher mortality rate he had observed among male than female newborns, and he believed that the explanation must lie in difficulties women experienced in giving birth which were caused by the larger size of males. Yet the significance of weight at birth, and therefore the purposes of measuring infant size, remained far from clear. According to the English man midwife Thomas Denman, whose midwifery text first appeared in 1782:

> Much industry hath likewise been used to determine the weight, length, and dimensions of the *foetus,* at different periods of uterogestation. The utility of this inquiry, if the truth could be discovered, does not appear. But as children born of different parents, or those born of the same parents, at the same or different births, vary at all periods of pregnancy, it is reasonable to believe, that there is an original difference in their size and in other respects. Many of the varieties may also depend upon the state of the health either of the parent or child before its birth, so that it seems impossible to bring this matter to a fair conclusion.[71]

The practice of systematically weighing newborns developed gradually during the nineteenth century, by and large in maternity hospitals, where large populations of infants were available for study. But during the first half of the century the purposes of these inquiries remained diffuse. The lingering curiosity about abnormally large fetuses yielded a continuing trickle of accounts in the medical literature about enormous newborns.[72] James Young Simpson, the famed Edinburgh professor of midwifery, pursued Clarke's interest in the relationship of sexual differences in fetal size to differential mortality patterns.[73] Others, such as the American physician Humphreys Storer, merely reported miscellaneous obstetric statistics.[74] The relationship of weight and length to fetal development was recognized in some circles, but according to the *Dictionnaire des sciences médicales* in 1816 these measures were insufficient to establish fetal age. Other physiological signs must be consulted to determine the stage of gestational development.[75]

It remained for the Belgian Adolphe Quetelet—mathematician, meteorologist, and early anthropometrist—to place the measurement of newborn weight and length in their modern context: the creation of baseline statistics against which further growth can be assessed. Quetelet played an important part in introducing statistical thinking to the study of human growth. In the early 1830s he collected the lengths and weights of 119 newborns (sixty-three males, fifty-six females) in the Brussels foundling hospital, and the heights of a much larger but unknown number of boys and girls of various ages from several institutions in the city, after which he constructed age-specific growth charts for each sex.[76] Apparently these were the first such tables to be compiled. Quetelet's statistics on neonatal size—in this case newborn length—provided the point of departure from which future physical growth could be measured.

By the late 1820s or early 1830s a number of European maternity hospitals, following the Paris example, had begun to weigh and measure newborns routinely. Contemporary and retrospective accounts note such practices in Berlin, Ghent, Göttingen, Jena, and Marburg, among other places.[77] While these reports seldom describe weighing procedures in detail, surviving accounts indicate that great care was taken to insure precise measurement. The German physician Eduard von Siebold, for example, noted that in his clinics each child was weighed naked, immediately after birth and cleansing, on an accurate scale.[78] But despite the growing quantity of information available, little more was done at the time to explore the significance of newborn weight and length.

From the 1850s through the 1870s, inquiry into fetal size (some of it based on data gathered before midcentury) followed one of several paths. Several investigators simply compiled further statistics about the physical dimensions of newborns.[79] Others recognized the diagnostic insights offered by measures of newborn size. During the early 1840s, the Württemberg physician M. Elaesser had restated the case for considering weight and length as measures of fetal maturity.[80] In the early and mid-1860s, Carl von Hecker, professor of obstetrics at the Ludwig-Maximilian University in Munich, undertook a wide-ranging investigation into the course of fetal development. Von Hecker defined length and weight standards of fetal growth for the middle and late stages of pregnancy according to the ten-month lunar calendar then commonly used in European medical circles to reckon gestational age. He regarded birth weight as the most useful among various neonatal measures of fetal development.[81]

Von Hecker was one of a growing number of researchers interested in the implications of newborn weight. In 1852 Natalis Guillot, a professor in the Faculté de Médecine de Paris, had been the first to encourage the daily weighing of infants as a means of assessing their nutritional well-being.[82] Later von Siebold and others also recognized the utility of birth weight as a means of monitoring infant growth and health. During the 1860s and 1870s, numerous studies examined the patterns of short-term weight loss and subsequent growth which characterize the early days of infant life, while another French physician, Louis Odier, energetically promoted the diagnostic value of routine weighing.[83]

Several investigators also began to explore the factors affecting size at birth. In 1855, having analyzed the records of some 2500 deliveries which occurred at a Berlin maternity clinic between 1836 and 1853, Gustav von Veit, professor of obstetrics at Rostock, noted that newborn weight varied with birth order as well as the sex of the child.[84] In a similar study, Frankenhäuser of Jena observed variation according to maternal height and length of gestation as well as sex and parity.[85] In the mid-1860s, the Edinburgh obstetrician Matthews Duncan argued that the influence of maternal age on weight and length at birth eclipsed that of birth order, while von Hecker, in Munich, disputed the point, demonstrating that parity had at least as much effect on birth size as did age.[86] By the late 1870s, poor maternal nutrition and health, as well as short intervals between pregnancies, had also been recognized as reducing weight at birth.[87]

The results of these inquiries slowly diffused throughout western medical thought during the late nineteenth and early twentieth centuries. Further studies broadened the geographic range of information about average birth size and confirmed earlier theories about factors affecting fetal growth, as well as the initial course of newborn life.[88] In 1887 E. Issmer, a physician at the university women's clinic in Munich, analyzed a sample of over 12,00 births in Dresden between 1872 and 1883 and noted much of what was by then generally accepted: that sex, birth order, and maternal age were the major factors affecting variations in fetal development, although the duration of pregnancy, maternal size, and parental social circumstances might also have an influence. He also observed regional differences in newborn weight and length.[89]

While merely one of many studies undertaken during these years, Issmer's work illustrated a growing ambiguity surrounding the question of the relationship between size at birth and fetal maturity. Issmer considered all newborns of 48 centimeters or longer to be mature (*reif*), and he limited his study population to that group. Von Hecker had used weight instead of length as the defining criterion of growth and had accepted only those weighing more than 2500 grams as fully developed; later investigators tended to follow von Hecker's lead, although most considered 2800 grams the lower weight limit of a mature infant.[90] In either case (and that of Issmer too) the assessment of newborn development was based upon the physical size of the infant, not its gestational age. In Issmer's case this meant defining almost 40 percent of the infants in his initial sample as premature. The confusion over the criteria used to determine newborn maturity persisted well into the twentieth century, size being one of several physiological features used to differentiate premature from normal newborns.[91] Gradually, however, birth weight came to be recognized as the principal index of fetal development, and the 2500-gram limit the lower bound of normal fetal growth.

Toward the end of the nineteenth century Adolphe Pinard, professor of obstetrics in the Faculté de Médecine de Paris, added further to the list of factors influencing weight at birth. Comparing the infants borne by women who worked until the eve of their delivery with those of mothers from similar backgrounds who had enjoyed institutional care for at least ten days before giving birth, Pinard discovered that the latter weighed significantly more than the former. He concluded that heavy work lowered weight at birth and that it also was closely associated with premature birth.[92] As a result, Pinard underscored the importance of rest during the later stages of pregnancy to maternal well-being and fetal development.

In succeeding years a number of French studies, several by students of Pinard, confirmed his findings and pursued their implications for public policy. They concluded that an extensive period of maternal rest prior to delivery added between 150 and 350 grams to newborn weight and that it also tended to increase the length of gestation.[93] Pursuing the logic of these conclusions, Pinard and his followers recognized the possibility that changes in a mother's prenatal environment might increase the weight of her unborn child and thus improve its life chances. In other words, they argued, birth weight could be influenced by human intervention and therefore by social policy. Citing examples in Switzerland, Germany, and the Netherlands, they called for laws in France to prevent the employment of women during the final weeks of pregnancy. Nor was the issue simply one of improved care for pregnant women and the unborn. The work of these medical scientists fed the flourishing pronatalist debate in fin-de-siècle France.[94] As the physician François-Charles Bachimont declared in a ringing cry endorsed by his mentor Pinard, "From the viewpoint of humanity, from the viewpoint of the increase of the population, from the viewpoint of the evolution of the French race, it is necessary, it is urgent, that the public authorities intervene to protect the pregnant woman during the last three months of her pregnancy, and the fetus during the last three months of its gestational life" (my translation).[95] These views did not go unchallenged. In one late nineteenth-century study, the German physician Karl Fuchs found no relationship between the physical demands of work and weight at birth.[96] But within a short time the importance of rest in the later months of pregnancy had gained widespread acceptance in medical circles throughout western Europe.[97]

By the end of the nineteenth century, weighing and measuring newborns had become a common medical procedure in both maternity hospitals and private obstetric practice in western Europe and North America. The search for a deeper scientific understanding of fetal growth had stimulated this development and had led to a broader understanding of the origins of variations in newborn size. But the motives underlying these routines had also shifted during the previous century. What had once been an activity prompted largely by curiosity had become a tool of pediatric diagnosis—a means of assessing the maturity of the newborn and a benchmark for the measurement of its further physical growth.

Medical care in pregnancy

The medical oversight of pregnancy is largely a twentieth-century phenomenon. As one historian of prenatal medicine has observed (with particular reference to Great Britain),

> In the eighteenth and nineteenth centuries, antenatal care as a concept did not exist. Neither the providers of health care, nor pregnant women themselves considered routine medical supervision necessary. There were no clinics or hospital departments set aside for that purpose. No professional body had successfully claimed the care of pregnant women as its expert territory. There was, furthermore, no systematic body of knowledge or techniques applicable to pregnancy which could provide a rationale for medical supervision.[98]

And what was true of Great Britain was in large part true of continental Europe and North America as well.

Although clinics and homes for indigent pregnant women predated the twentieth century—Clinic III had functioned at the Allgemeines Krankenhaus in Vienna since at least the 1860s—Pinard was among the first to promote the idea of prenatal medical care, or what he called *puériculture*. Unlike maternity refuges, which offered women little more than shelter and regular meals, the new concept embodied the routine medical examination and advising of mothers-to-be. Pinard's concerns were shared not only by his students but also by medical men in other countries. Even before he published his call for more effective prenatal care in 1892, the American physician Charles M. Green had deplored the lack of medical supervision during pregnancy, terming it "a misfortune, and a detriment to the best interests of the race."[99] The influential Edinburgh obstetrician J. W. Ballantyne approached this question from the viewpoint of medical science. In 1901 he called for the founding of a pre-maternity hospital, where pathologies of pregnancy could be investigated and treated scientifically.[100] (At this point, however, Ballantyne had no vision of a program of prenatal care aimed at all expectant mothers.) Similarly, in 1911 the German physician Otto von Franqué declared that every pregnant woman should receive a medical examination several weeks before delivery and that it should be offered free of charge to women who could not afford the cost.[101]

But it took some time to translate conviction into action. In most countries prenatal medical services were slow to develop. One early example was the home-visiting program for pregnant women established by the Boston Lying-in Hospital in 1901; over the next decade several other prenatal care programs were created in eastern American cities.[102] The first British outpatient clinic for expectant mothers was founded at the Edinburgh Royal Maternity in 1915. Similar services, funded by local governments, soon were established in many parts of Great Britain. Still, throughout the 1920s only a small proportion of British and American mothers-to-be (and presumably those in other countries as well) received any prenatal care whatsoever.[103]

Diet was one subject touching on pregnancy which doctors spoke of freely. Most obstetrics texts included some brief bits of nutritional wisdom intended for women in pregnancy, as did many popular self-help manuals aimed at the female market. The American physician G. H. Napheys, author of a highly successful guide for women first published in 1869, offered some unusually extensive counsel:

> The nourishment taken should be abundant, but not, in the early months, larger in quantity than usual. Excess in eating or drinking ought to be most carefully avoided. The food is to be taken at shorter intervals than is common, and it should be plain, simple and nutritious. Fatty articles, the coarser vegetables, highly salted and sweet food, if found to disagree, as is often the case, should be abstained from. The flesh of young animals, as lamb, veal, chicken, and fresh fish, are wholesome, and generally agree with the stomach. Ripe fruits are beneficial. The diet should be varied as much as possible from day to day. . . . The taste is, as a rule, a safe guide, and it may be reasonably indulged. But inordinate, capricious desires for improper, noxious articles should, of course, be opposed. Such longings, however, are not often experienced by those properly brought up.[104]

Nutritional homilies like this one were fixtures of obstetric literature through-out the nineteenth century and on into the twentieth, and their content varied little from one author to the next.[105]

Nonetheless, two innovations left some imprint on medical thinking about nutrition in pregnancy during the early twentieth century. One was the so-called Prochownick or reducing diet. Prochownick was a German obstetrician from Hamburg concerned with the high infant mortality rate associated with cases of prematurely induced labor for women with contracted pelves.[106] Early induction was intended to produce a smaller child, one which was easier for a woman with a small pelvis to deliver. It was an increasingly common practice toward the end of the nineteenth century, preferred to the Caesarean section or symphyseotomy with their attendant high rates of maternal mortality. But the mortality of newborns following early induction also ranged around 50 percent.

Prochownick hoped to avoid both problems by placing women who were at risk on restricted diets.[107] The diet he prescribed was high in protein and low in carbohydrates, it restricted the intake of fluids, and it had a daily energy value of between 1800 and 2000 calories. Its purpose was to limit the forma-tion of fat tissue, thus reducing the size of the fetus and easing its delivery. He prescribed it for a small number of patients with narrow pelves and, in his major paper on the subject (published in 1901), claimed success for his ef-forts. He has since been widely, and erroneously, acknowledged as the author of the theory that birth weight can be controlled through nutrition during preg-nancy. In subsequent years the Prochownick diet stirred some controversy among medical professionals.[108] But obstetric textbook authors continued to offer variations on Napheys's advice long after Prochownick had published his findings.

After the turn of the century, the growing scientific understanding of food also began to penetrate medical thinking about nourishment in pregnancy. The concept of an adequate diet, one which identified the essential elements of human nutrition, gradually took form in biochemical circles during the later nineteenth century, and by the early twentieth century some of its most impor-tant constituents were well known.[109] Prochownick himself used the language of nutritional science when describing his patients' diets. He wrote of pro-teins, carbohydrates, and fats, not simply meat, fruit, and vegetables. And others did likewise. In a popular guide to prenatal care published in 1914, J. W. Ballantyne (presumably now converted to a public health view of pre-natal care) advised his readers:

> I approve of a full healthy mixed dietary during pregnancy; it will
> not necessarily be the food the mother has been in the habit of taking,
> but it should contain within its range proteins, water, and mineral

matters which together make up the building materials, fats which are heat producers, and carbohydrates which supply energy, especially muscular energy. These should all be present in the dietary, although of them all the proteins, such as meat and milk, are the most important, for to some extent they can give likewise heat and energy.[110]

Another readily accessible work of this period, this one addressed by a doctor to public health, school, and local government officials, spoke much the same language.[111] Some research also examined the relationship between specific dietary elements and fetal growth. One early study, for example, explored the effects of low-fat and low-protein diets on newborn weight in the period before and during World War I. It found none.[112]

But in the short run, at least, the new science of nutrition had little more influence on the unborn than had the physician's homely wisdom before it. Until medically supervised prenatal care touched the lives of most mothers-to-be, no doubt most women ate what they liked and what they could afford. Certainly, few of the women considered in this study could have been informed by medical dietary advice. Only a small proportion would have received medical attention before they went into labor and, even had they done so, many could not possibly have afforded the diets which doctors commonly advised.

Institutional childbirth

Childbirth in hospital, like prenatal care, is a comparatively recent development. Until well into the twentieth century, most children in western Europe and North America were born in their mother's home. Most premodern hospitals were intended for the poor and indigent sick; thus they seldom provided for women in childbed and for their newborn infants. Apart from the Hôtel Dieu in Paris, a general hospital which had admitted maternity patients since at least the 1630s, the earliest European lying-in institutions were not established until the mid-eighteenth century.[113] Over the next 150 years they became a common feature of the urban landscape throughout the western world, their founding inspired by a mixture of philanthropic and medical motives. Charitably minded men and women (and sometimes benevolent agents within church and state as well) encouraged them because they aided the poor in childbirth. Physicians supported them because they provided opportunities to study human reproduction and parturition, as well as a ready supply of clinical subjects with which to teach student doctors and midwives.

The patients cared for in nineteenth-century maternity hospitals came from the lowest ranks of urban society. Only the poor, the unmarried, the destitute, and the homeless—those who could not afford the financial or social costs of childbirth in their homes—sought refuge in lying-in hospitals. Most of these institutions were charities supported by private donations or funds from the state; the fees they charged patients were nominal and usually were waived in cases of need. Hospital childbirth in the nineteenth century thus carried with it the stigma of taking alms. It also bore the moral taint of sexual laxity. Maternity hospitals usually admitted a disproportionately large number of unmarried mothers and, in consequence, the odor of license and righteous condemnation clung to them and their clients. Two institutional alternatives for childbirth remained. One was the private maternity boarding house, a fixture in most larger cities, where expectant (usually single) women received discrete care for a fee. The other was the outpatient service offered by some lying-in hospitals to women in their homes. But for the most part these services, when and where available, could only assist married women with settled home lives. For these reasons, then, the woman who delivered her children in a nineteenth-century charity hospital did so only as a last resort.

After the turn of the twentieth century, the character of maternity hospitals in western Europe and North America began to change. The most obvious sign was the gradual transformation of the hospitals' patient body. In slowly growing numbers women from all social ranks began to seek institutional care when delivering their children. This process moved at varying rates in different societies, but by the 1930s it was well advanced in most western nations. In England and Wales, for example, the proportion of live births occurring in institutions rose from 15 percent in 1927 to 35 percent ten years later, while by 1935 some 37 percent of American newborns were delivered in hospitals.[114]

The removal of childbirth from home to hospital during these years was accompanied by rapid growth in the knowledge base of obstetrics and gynecology, as well as that of related medical sciences. Among the most important were the developing fields of embryology and endocrinology, which offered major additions to an understanding of human reproduction and the physiology of the female reproductive system. Improvements in anesthesia and bacteriology also influenced obstetric practice, though the antibiotic revolution ushered in by the discovery of the sulphonamides—and which provided the first effective therapy for the greatest scourge of the lying-in hospital, puerperal sepsis—lay ahead in the 1930s. New techniques in radiology offered obstetricians and gynecologists a wider range of diagnostic tools after the turn of the century, while the development of safer blood transfusions increased the safety of childbirth for mothers and children alike. These innovations, associated as they were with the growth of scientific clinical medicine, were among the leading influences behind the growing popularity and gradual extension of childbirth in hospital.[115]

Before the age of prenatal care, expectant mothers usually presented themselves for admission to a lying-in hospital when in the early stages of labor. Indigent women would sometimes seek earlier entry in hopes of finding shelter. But nineteenth-century maternity hospitals often were small, crowded places, faced with demands for beds which they sometimes could not satisfy. As a result, most of them routinely discouraged early admission, with greater or lesser degrees of success depending on institutional practice. Lengthy hospitalization after delivery was also the common pattern, ten days to two weeks being normal, during which time the mother's recovery and the newborn's progress could be observed and recorded.

But while some pregnant women found the lying-in hospital a place of refuge and much-needed assistance, they also faced grave dangers when entering its doors. Throughout the nineteenth century, recurrent outbreaks of puerperal fever swept lying-in hospitals on both continents, with attendant high rates of maternal death. Puerperal (or childbed) fever was commonly caused by a streptococcal or staphylococcal invasion of tissues wounded at birth. Because the body hosts many organisms which can cause a puerperal infection, one may occur spontaneously. But these bacteria are highly infectious and contagious, and therefore are easily spread by medical attendants. For this reason, the lying-in hospital, which concentrated patients, nurses, midwives, and doctors in a single institution, greatly increased the ease of transmitting the infection. This fact helps account for the fact that childbed mortality rates among hospitalized maternity patients were far higher than among women delivered at home. The bacteriological and antiseptic revolutions of the late nineteenth century provided an understanding of the infection and techniques for its prevention. But no effective control was possible once the disease was present in its victim until the introduction of antimicrobial drugs during the 1930s.

As to the hospital care of infants, the only subject of relevance here concerns the initial assessment of newborn size during the first minutes of life. Unfortunately, no record survives of the procedures or instruments used to weigh and measure newborns in the hospitals with which this study is concerned. Nonetheless, enough information is available from comparable institutions to draw reliable inferences about common practices. The procedures employed by von Siebold in Marburg and Göttingen before midcentury have already been noted. Those described by Issmer, which were followed in Dresden and Munich during the 1870s and 1880s, differed very little.[116] Soon after birth, each child was bathed and then carefully weighed and measured by the physician on duty, the results being recorded in the hospital's birth journal. By the second half of the nineteenth century these routines likely were common, at least in lying-in hospitals directed by doctors with an interest in fetal growth. And as the diagnostic value of newborn size became ever more widely recognized, the custom of infant weighing gradually spread throughout the maternity hospital system, as well as among obstetricians and general physicians in private practice.

Concerning accounts of the scales commonly used to weigh newborns, the sources of information vary. Von Siebold employed one devised by the obstetrician Osiander and another set up by his own father. The two proved equally accurate after scrupulous comparison, but the Siebold scale was portable while the other was not.[117] In the later 1860s the French interns Odier and Blache designed a light, portable balance scale intended for newborns and infants weighing up to 10 kilograms.[118] They claimed that it was accurate to within 20 grams. During the second half of the nineteenth century, the manufacturers of weighing devices and the makers of medical and scientific equipment sold a range of scales for infants.[119] Some machines used spring balances while others employed beams and weights. They normally included a wicker basket or metal pan in which the child could be placed while its weight was being taken. Most likely the hospitals in this study routinely weighed newborns on one or more of these commercially available scales.

2

EDINBURGH, 1847–1920

Population and economy

The population of Edinburgh grew slowly at best during the period under review. In keeping with the rest of western Europe and North America, birth and death rates declined in the city from the mid-nineteenth century onward, with crude birth rates continuously exceeding crude death rates by between six and ten per thousand. During the second half of the nineteenth century the urban population increased by a bit more than a third to just over 300,000, the average rate of increase a modest 10 percent per decade. Over the next twenty years it did not grow at all, an insignificant increase of 1 percent during the first ten years of the new century offset by an equal decline during the second.[1] The leading source of what growth did occur was natural increase, for like all of the eastern Scottish Lowlands Edinburgh bred more people than it could support.[2] While immigration brought many Scots, Irish, and English to the city, their numbers were offset by a substantial out-migration. Between 1900 and 1920, in particular, the city suffered a serious population outflow, losing the equivalent of all of its natural increase to emigration.

Yet seen in its regional economic setting, Edinburgh was comparatively prosperous. Together with Glasgow it had higher earnings rates than all other parts of Scotland. According to one historian it likely had "a greater *per capita* income and more widely spread affluence" than any other Scottish city.[3] In their national economic context, however, the circumstances of Edinburgh were rather more complex. At midcentury, Scotland was a low-wage region, but during the next fifty years its relative wage rates rose steadily. By the early twentieth century, Scotland—or at least the central belt in which Edinburgh was located—was one of the highest-wage areas in the United Kingdom (although the Scottish social historian T. C. Smout has questioned whether earnings actually reached the level of wage rates reported at the time).[4] Indirect evidence also suggests that Scottish purchasing power increased steadily from the 1870s to the eve of World War I.[5] But despite this improvement, living costs in the principal Scottish cities remained above those in the larger English boroughs. Thus, real wages were lower north of the border than south. In 1912 rent and food (about 80 percent of weekly working-class expenditures) cost 10 percent more in Edinburgh than in major English provincial cities.[6] More generally, Scottish real wages were 13 percent lower than those in London, and 10 to 12 percent lower than those in the Midlands and the northern English counties, both before and after World War I.[7]

Closely integrated into the national economy, Edinburgh experienced the same broad cycles which characterized economic growth in Great Britain as a whole. The business cycles of Edinburgh's construction and capital goods industries, in particular, followed national trends.[8] When discussing national economic trends, some historians divide the prewar era into two broad phases: a mid-Victorian era of quite rapid development and a late Victorian and Edwardian era of much slower growth.[9] During the third quarter of the nineteenth century Britain's gross domestic product grew rapidly, led by expansion in the coal, textile, and iron and steel industries. But the growth rate fell abruptly after the crash of 1873 and remained lower until 1900, after which it fell even further. Shorter business cycles occurred within these broad phases, including a period of decline from 1873 to 1882, two phases of recovery between 1882 and 1899, followed by a further depressed cycle after the turn of the century which reached its nadir in 1913. The war itself brought the greatest setback to the growth of real gross domestic product in Great Britain since the industrial revolution.

At the same time, local factors in Edinburgh also affected economic activity. Seasonal and other short-term fluctuations distinguished some trades— tailoring and shoemaking, for example, which were particularly sensitive to volatile consumer demand.[10] Other consumer industries, such as the food and drink trades, were much more stable.[11] The ongoing demands of Edinburgh's large middle and upper classes for services and the products of skilled labor tended to dampen fluctuations in the business cycle. At the same time, incomes among the poor were augmented by the large philanthropic effort of the city's well-to-do residents, some £250,000 a year in the early 1900s.

The economy of Edinburgh reflected the city's role as a regional metropolis. It was the administrative, judicial, banking, and educational center of Scotland, and many of the goods and services it produced were intended for its comparatively large and prosperous bourgeois market. C. H. Lee has noted the service orientation of the regional economy, particularly the large numbers of occupations in professional, government, banking, and commercial activities centered in the city and district.[12] Services were the leading edge of the regional economy, accounting for 45 percent of all new jobs in expanding employment sectors between 1851 and 1911. The same local orientation can be seen in urban manufacturing, directed as it was toward the consumer industries. Its principal goods (clothing, food products, and books and printed matter) were produced in small shops and factories. While the metal and textile trades were not wholly absent from Edinburgh, for the most part the city lacked the heavy industries of Glasgow, Dundee, and the great English industrial cities to the south. Its economy more closely resembled that of southeast England than any other part of the British Isles.

The strong service orientation of the local economy created an ongoing demand for female labor. Between 1841 and 1921, women comprised between 35 and 40 percent of urban workers, but, as table 2.1 reveals, the structure of the urban female labor force changed gradually over time. In 1841 nearly 70 percent of all female wage earners worked in domestic or personal service, but by 1881 the proportion had fallen to 50 percent and by the end of World War I it had sunk to 30 percent. The clothing and textile trades were by far the largest industrial employers of women. But although the proportion of women at work in this sector rose during the 1840s and 1850s, thereafter it fell—from just under 30 percent in 1861 to well below 20 percent by the dawn of the new century. The other major concentrations of women factory workers were found in the food and drink trades and the publishing sector, each of which offered expanding job opportunities and absorbed between 8 and 9 percent of the female labor force by 1901.[13] Together with teaching and commerce (the latter increasingly open to female clerical labor) they constituted the leading areas of growth for women workers in the nineteenth-century urban economy. But even though female job opportunities grew more diverse over time, women's work remained predominantly low paid throughout the entire period.

The hospital and its patients

The Edinburgh Royal Maternity Hospital was one of the famous maternities of Europe during the nineteenth century. It was here in 1847 that James Young Simpson first used chloroform as an anesthetic in childbirth. The maternity hospital was the larger of two charities in the city which aided women in childbirth during the nineteenth and early twentieth centuries.[14] From its founding in 1844, the hospital moved among several locations in the Old Town before finding permanent quarters in 1879 in a purpose-built building on its southern edge. It remained there until 1939, when it merged with the

Table 2.1   Edinburgh: occupational categories of female workers, 1841–1921 (Percentage)

	1841	1861	1881	1901	1921[a]
Professional	1.9	3.6	5.7	7.4	9.9
Domestic & personal service	67.4	50.8	52.1	42.5	30.1
Commercial	4.7	1.7	1.5	5.4	13.4
Clothing, textiles	17.6	29.1	17.7	17.2	10.3
Food, tobacco, drink, lodging	5.1	3.8	6.5	8.8	2.8
Paper, prints, books	0.7	3.1	6.3	8.4	6.0
Other manufacturing	2.6	5.5	8.0	8.4	6.0
Other occupations	0.4	2.5	2.2	1.9	21.2
Total female work force	10,248	31,684	36,315	53,712	70,579
% Total employment female	40.6	39.0	35.3	36.3	34.4

Source: Great Britain, Census of Scotland, 1841–1921.

[a]Occupational categories for the 1921 census are not wholly consistent with those from earlier years, particularly for some forms of manufacturing.

Royal Infirmary, Edinburgh's major general hospital. During the 1870s the Royal Maternity also introduced clinical services to patients in their homes, and in 1907 it opened an outpatient branch in neighbouring Leith.

Throughout its long history, the hospital placed few restrictions on the admission of patients. A charity, it required no fees from most of the women it served until well after the turn of the century, when it began to charge patients more systematically. In 1895 the hospital matron reported that those who could afford to usually gave sixpence or one shilling a day, but that fewer than half of the previous year's admittees had paid anything at all.[15] The two major exceptions were the wives and daughters of soldiers and sailors in the British forces, who after 1896 were charged a small fee, and private patients accommodated in the Married Women's Pavilion, opened in 1895, who paid upwards of a pound a week for their care.[16]

This open admission policy was not without its critics. In 1876 the Maternity's Ladies Committee recommended that prostitutes not be accepted as patients, arguing that allowing them entry prejudiced the hospital's best interests, presumably by discouraging respectable women from coming to the institution. But the medical directors refused the recommendation, citing the practical difficulties of excluding any class of patients and the good they believed the hospital had done for prostitutes in the past.[17] Undeterred, the Ladies Committee chose another tack in 1881, proposing to raise money for a new wing of the still incomplete hospital if it were set aside for "respectable married women." Their purpose, they reiterated three years later, was to accommodate married women entirely apart from other patients.[18] After a further decade of fund raising, the committee won its goal and the maternity opened a wing dedicated to married women. Evidently the innovation altered the public's perception of the hospital. The proportion of married patients more than doubled over the next quarter century, in part, no doubt, because the hospital no longer appeared to many as the last resort of the poor and dissolute.[19]

The chief restriction imposed by hospital admission policy was that patients only be given a bed when their expected due date was imminent. The rule was intended to keep indigent women from using the hospital as a shelter while awaiting delivery. On giving sufficient reason, a woman might be admitted two weeks before her child was expected, but she was to support herself until giving birth.[20] The hospital seems to have pursued this policy with some rigor. In 1874 the Inspector of the Poor in North Leith complained that a pauper sent to the hospital had been refused admission and had delivered the following day. The house surgeon explained that she had been turned away because she had told him that she was only in her eighth month of pregnancy and he had thought it best that she not be admitted until nearer her due date.[21] Two decades later the hospital directors reaffirmed the policy on admission just prior to delivery, although several of them recognized the need to accommodate some women well before they were due.[22] Perhaps for this reason, in 1899 the hospital established a home nearby where unmarried women might live before and for a short time after their delivery, although only those with their first child and of good character were admitted.[23]

Yet practice differed from policy in some important respects, for despite official policy many patients were admitted well in advance of childbirth. Before 1876, the period for which this information is available, almost two-thirds of patients delivered within a day of their admission while another 12 percent did so within a week of hospitalization. A further 11 percent bore a child between one and three weeks after entry, while the remaining 13 percent had still longer hospital stays.

During the early twentieth century, two further developments affected admissions to the hospital. The National Insurance Act, introduced in 1911, provided maternity benefits for insured women or the wives of insured men. Two years later the Royal Maternity signed the first of many agreements with fraternal, friendly, and working men's societies to administer the maternity benefit for their members.[24] Working-class families were the primary beneficiaries of this program. At first the law required that women receiving the benefit were to employ a registered physician or a qualified midwife, a measure which precluded them from attending the hospital. As a result the numbers of patients in the Royal Maternity dropped sharply, a decline of 22 percent by 1914, particularly among married women.[25] The directors feared that the decline in the number of patients would interfere with the supply of cases needed to teach student doctors and midwives, but after an appeal the insurance commissioners amended the plan to allow hospital participation. Thereafter, working women and working men's wives had greater access to the hospital than ever before. In the long run, the National Insurance Act reinforced the growing tendency of pregnant women to seek hospital deliveries, widening the social and occupational base of the institution. Thus, from the early twentieth century onward the Royal Maternity was less and less a last resort for poor women in childbirth, and more and more a hospital for the growing numbers of women who chose to deliver their children with the help of skilled medical aid.

One final innovation is also worthy of note, perhaps for its effects on the patients in this study and certainly because of its long-term implications for prenatal maternity care. In 1912 one of the hospital's doctors, J. H. Ferguson, noted the importance for both mother and child of good maternal care during pregnancy. Ferguson had been a visiting physician at the hospital's home for unwed mothers and had noticed the benefits of rest, good diet, and routine medical care for women and their newborns alike. In particular he believed that proper prenatal care increased birth weight and decreased prematurity and infant mortality.[26] In 1915, at his urging, the hospital established a prenatal outpatient clinic, and over the next five years it participated in schemes funded by national and local government agencies, as well as the Carnegie United Kingdom Trust, to establish similar clinics throughout the city. By the end of World War I there were seven prenatal clinics in Edinburgh, with a consultative center at the hospital.[27] This innovation, the first of its kind in the United Kingdom, may have had an influence on some of the patients examined here. And as prenatal maternal care became increasingly common in the 1920s and 1930s it altered the experience and outcome of pregnancy for growing numbers of childbearing women in Edinburgh and elsewhere in Great Britain.

During the second half of the nineteenth century, between 3 and 5 percent of all births in the city occurred in the Royal Maternity. After 1900, however, the proportion of hospital births began to rise, reaching 18 percent by the end of the war. The Edinburgh women who sought hospitalization for childbirth came by and large from the bottom ranks of the urban social structure. Well over 90 percent of the unmarried women either were unemployed or were servants, clerks, or unskilled and semiskilled laborers. On average, the husbands of married patients were perhaps slightly better placed—as many as one-third were skilled laborers. Still, the substantial majority of them also lived by menial laboring, service, and clerical tasks. Fewer than 2 percent of all patients came from the professional and managerial strata of Edinburgh society.

Three other characteristics of the patient population are also noteworthy. Most striking of all is the great disproportion of single mothers among the patients. At a time when illegitimacy in the city gradually fell from 10 percent to 7 percent of all births, some two-thirds of women attended in the hospital were unmarried. Newcomers to the city, especially those born in northern Scotland, England, and abroad (excluding Ireland), were overrepresented, while the Edinburgh born were markedly underrepresented. Finally, 96 percent of all women who delivered at the Royal Maternity were living in Edinburgh or the surrounding district at the time their child was born. Not surprisingly, the majority of them lived in the city's working-class districts, which included some of the classic slums of Victorian and Edwardian Britain.[28]

The social composition of the patients attending the hospital altered in several respects during the years of this study. The average age declined from 25.5 to 24.1 between the later 1840s and the early 1870s, after which it gradually rose to its former level and remained there until late in World War I, when it suddenly increased a further two years. The proportion of patients who were married (itself an age-related phenomenon) followed much the same course, declining to 1880 and rising thereafter. By the close of the period under review, only 36 percent of all women who delivered in the hospital were unwed, whereas in 1880 some 83 percent had been so. Concerning birthplace, the numbers of the Edinburgh born gradually rose after 1860, while newcomers to the city attended the hospital less often over time. The occupational structure of the patient body reveals three significant trends: a rising proportion of laborers, a falling one of those employed in domestic and private service, and a peak of workers in food-handling occupations between 1890 and 1910.

Weight at birth

Figure 2.1 depicts the trend in the annual birth weight mean for the infants in the Royal Maternity sample. It includes 8891 live-born singletons weighing 1500 grams or more. The fragmentary evidence for the midcentury decades indicates an annual average fluctuating around 3300 grams. The higher peaks of the 1860s and early 1870s coincide with years in which the sample size is unusually small and therefore may be anomalies. Nonetheless, mean birth weight was slightly higher during this period than it had previously been. From the mid-1870s to the early 1890s, the mean varied around 3300 grams once more. For the most part it moved between 3000 and 3200 grams thereafter, with a slight upward trend over time. These means also accord generally with average Scottish birth weights published during the nineteenth century.[29]

Multiple regression analysis was performed on the weights of all infants in the Edinburgh sample. The results are summarized in table 2.2.[30] The variables entered into this regression fall into three categories: biological, medical, and socioeconomic. Turning first to the biological variables, male sex, birth order, and maternal age contributed to an infant's weight—by 107.7 grams, 13.3 grams for each birth increment and 3.8 grams for each additional

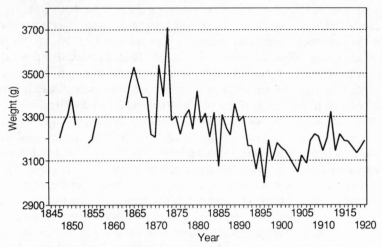

Fig. 2.1   Edinburgh, 1847–1920: mean birth weight

year, respectively. These results are broadly consistent with the findings of modern studies, which note superior weight performance for males, second or later-born infants, and infants born to mothers over twenty.

With one qualification, birthplace—the variable associated with ethnic and cultural origins and therefore possible gene pool influences—had no association with birth weight variation. Women born in the Scottish Highlands were the exception; their children weighed 78.6 grams more than average. Two explanations for this exception are possible. They may well have been rooted in genetic differences, for many Highlanders were of Gaelic stock. Alternatively, the cause may have lain in differing dietary customs in the Highlands, where the traditional Scots diet persisted longer than it did in the south.[31]

Two medical variables—major illness and pregnancy history—are identified in the clinical records. For purposes of analysis the various complaints were grouped into a single category, but by far the most common among them was eclampsia. The regression reveals that serious maternal illness reduced the average weight of newborns by 410.2 grams. Eclampsia, venereal diseases, and other major complaints have long been known to be detrimental to fetal growth. In this instance, smaller size at birth may have been due to growth retardation *in utero,* to premature birth, or to a combination of the two. Concerning the patient's earlier pregnancies, a record of one or more miscarriages was associated with an average weight deficit of 53.7 grams. This result, too, is consistent with recent findings, which note that women with histories of preterm birth or intrauterine growth retardation are likely to deliver somewhat lighter infants.

Table 2.2   Edinburgh birth weight sample multiple regression analysis

Variable	Coefficient (g)	t
Biological		
Male child	107.7	7.483
Birth order	13.3	2.687
Mother's age	3.8	2.327
Mother's birthplace Highlands	78.6	2.930
Medical		
Mother ill at delivery	−410.2	−5.317
History of previous miscarriage(s)	−53.7	−4.018
Social and economic		
Father's occupation clerical, bureaucratic	124.9	4.297
Father's occupation unskilled, semiskilled	93.7	3.550
Father domestic servant	140.9	2.798
Father's occupation skilled	63.4	2.457
Father's occupation food handling	85.8	2.153
Mother domestic servant	111.4	5.275
Mother's occupation food handling	97.4	2.656
Birth in autumn	36.9	2.177
Year of birth 1863 to 1873	164.3	5.272
Year of birth 1900 to 1913	−66.8	−3.970
(Constant)	2950.5	76.122

$N = 5449$; adjusted $R^2 = .040$; standard error $= 530.7$.

The remaining variables entered into the equation reflected the social and economic condition of the mothers in the sample. Birth in autumn added 36.9 grams to neonatal weight. Most likely, this difference was related to the lower cost, greater abundance, and wider accessibility of food in the autumn months. Business cycle effects are also evident. Birth between 1863 and 1873 added 164.3 grams to newborn weight. Conversely, children born between 1900 and 1913 weighed 66.8 grams less than average. The weights recorded during the disturbed conditions of the war and postwar years, however, did not differ significantly from those experienced throughout this period, excepting the two intervals already noted. Thus, year of birth itself had an influence on weight at birth, although in this analysis time is obviously a proxy for those prevailing social and economic circumstances which influenced living standards.

These results conform generally to the course of the British business cycle in the period under review.[32] In the decade prior to the collapse of western capital markets in 1873—when the rate of economic growth in Britain was higher than at any other time in the century—mean weight at birth was significantly above the average for the entire period. After 1873, however, when the

British growth rate declined sharply, neonatal weight fell off somewhat, especially between the turn of the century and the outbreak of the war—a period of very slow economic growth. The war years themselves saw some increase in birth weight levels, perhaps because of improvements in diet as well as concerted public efforts to raise standards of maternal and infant health.[33] Overall, the evidence thus indicates that the fluctuation of birth weight means coincided with broad national cycles of economic growth.

The only other variables in the regression which influenced weight at birth were related to employment. In the case of married patients, all of the major occupational categories of their husbands were associated with superior birth weights. In effect, among married women the regression measured the benefits of marriage itself rather than that of their husbands' particular occupational groups.

Among unmarried women, however, significant variation in birth weight was associated with occupational differences. Children born of domestic servants weighed 111.4 grams more than those of most other workers, while those whose mothers worked in tasks involving food handling enjoyed an advantage of 97.4 grams. Servants usually dined in the households of their employers and therefore derived at least some of the superior nutritional benefits enjoyed by their social betters. They also may have had physically less demanding tasks than those performed by other working women. The perquisites of women employed in food processing, preparation, or serving scarcely require comment. It seems hard to believe that poorly nourished women would not help themselves to meat and drink when the opportunity presented. Overall, then, the regression underscores the important contribution of nutrition to superior birth weight performance.

All low birth weight infants (those weighing under 2500 grams and including all live newborns excluded from the earlier multiple regression) were singled out for further analysis. Figure 2.2 indicates that, while the proportion of low birth weight infants in the sample fluctuated somewhat between the mid-nineteenth century and the end of World War I, the overall trend was upward. Until the early 1880s, around 8 percent of newborns were of low birth weight, a proportion comparable to that found in most developed countries today.[34] Thereafter it rose sharply, approaching levels experienced in some parts of the contemporary underdeveloped world. This rise seems not simply to have been the consequence of a greater proportion of pregnancies resulting in live births. Quite the contrary, as figure 2.3 reveals, the proportion of stillbirths in the hospital was also increasing at the time, if anything slightly more sharply than the rate of births at low weight.

The causes of these parallel trends are not wholly clear. No information is available on the general rate of stillbirths in the community at large, and as a result we cannot rule out the possibility that, over time, the hospital attracted

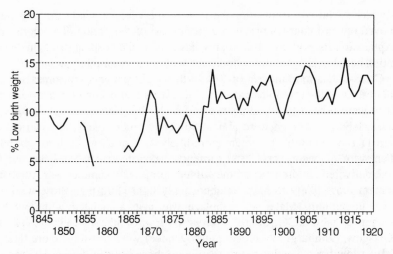

Fig. 2.2   Edinburgh, 1847–1920: percentage low birth weight (3-year running average)

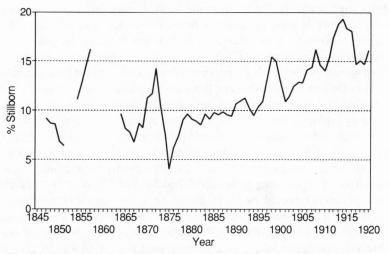

Fig. 2.3   Edinburgh, 1847–1920: percentage stillborn (3-year running average)

an increasing proportion of urban women who suffered from pregnancy complications leading to fetal death. The medical notes in the records reveal no trends in the state of maternal health over time, but because of their subjective nature they are not a reliable guide to trends in any event. Nor did the gradual rise in low birth weight and stillbirths coincide with shifts in patterns of hospital attendance. The maternity hospital only began to attract a clientele from a wider social spectrum after the turn of the century, while the two trends moved upward continuously throughout most of the period. The more likely explanation for both trends probably lies outside the hospital itself, in deteriorating health and nutritional conditions within the community at large.[35]

Cross-tabulation analysis of low birth weight patients reinforces some of the results of the multiple regression. It reveals that occupation and season of birth were related to the incidence of low birth weight. As table 2.3A indicates, laboring women were almost 50 percent more likely, and clerical and bureaucratic workers 46 percent more likely, to bear a low birth weight infant than were domestic servants.[36] Similarly, according to table 2.3B, women who delivered children during the winter, spring, and summer were almost 20 percent more likely to have an abnormally light child than those who gave birth in autumn. Maternal birthplace was also associated with low birth weight, as table 2.3C reveals. Women born in Scotland's four largest cities (Glasgow, Edinburgh, Aberdeen, and Dundee) were one-third more likely to deliver low birth weight infants than were those born in the north, the Lowlands, or the border counties. In this instance, however, birthplace masks some important occupational differences which had a bearing on weight at birth. Migrants to Edinburgh from the Scottish countryside were much more likely to work in food handling or domestic service than were locally born women, who were overrepresented in laboring and clerical jobs. In other words, those born outside the city worked at tasks which gave them a nutritional advantage over their counterparts from Edinburgh, and this is the likely cause of their more favorable low birth weight record.

The relationship between economic change and newborn size can also be tested by exploring the association between the annual birth weight mean and other statistical measures of economic performance. The most desirable measure would be a real wage index for the city, but in this case none exists. Instead, three measures of national economic change were employed: a real wage and a cost of living series published by A. L. Bowley in 1937 and an earnings series reported by C. H. Feinstein in the early 1970s.[37] Linear regression analysis was used to test the relationship between the birth weight mean and each of these indices. A statistically significant association was established in only one case, that of the annual rate of change in Feinstein's index of British earnings. The regression indicated that 48.5 percent of the year-to-year variation in mean birth weight might be attributed to the annual rate of change in earnings, as well as to advancing time in general.[38] An increase in weekly earnings raised birth weights, while a decrease produced the opposite effect. The absence of a relationship between the Bowley indices and the birth weight mean is not necessarily a telling problem; it may result from limitations in these long-established measures of well-being.[39]

Table 2.3   Edinburgh: proportion of infants of normal and low birth weight

A. By occupation

	Laborer	Domestic	Clerical	Food	Other	N
≥ 2500 g	84.7	89.7	85.0	87.6	84.4	2633
< 2500 g	15.3	10.3	15.0	12.4	15.6	367
N	561	1671	226	298	244	3000

Chi-square = 28.641; significance = .000.

B. By season

	Autumn	Other	N
≥ 2500 g	89.9	88.0	5530
< 2500 g	10.1	12.0	721
N	1465	4786	6251

Chi-square = 3.844; significance = .050.

C. By maternal birthplace

	North	Borders & Lowlands	Major Cities	Other	N
≥ 2500 g	90.3	90.0	87.0	88.6	5530
< 2500 g	9.7	10.0	13.0	11.4	721
N	853	1685	2966	747	6251

Chi-square = 12.856; significance = .005.

Birth length

A separate multiple regression was performed on the lengths of some of the newborns examined in the analysis of weights. Here, however, the problem of measurement must be addressed, for the lengths noted in the hospital records appear not to be as reliable as the weights. No account exists of the procedures used to measure newborns at the Royal Maternity during these years. The lengths noted before 1886, however, seem unduly low.[40] For this reason, analysis of birth lengths has been confined to the period from 1886 to 1920.

The results of this second regression are summarized in table 2.4. As before, the regression considered three groups of variables: biological, medical, and socioeconomic. In this instance the results differed somewhat from those of the regression on weights. Considering the biological variables first, male sex conferred a benefit of 0.75 centimeter while maternal maturity also bestowed a small advantage, 0.02 centimeter for each year of a mother's age. The former reflects the fact that male newborns are slightly larger than females on average, while the latter agrees with the results of the regression on weights as well as with modern findings indicating that women tend to deliver larger babies as they age. Maternal birthplace, with its possible gene pool

Table 2.4   Edinburgh birth length sample multiple regression analysis

Variable	Coefficient (cm)	t
Biological		
Male child	0.75	7.088
Mother's age	0.02	2.463
Mother's birthplace Highlands	0.52	2.539
Medical		
Mother ill at delivery	-1.42	-3.476
Social and economic		
Birth in autumn	0.31	2.497
Year of birth 1900 to 1913	1.32	11.288
Year of birth 1914 to 1920	0.80	5.215
(Constant)	48.71	193.165

$N = 4242$; adjusted $R^2 = .046$; standard error $= 3.45$.

implications, was the only other biologically related factor which influenced newborn length. Here, too, the Highland Scots were significantly different, their children being on average 0.52 centimeter longer than the others in the sample. Again, the explanation might encompass either or both nutritional or genetic influences.

As to medical factors, women afflicted with serious illnesses delivered children who were 1.42 centimeters shorter on average than those of healthy mothers. When socioeconomic variables are considered, several differences between the two regression results are immediately apparent. Most obvious is the fact that far fewer social and economic factors affected neonatal length. No occupational variables were associated with birth length differentials. Seasonality apart, the remaining social and economic variables associated with significant differences in length were related to year of birth. Taking the period from 1886 to 1899 as the basis for comparison, a clear upward trend is evident. Infants delivered between 1900 and 1913 enjoyed a considerable advantage (1.32 centimeters while wartime and postwar infants shared almost as great a benefit (0.8 centimeter).

While some of these findings support conclusions based on the first regression, others seem clearly at odds with the general downward trend identified in weight at birth during the late nineteenth and early twentieth centuries. In particular, why would mean birth length increase when mean birth weight was falling? Given the state of present knowledge about the factors affecting fetal growth any explanation must be highly tentative, but the most likely one is that the weight and length reflect somewhat different environmental and nutritional conditions.

The primary influences upon birth weight act during the last third of pregnancy, when fetal weight gain is most rapid. Thus, weight at birth is likely to be particularly affected by immediate environmental factors. The skeleton, however, is laid down early in pregnancy, and growth is most rapid during the middle third of gestation. The nutritional mechanisms which support skeletal growth are not yet fully understood, but the likelihood is that both long- and short-term factors are influential, and therefore it may be affected by the maternal nutritional legacy in ways which birth weight is not.[41]

The results of these two regressions support this hypothesis. While birth weight was affected by a series of social and economic factors, the primary socioeconomic variable which influenced length was year of birth. Had length been sensitive to short-term influences, one might expect to find more variation—by occupation or marital status, for example—within the patient population. The fact that such variation was not evident, and that time was related to the greatest differences in birth length, suggests that the increase in mean length among the Edinburgh newborns reflected gradual, general improvements in those elements of nutrition responsible for fetal skeletal development. At the same time, the downward trend in birth weight indicates that the caloric value of diets, and perhaps other environmental influences as well, deteriorated somewhat during these years.

Nutrition and the disease environment

Finally, some nonquantitative sources offer further indications of the state of nutrition in Edinburgh at this time. Unfortunately the evidence is rather slight. The findings of the earliest survey of food consumption patterns in Edinburgh, conducted for the Scottish Poor Law Commissioners in 1843, have been lost, although those for the surrounding area of the city have survived. They indicate that the working-class diet of the Edinburgh area included large amounts of tea, wheat bread, oatmeal, and potatoes, but very little meat.[42] Some twenty years later Dr. Henry Littlejohn, the great Scottish sanitary reformer, confirmed the fact that the Edinburgh poor seldom ate meat, though he had little else to say about dietary matters.[43]

Further information on living standards in Edinburgh became available soon after the turn of the century. Military recruitment during the Boer War revealed disturbingly low standards of health and stature among potential enlistees, a fact which raised serious concern in British government circles. The government and private inquiries conducted in Edinburgh in the wake of these discoveries underlined the poor quality of diet, housing, and health within the urban working class. In 1903 the *Report of the Royal Commission on Physical Training (Scotland)* noted that almost 20 percent of Edinburgh children were in apparent bad health and 30 percent were poorly nourished.[44] While a later inquiry questioned the statistical basis of these claims, it left little doubt of their essential validity.[45]

Another survey of dietary patterns among laboring people in Edinburgh, conducted by Noël Paton and two associates in 1902, also emphasized the poor quality of the common Scottish diet. On the basis of a sample of fifteen families, the Paton group concluded that the principal foodstuffs in the working-class regime were (in order of importance) bread, potatoes, milk, vegetables, sugar, and small quantities of beef.[46] They also noted the infrequent use of some nutritionally rich foods, in particular oatmeal, peas, and barley, oatmeal at one time having been the staple of the Scottish laborer's diet. "Looking over the dietaries studied," Paton and his associates concluded, "the outstanding feature is the great use of bread combined with butter, tea, and sugar." In their eyes, the laboring classes in Edinburgh enjoyed a standard of nutrition which compared satisfactorily with that of their counterparts in Philadelphia and New York but unfavorably with that of the poor of Chicago. Edinburgh's workers also ate more poorly than did most inmates of poorhouses, prisons, and pauper lunatic asylums in the British Isles.

Considering the foregoing, it is not surprising to learn that the historians of Scottish nutrition have emphasized the deterioration of the urban laborer's diet during the industrial era. In particular, A. H. Kitchin and R. Passmore noted five basic features of food consumption patterns which worked to the detriment of laboring families: the substitution of white roller-milled flour for oatmeal, of margarine for butter, and of tea for ale, as well as the great increase in sugar consumption and the inadequacy of fruit, vegetable, and milk supplies in urban areas.[47]

A broader study of nutrition and living standards in early twentieth-century Great Britain also supports the Edinburgh findings. According to P. E. Dewey, the national diet was only barely adequate nutritionally during the prewar years.[48] Moreover, the social distribution of nutritional benefits was decidedly uneven: working-class diets were markedly inferior and working-class husbands often enjoyed more and better food than did their wives and children. In contrast to the experience of the Central Powers, however, the war had relatively little impact on the nutritional value of the British diet. Although patterns of food consumption altered somewhat, the energy value of the national diet changed relatively little. What deterioration occurred was short in duration and it did not affect working-class families disproportionately.[49]

Whether contemporary or retrospective, none of these inquiries rested on a broadly based survey of Scottish food consumption habits, and for this reason they do not inspire as much confidence as one would like. Yet together they reveal the broad outlines of low and declining nutritional standards among laboring people in nineteenth- and early twentieth-century urban Scotland. In general terms they, too, confirm the results of the birth weight analysis.

The possibility that changes in the urban disease environment also affected mean birth weight and length over time must also be addressed. In Edinburgh, as elsewhere, the best available statistical measure of the disease environment as it affected women of childbearing age is the tuberculosis mortality rate for women aged fifteen to forty-four.[50] Data for this series are available between 1861 and 1910, during which time the mortality rate fell from 38.6 to 12.3 per ten thousand. When this annual mortality rate was regressed against the annual birth weight and length means, however, no statistically significant results were obtained. This finding suggests that the general disease climate had no appreciable influence on size at birth in Edinburgh.

The relationship between the annual birth weight mean and the course of economic development in Edinburgh between the mid-nineteenth century and the end of World War I thus seems clear. It fluctuated in harmony with the business cycle, save perhaps for the war and postwar years, when state intervention and private philanthropy combined to improve the lot of poor pregnant women, young mothers, and children. In particular, mean birth weight declined gradually between 1874 and 1913, a period of falling economic growth rates throughout Great Britain. This decline was accompanied by rising low birth weight and stillbirth rates among the hospital's patient population, facts which, when taken together, point to declining standards of nutrition and health among poor women in the city. It was also broadly consistent with nineteenth- and early twentieth-century dietary surveys, as well as accounts of Scottish food history, which emphasized the poor quality of working-class nutrition in Edinburgh and elsewhere in urban Scotland. The analysis of newborn weight in relationship to occupation also underscores the importance of nutrition to birth weight outcomes. In sum, the gradual deterioration in the nutritional condition of Edinburgh's working-class women caused a decline in mean birth weight between the early 1870s and the eve of World War I. Thereafter, wartime improvements in maternal well-being raised the average newborn weight somewhat.

3

VIENNA, 1865–1930

Population and economy

Two basic processes characterized the population history of Vienna during these years, the demographic transition and a distinctive pattern of growth and stagnation. While the beginnings of the transition predate the first years of this study, Vienna moved from high to low birth and death rates during the period examined here. Between 1869 and World War I, the city's population more than doubled, from 850,000 to just over 2 million. Estimates indicate that slightly more than half of all prewar growth was attributable to net migration.[1] During the war decade, however, Vienna experienced a sharp fall in its birth rate and a death rate persistently higher than the birth rate. The city also suffered a net population outflow which, together with its natural decrease, reduced the urban population by as much as 10 percent by the early 1920s. Thereafter, shorn of its empire, Vienna grew exceedingly slowly until 1930, the effects of its continuing excess of deaths over births offset only slightly by the greatly diminished numbers of migrants who came to the city.

Economic growth in the Habsburg domains lagged behind that of most of northwestern Europe during the nineteenth century. The economic historians Berend and Ranki indicate that in 1900, per capita industrial productivity in Austria-Hungary was below that of Britain, Germany, the Low Countries, Switzerland, France, and all of Scandinavia save Finland, though it ranked above that of the Mediterranean and Iberian world and even higher above that of the eastern European nations.[2] From the late eighteenth century to the early twentieth, the level of economic development was extremely uneven through-

An earlier version of this chapter appeared in *The Journal of Interdisciplinary History* 19:203–29; excerpts are reprinted here with permission of the editors and the MIT Press. © 1988 by The Massachusetts Institute of Technology and the editors of *The Journal of Interdisciplinary History*.

out Franz Josef's lands. The highest levels existed in Bohemia, Moravia, and the Vienna basin, where production and consumption approached northwestern European patterns, while the lowest occurred in the eastern reaches of the empire.

Regarding the timing of Austrian industrialization, several historians have recently questioned earlier attempts to identify a growth spurt later in the nineteenth century leading to sustained industrial development. They have concluded that industrialization in Austria was a prolonged and gradual process. Its first stirrings occurred in the mid-eighteenth century, and its primary roots lay in the *Vormärz* period before the revolution of 1848.[3] But while the revisionist historians argue that no time lag separated Austrian industrialization from that of northwestern Europe, they do admit that its initial growth rate was somewhat lower. Relatively high rates prevailed from 1870 onward, especially between the turn of the century and the eve of World War I.[4] The evidence suggests that the gap between development levels in Austria and the more advanced regions of Europe was closing at this time.

Prewar economic cycles can be described quite briefly. The so-called *Grunderzeit,* a period of rapid economic expansion, occurred between 1867 and 1873. It culminated in a crash on the Vienna stock exchange in May 1873 which Milward and Saul consider "the most spectacular in modern history after the Wall Street crash of 1929."[5] The subsequent crisis persisted throughout the decade, although older assumptions about its great depth have recently been questioned.[6] Recovery occurred after 1880 but growth remained sporadic, with upswings from 1880 to 1883, 1888 to 1891, and 1896 to 1899. A short but severe depression in 1900–1901 was followed by a decade of rapid growth, from 1903 to 1913, interrupted only by a brief recession in 1908–9.[7]

The outbreak of war profoundly affected the Austrian economy. As the war crisis deepened, production in Austria declined substantially and growing shortages of major commodities occurred. Despite price regulation of staple foodstuffs, inflation ranged between 58 percent and 115 percent annually during the war and remained at these levels until 1921. In 1922 it rose to catastrophic heights and virtually destroyed the value of the Austrian krone.[8] Inflation was one product of the fundamental economic problems which beset postwar Austria. Major shortages of essential commodities continued long after the armistice as government budgetary problems, a balance of payments deficit, a flight of capital, inadequate transportation, and severe trade restrictions aggravated the problem of low production. In 1923, however, international financial aid encouraged a new measure of stability in the beleaguered Austrian economy; the years until 1930 were ones of readjustment and slow recovery.[9]

These cycles characterized the Austrian economy as a whole, that of Vienna included. At the same time, major structural change affected the Viennese

Table 3.1   Vienna: occupational categories of female workers, 1880–1934 (Percentage)

	1880	1890	1900	1910	1923	1934
Domestic service	52.3	33.7	33.4	26.5	26.3	25.0
Manufacturing	33.1	46.1	41.7	40.2	39.1	39.7
Clothing, textiles	—	28.9	23.5	25.3	—	—
Trade & commerce	5.1	15.3	18.5	26.3	24.3	23.2
Public service	5.0	4.1	6.1	6.5	9.7	11.4
Other occupations	4.5	0.8	0.4	0.5	0.6	0.7
Total female work force	143,845	256,513	297,424	374,651	342,234	356,719
% Tot. employment female	35.9	36.1	35.4	36.3	36.4	38.5

Sources: Austria, *Die Bevölkerung der im Reichsrathe vertretenen Königreiche und Länder nach Beruf und Erwerb,* 1880; Austria, *Berufsstatistik nach den Ergebnissen der Volkszählung von 31. December 1890;* Austria, *Berufsstatistik nach den Ergebnissen der Volkszählung von 31. December 1900;* Austria, *Berufsstatistik nach den Ergebnissen der Volkszählung von 31. December 1910;* Rigler, *Frauenleitbild und Frauenarbeit in Österreich,* 57, 147.

economy and this, too, forms part of the economic background against which the urban birth weight trend must be viewed. Despite the gradual spread of the large-scale factory and corporate business organization in the monarchy, manufacturing in Vienna remained predominantly small scale until well into the twentieth century. One reason for the persistence of traditional forms of manufacturing was the importance of luxury products in the urban economy. Vienna's imperial court, its aristocratic aureole, and the large urban bourgeoisie created a high demand for handcrafted goods. The Austrian historian Peter Feldbauer believes that the growth of Vienna owed more to its political, governmental, and financial functions than to industrialization.[10]

Household production waned during the last third of the nineteenth century in the face of the rising power of industrial capitalism. The growth of white collar and public service occupations after the turn of the century provided other signs of this restructuring in the labor force. These changes affected men and women somewhat differently. Household manufacture declined more slowly in traditional areas of female employment than male. Women's work in mid and late nineteenth-century Vienna was concentrated in garment production and domestic service, and while industrialization gradually transformed the needle trades toward the end of the century it left less of a mark on the service sector (table 3.1). Female employment grew rapidly in the new electrotechnical and machine construction industries founded in Vienna during the two decades before World War I. The war itself greatly expanded the range of women's industrial work and many of these gains became permanent in the postwar world, as women filled the gaping holes in the male labor force left by military recruitment and high casualty rates. By the eve of the depression the service sector, long a preserve of female labor, had shrunk somewhat but women constituted a large proportion of the labor force in the new electrical, machine, metalworking, and communications industries while retaining their predominance in most traditional areas of female work. Meanwhile, after the war, working-class wives tended increasingly to labor in their homes at unpaid housework.[11]

The hospital and its patients

The Vienna patient records come from the Allgemeines Krankenhaus, one of the leading hospitals in the western world during the nineteenth and early twentieth centuries. It was here during the later 1840s that Ignaz Semmelweis pursued his inquiries into the etiology of puerperal fever—using some of the same records employed here, though for an earlier period—and made his important contribution to the evolving germ theory of disease transmission. In 1865 the hospital operated three maternity clinics, where virtually all institutional births in the city occurred.[12] These constituted approximately 20 percent of all Viennese births until 1910, the proportion rising to about 40 percent by the later 1920s. Thus the data used here were drawn from a broad segment of the urban populace, one which widened over time. The clinics were patronized almost exclusively by poor and working-class women until after the turn of the twentieth century, when the social base of the hospital began to widen.

The extent to which medical insurance benefits affected the character of the hospital's patient population is not clear. Austria was a pioneer in the provision of social insurance benefits, and the first health insurance scheme—adopted in 1888—included maternity cases. The plan only included industrial workers, however, and its initial reach was not particularly broad. By 1901 it covered no more than 9 percent of the Austrian population, although it expanded to include all employed persons during the last years before the war.[13] But because the hospital accepted maternity cases free of charge, these innovations likely had little effect on the social composition of the patient population.

The hospital accepted all women who sought admission and normally assigned them to one of two obstetric wards (Clinics I and II). It made no attempt to exclude patients on moral grounds. The single limitation it imposed on admission was a regulation which allowed lengthy hospitalization before delivery only in exceptional cases. All applicants except those already in labor were examined on arrival by a physician to determine whether they should be received or dismissed.[14] The hospital also operated a separate unit intended as a shelter for destitute pregnant women (Clinic III). Unlike the two main obstetric departments, this one often accepted patients well in advance of delivery.

The Viennese birth weight data base was gathered from the patient records—the *Geburtsprotokolle*—from Clinics I and III. The *Geburtsprotokolle* for Clinic I exist in continuous series from 1872 to 1930. They were augmented by the records of Clinic III for 1865 to 1870, the first maternity unit in the hospital to record birth weights on a regular basis. The social structure of the patient bodies in the two clinics have no significant differences save that nonresidents of the city were underrepresented in Clinic III and its patients stayed in hospital somewhat longer on average than those in Clinic I. Slight though they are, these differences also encourage caution when combining data from the two clinics in a time series.

Like women everywhere in the western world, Viennese women seldom enjoyed medical advice during pregnancy until after the turn of the twentieth century. No doubt they learned the folk wisdom of prenatal care from female relations and friends, but the medical profession could offer them little until they went into labor. In Vienna, concern for infant welfare gradually broadened in the first years of the new century. But maternal advisory bureaus were not established until the early war years, by which time the gathering crisis of war must have rendered most nutritional advice to pregnant women virtually pointless.[15] Wartime conditions brought a growing recognition among some physicians of the possible connection between maternal diet and newborn size.[16] But any effect the medical profession might have had on the overall quality of public prenatal care in Austria must have been negligible before at least the mid-1920s.

When compared with the entire Viennese population, the Allgemeines Krankenhaus maternity patient sample had five major distinctive characteristics:

1. Like the urban population, the sample was overwhelmingly Roman Catholic; but the city's small Protestant and Jewish minorities were significantly underrepresented.
2. Three-fourths of the sample were unmarried. The proportion of unmarried mothers in the sample declined with the fall in illegitimacy in Vienna, but at all times it was about twice that of unwed mothers in the general population. At present, however, we know little about pregnancy and illegitimacy in the working class of Vienna apart from one claim that unmarried motherhood had no clear association with lack of respectability.[17] Within the clinic itself the social characteristics of unmarried patients changed little over time, except for a sharp decline in domestic service occupations and the rising numbers of the unemployed during the 1910s and 1920s.

3. All but 2 percent of patients lived in Vienna or in neighboring areas of Lower Austria. In general the sample reflected the overall pattern of population distribution throughout the city's twenty-one *Bezirkes* (administrative districts).[18]

4. Unmarried patients were heavily concentrated in domestic service and unskilled or semiskilled labor or, from 1910 onward, were unemployed. Compared with the general pattern of women's work in Vienna, domestic service was substantially overrepresented in the sample and other occupational groups were underrepresented. The hospital thus served single women from a narrower range of occupations than was generally open to female workers, and these were among the most menial and least remunerative jobs available to them. After 1900 half of the married patients' husbands worked in professional, managerial, mercantile, clerical, and bureaucratic occupations. In other words, the great majority of patients came from the lowest economic ranks of Viennese society, though somewhat less so over time.

5. The proportion of patients whose origins lay outside Vienna—most of them from Lower Austria, the province where Vienna is located, and from Bohemia and Moravia—was considerably higher than that of the "foreign-born" portion of the urban population, especially before 1914.[19]

Six fundamental changes occurred in the structure of the patient sample over time, three of which had potential implications for analysis of the birth weight trend. First, the proportion of married patients grew substantially. At the beginning of the period under study, over 95 percent of the patients were single, but toward the end of the nineteenth century the ratio of the unmarried to the married began to decline. By the 1920s only a third of all patients were unwed, a reflection of changes in the maternity's social and medical functions and the sharp decline in illegitimacy throughout Austria which commenced toward the end of the nineteenth century. Second, very few women from higher income backgrounds delivered children in the clinics before the early twentieth century. From that time onward, however, they formed a small but growing segment of the patient population. In part the change derived from the increasing proportion of married women who attended the maternity clinics. The husbands of married women worked in a much broader range of occupations than did unmarried, wage-earning women. In part this change also stemmed from the widening tendency toward hospital birth, especially pronounced from 1914 onward. Third, after the turn of the century, a rising number of patients, most of them single, were unemployed. In fact, by the 1920s one-third of unmarried patients were without work.

The remaining three structural changes were of lesser consequence. The proportion of the Vienna born jumped sharply after the end of World War I;

once Austria had been shorn of her former empire, migration into the city dropped off sharply. In addition, the great Catholic preponderance of the earlier years dwindled somewhat as the numbers of Protestants and Jews attending the hospital grew slowly over time. A final minor trend was the slight ageing of the hospital patient population during and after World War I.

Weight at birth

The Viennese annual birth weight mean is depicted in figure 3.1. Apart from the period between 1865 and 1870, for which the data are somewhat problematic, the annual mean moved between 3100 and 3200 grams in most years until the outbreak of World War I. No trend in the mean can be discerned. Between 1916 and 1922, however, the mean dropped sharply in the protracted economic collapse which beset Austria during and after the Great War. It fell below 3000 grams in 1921, during the most acute stage of the postwar inflationary spiral. In 1923, after international intervention and currency stabilization had resolved the crisis, mean birth weight rose to just over 3200 grams, an unprecedented level, above which it remained until the eve of the depression.

Two multiple regression analyses were performed on the weights of the Viennese newborns. The first examined all live, singleton infants weighing 1500 grams or more. Because birth weight proved sensitive to the duration of institutional care, a second regression was performed on a restricted sample of infants whose mothers had been in hospital seven days or less before delivery. The results of these analyses are summarized in table 3.2.

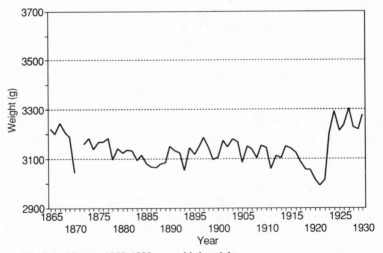

Fig. 3.1   Vienna, 1865–1930: mean birth weight

Table 3.2   Vienna birth weight sample multiple regression analysis

	All patients[a]		Patients 0–7 days[b]	
Variable	Coefficient (g)	t	Coefficient (g)	t
Biological				
Male child	130.7	13.470	120.3	10.847
Birth order	35.4	10.094	32.4	8.401
Mother's age	6.2	5.827	6.7	5.580
Social and economic				
Days in hospital before delivery	4.1	10.598		
Professional, managerial occupation	102.8[c]	1.877	137.9	2.329
Food handling occupation	67.7	2.486	82.5	2.665
Domestic servant	37.3	3.408	38.5	3.120
Birth in autumn	46.4	4.059	55.4	4.247
Lower Austrian address	−33.4	−2.485	−61.2	−3.518
Year of birth 1865 to 1873	50.4	2.728	38.9[c]	1.821
Year of birth 1916 to 1919	−44.1	−2.038	−78.1	−3.037
Year of birth 1920 to 1922	−127.5	−4.944	−147.7	−5.139
Year of birth 1923 to 1930	125.3	7.570	114.7	6.156
(Constant)	2773.6	105.714	2773.3	93.603

[a]N = 9213; adjusted R^2 = .070; standard error = 465.2.
[b]N = 7227; adjusted R^2 = .061; standard error = 471.0.
[c]Between a critical level of .05 and .07.

The regression performed on the larger sample indicates that the biological variables infant sex, birth order, and maternal age influenced birth weight. Male sex added 130.7 grams, each birth increment added 35.4 grams, and each year of a mother's age added 6.2 grams to mean weight at birth. These findings are consistent with those of modern studies, which associate higher birth weights with males, multiparous births, and women aged twenty or older.[20] Ethnicity, the only additional biologically related variable entered into the regression, had no statistically significant relationship to birth weight outcomes. This finding is a strong indication that gene pool influences—differences in the genetic composition of the sample's major ethnic groups—had no effect on birth weight means. It is unlikely that ethnogenetic factors influenced variations in neonatal weight.

The remaining variables entered into this regression were associated with the social and economic circumstances of the mothers in the sample. Among the most revealing is the length of time a patient spent in hospital before delivering her child. For each day of a woman's hospitalization her child gained 4.1 grams on average. While 78 percent of all mothers delivered within a week of entering the clinic, 11 percent were hospitalized between one and three weeks, and another 11 percent more than three weeks before giving birth. The duration of institutional care thus had a particularly important bearing on the weights of the children of patients who spent at least one prenatal week in hospital.

The clinical records provide no indication that medical need brought long-staying patients to hospital well before they were due (though the mere absence of information is not enough evidence to rule out this possibility entirely). Apart from women admitted while in labor, all patients were examined before admission to determine whether their due dates were sufficiently close to justify hospitalization. Only place of residence, marital status, and occupation had a strong association with the likelihood that a woman would have a prolonged prenatal hospital sojourn. On average, women from outside the city stayed three times as long as city dwellers, the unmarried twice as long as the married, and servants and the unemployed twice as long as those in other occupations. The vulnerability of unemployed and unmarried pregnant women needs little further comment. That of domestic servants is also readily explained; as was common in most western communities, unmarried pregnant servants in Vienna were often dismissed when their employers learned of their condition. Thus, long-staying hospital patients most likely came early to the hospital because they lived at a distance or because they needed charitable aid. The effects of institutional care itself offer the best explanation for the higher birth weights associated with prolonged care patients. The hospital provided them with rest and regular meals and, in doing so, increased their net nutritional intake. This benefit was passed on to the growing fetus and reflected in its birth weight.

Two groups of occupations, domestic service and tasks involving food handling, also were associated with birth weight variation while a third, professional and managerial employments, approached statistically significant influence in the first regression and established it in the second. On average these groups bore children respectively heavier by 37.3 grams, 67.7 grams, and 102.8 grams than all other groups in the sample. But the relationships of all other occupational groups to birth weight variations were statistically insignificant. The absence of any occupational variation in birth weight among laborers, clerks, and women with minor bureaucratic jobs perhaps derived from, and therefore reflected, the relatively homogeneous living standards within the lower ranks of the Viennese working class. The comparative economic advantages of women in the highest occupational category are self-evident. Those of servants were rooted in the fact that, while their job status might be low, perhaps 95 percent of servants in Vienna lived and ate with their employers and therefore enjoyed the superior diets of a more privileged social group.[21] Those who worked in the food trades enjoyed an obvious nutritional advantage as well.

This regression also detected a seasonal effect upon newborn weight. Birth in autumn contributed 46.4 grams to the mean weights of infants, although the other seasons had no statistically significant effect upon them. Here the likely explanation is economic, for food prices normally were lowest in the fall when supplies were most abundant. A breakdown of seasonal differences in birth weights by occupational group supports this hypothesis. The mean weight of servants' infants varied little throughout the year while that of non-domestics fluctuated somewhat more widely, again reflecting the advantages which domestics enjoyed.[22] Dining in their employers' households insulated servants from the annual price cycles to which other workers were exposed.

In one instance place of residence, another factor with social and economic implications, also was associated with weight at birth. The children of women from Lower Austria outside Vienna weighed 33.4 grams less than the others. The inferior weights of country women are somewhat puzzling. Perhaps they were a sign of some combination of lower living standards, poorer working conditions, and heavier physical labor in the countryside than in the city. Somewhat less likely, they may have resulted from medical conditions not noted in clinical records which impelled these women to seek hospital care during childbirth. Whatever the reason, none of these differences are large and, if anything, the absence of great differences in birth weight among residential groups requires explanation more than do the differences themselves. Most of it lies in the overwhelmingly proletarian character of the hospital's patient population. In addition, residential patterns in Vienna were rather less socially differentiated than in some other European and North American cities, and as a result Viennese housing mingled residents of differing occupations and income levels in many neighborhoods. Within the working-class population, servants were particularly widely dispersed throughout the city.

One final variable, year of birth, also correlated strongly with newborn weight. The regression identifies six time intervals which accord with broad peacetime economic cycles and the two stages of economic collapse during and after World War I: 1865–73, 1874–99, 1900–15, 1916–19, 1920–22, and 1923–30.[23] Table 3.2 indicates that those born between 1865 and 1873 seem to have enjoyed a slight advantage, but when the analysis is restricted to those hospitalized for a week or less the significance of the advantage is qualified. Most of the patients in this part of the sample came from Clinic III, which admitted a larger proportion of patients well in advance of their due dates. The advantage enjoyed by this cohort came from its institutional care, not its social and economic circumstances.

The remaining time intervals significantly associated with birth weight differentials were found in the last years of the sample. As the results for the 1916 to 1919 group indicate, the mounting crisis of war reduced birth weight means by 44.1 grams. The weight of those born during the economic collapse between 1920 and 1922 fell even further, by 127.5 grams. During the recovery of the mid and late twenties, however, mean birth weight rose to new peaks, 125.3 grams above late nineteenth- and early twentieth-century levels. Considering birth year as a proxy for current living standards, the regression reflects significant changes which occurred in levels of well-being from one time interval to the next. It indicates that birth weight levels declined slightly after the economic crisis of 1873, and remained at somewhat lower levels until the outbreak of World War I. The profound economic crisis of 1916 to 1922 produced a substantial birth weight deficit, while the postrecovery economy of the mid and late twenties yielded birth weight means of unprecedented height.

When patients who spent more than a week in hospital before delivery are set aside, the relative contributions of the biological and most socioeconomic variables remain largely unchanged. But the few changes which did occur are of some importance. The second regression indicates that the birth weight deficits of the crisis years and those of Lower Austrian patients were greater among short-staying patients than among the total sample population. The institutional effect had masked some of the environmental influence upon these patients. To put the matter in slightly different terms, the benefits of hospital care were particularly evident during the war and postwar emergency and among those who came farthest to find hospital care.

Overall, multiple regression analysis indicates that a cluster of biological variables—infant sex, birth order, and maternal age—influenced the weights of children born in this Viennese hospital. Because these relationships are biologically determined, their interest to historians is limited. But one additional biological variable, ethnic or gene pool origin, had no effect on birth weight means and this finding is more significant. It indicates that there were no differences in the ethnogenetic legacies of these children which affected their weight at birth. The environmental circumstances of both the fetus and the mother also influenced the weights of these newborns. The hospital patient records indicate some but not all of these influences. All of those most clearly identified here were directly related to the economic well-being and living standards of the hospital's patients, their nutrition in particular.

The annual low birth weight rate is graphed in figure 3.2. Although the proportion of low birth weight infants in the sample fluctuated from year to year, the trend moved upward from 1865 until the early 1920s, after which it began to decline. The low birth weight ratio was especially high during the late war years and the ensuing economic crisis, a further reflection of the depth of economic distress experienced in Vienna during this period.[24] The stillbirth rate, another index of pregnancy problems, was rising at the same time, both in the sample population and as a proportion of all civic births (fig. 3.3). These parallel increases in the incidence of low birth weight and stillbirth are further signs of deterioration in the health, well-being, and living standards of working-class Viennese women.[25]

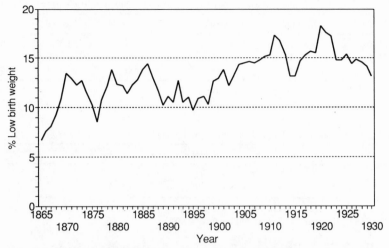

Fig. 3.2   Vienna, 1865–1930: percentage low birth weight (3-year running average)

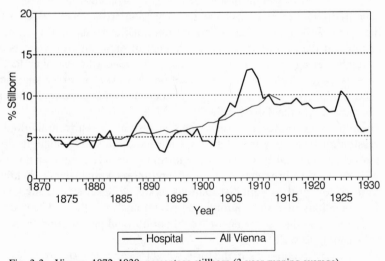

Fig. 3.3   Vienna, 1872–1930: percentage stillborn (3-year running average)

Cross-tabulation analysis reveals two statistically significant relationships between sample variables and the proportion of low birth weight infants. Table 3.3 indicates an association between a patient's occupational category and the likelihood that she would deliver a low birth weight child. Women from laboring occupations were almost 40 percent more likely, and the unemployed over 90 percent more likely, to deliver a low birth weight child than were domestic servants.

Table 3.3   Vienna: normal and low birth weight infants by occupation (Percentage)

	Laborer	Domestic	Unemployed	Other	N
≥ 2500 g	89.9	92.5	86.4	90.2	8646
< 2500 g	10.1	7.5	13.6	9.8	835
N	3404	5198	390	489	9481

Chi-square = 29.242; significance = .000.

Table 3.4   Vienna: normal and low birth weight infants by season, 1916–1922

	Fall	Other months
≥ 2500 g	37	113
< 2500 g	0	33

Note: These women were laborers living in working-class districts.
N = 183; chi-square = 8.731; significance = .003.

In addition, a strong association existed between season of birth and the number of low birth weight infants delivered by women from laboring occupations living in working-class Vienna during the crisis years, 1916 to 1922 (table 3.4). While these women bore no light babies in autumn, even during the depths of the economic crisis, 29 percent of their children were born at low weight during the remaining months, when food was less abundant and more expensive. With one minor exception, however, no other statistically significant higher-order relationships were detected among the social and economic variables in the data sample.[26]

These findings reinforce some of the conclusions drawn from the multiple regression analysis. In particular they underscore the strong relationship between occupation and birth weight, confirming the advantages of domestics as well as the disadvantages of laborers and those without work. While the analysis of low birth weight distributions produced fewer statistically significant associations than did multiple regression analysis, those detected were directly linked to the economic well-being of hospital patients and their nutritional standing as well.

The primary fluctuations in the birth weight mean seem to correspond with some major changes in Austrian economic performance.[27] In order to test the strength of this relationship, the annual birth weight mean should be compared with other significant measures of economic behavior. Here, as elsewhere, the most satisfactory measure would be an index of real per capita income. As no such index for Vienna exists, the mean was regressed against the annual rate of change in an Austrian cost of living index for these years.[28] The regression also entered the war and postwar crisis years as a dummy variable and introduced time as a separate variable. According to the regression,

46 percent of the annual variation in mean birth weight can be attributed to a combination of changes reflected in the cost of living index and the social and economic circumstances of wartime and postwar Vienna.[29] A decline in the cost of living raised the birth weight mean while an increase in living costs yielded the opposite result, although in both instances the effect was rather small. While the influence of the period from 1916 to 1923 was strong, that of time in general was statistically insignificant.

With few exceptions the mean weights of infants from all social and economic groups identified in the sample did not deviate significantly from the birth weight trend. The exceptions themselves are revealing, however, for they shed further light on the socioeconomic factors which influenced weight at birth. This evidence comes from analysis of different segments of the hospital population during the economic crisis of 1916 to 1922 when the birth weight mean fell to unprecedented lows. As figure 3.4 indicates, three groups of patients did not share these declines: domestic servants, long-staying hospital patients, and residents of Lower Austria. The most likely explanation for the experience of servants is that, by the late war and early postwar years, the decline of service had confined servants largely to the homes of the wealthy, sheltering them from the worst of the economic crisis.

In contrast to their general experience, women who lived in lower Austria fared somewhat better through most of this period. The three residential groups in the sample all experienced significant declines in mean weights as the crisis progressed. But at least until 1920, the children of Lower Austrian women were on average as heavy as they had been for the previous four dec-

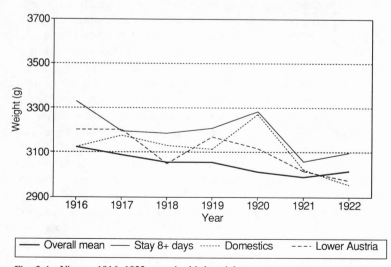

Fig. 3.4   Vienna, 1916–1922: superior birth weight

ades while those of urban residents had fallen to unprecedented lows. Only in the final year of the postwar collapse did they share in the general birth weight decline. In this instance the explanation appears to be that those who lived in rural communities, and who therefore had direct access to food, had the advantage over city dwellers.

Long-staying hospital patients also maintained weight means at levels higher than all but a few prewar years. (Lower Austrians and domestics, who remained in hospital far longer than other segments of the patient population, were excluded from this analysis.) The sharp declines in the mean weights of short-staying patients were not reflected in those of women who spent more than a week in hospital before delivery. At the depth of the crisis their infants weighted 360 grams more than those with little or no institutional prenatal care.

Birth length

The patient records of the Allgemeines Krankenhaus listed the lengths of the newborn children as well as their weights and, unlike the other hospital records surveyed in this study, these lengths were measured and recorded with care throughout the whole period.[30] For this reason, multiple regression analysis was also performed on the Vienna patient sample using birth length as the dependent variable. As before, two regressions were run, one on all patients and a second only on those hospitalized a week or less before giving birth. The results are summarized in table 3.5.

The regression analysis of birth length generally supports that of newborn weight, although the range of systematic variation in length was small—invariably less than 2 percent above or below the mean. Among the biological factors male sex, birth order, and maternal age all had a small effect on length. Boys were 0.71 centimeter longer than girls, each parity increment added 0.14 centimeter to length and advancing age added 0.03 centimeter per year to the size of a newborn child. Maternal birthplace in Lower Austria also added 0.1 centimeter to infant dimensions—although in this case the statistical relationship is not especially strong—an influence which might suggest possible gene pool effects. But Lower Austrians did not constitute a unique gene pool and therefore the genetic explanation must be set aside. On the contrary, the superior lengths of these newborns probably had nutritional origins. Lower Austrian-born women were much more likely to undergo lengthy hospitalization before delivery than were urban-born patients, widely employed in domestic service and the food trades. Such hospitalization, with the attendant nutritional benefits that have already been discussed, may well explain the greater length of their infants.

Most of the social and economic characteristics which affected newborn

Table 3.5   Vienna birth length sample multiple regression analysis

	All patients[a]		Patients 0–7 days[b]	
Variable	Coefficient (cm)	t	Coefficient (cm)	t
Biological				
Male child	0.71	13.621	0.65	10.811
Birth order	0.14	7.296	0.14	6.709
Mother's age	0.03	5.391	0.03	4.699
Lower Austrian origin	0.10[c]	1.767	0.13[c]	1.931
Social and economic				
Days in hospital before delivery	0.02	9.107		
Food handling occupation	0.31	2.140	0.37	2.205
Domestic servant	0.29	5.224	0.31	4.792
Birth in autumn	0.15	2.252	0.17	2.320
Birth in winter	−0.11[c]	−1.781	−0.14[c]	−1.939
Lower Austrian address	−0.26	−3.363	−0.41	−4.124
Year of birth 1900 to 1915	0.28	4.495	0.22	3.069
Year of birth 1916 to 1919	−0.23	−2.014	−0.37	−2.700
Year of birth 1920 to 1922	−0.42	−2.925	−0.47	−2.909
(Constant)	48.20	331.266	48.25	289.549

[a]$N = 8829$; adjusted $R^2 = .055$; standard error $= 2.43$.
[b]$N = 6925$; adjusted $R^2 = .046$; standard error $= 2.48$.
[c]Between a critical level of .05 and .08.

weight also were related to variation in birth length. Duration of predelivery hospital care added 0.02 centimeter per day. Some of the same jobs linked to higher birth weights were also associated with longer infants: domestic servants (0.29 centimeter) and food-related occupations (0.31 centimeter). Seasonality also had a slight effect, birth in autumn adding 0.15 centimeter to mean length; conversely, birth in winter subtracted 0.11 centimeter from length (although here, too, the statistical relationship is somewhat weaker). With a single qualification, however, place of residence had no association with differences in newborn dimensions, no doubt for the same reasons that it was unrelated to birth weight differentials. Residents of Lower Austria were the sole exception, these women bearing infants shorter as well as lighter than the norm. The reasons for this fact are unclear, but they likely are the same as those noted above, which perhaps explain the shortfall in newborn weight.

Year of birth is the one area in which some significant differences exist between the regressions on newborn weight and length, and these differences lay in the twentieth century. Both weight and length declined during the crisis years 1916 to 1922. In both cases, as well, between 1916 and 1919 the decline was associated only with women who had short hospital stays (and whose children therefore did not share the benefits of institutional care), while all patients bore shorter infants on average during the inflationary spiral of the early 1920s. But in the first fifteen years of the century, newborns measured on average 0.28 centimeter more than they had in the nineteenth century—a small but significant increase—although no change in birth weight can be detected. And the lengths of children born during the mid and late twenties did not differ at all from those recorded before 1900, while birth weights rose to new heights.

The explanation for these seeming anomalies is far from clear. As noted in chapter 2, skeletal development and rapid body mass growth occur at different phases of gestation. They may respond rather differently to the same nutritional stimuli, and they may also require somewhat dissimilar nutritional sources. As a result, these contrasting growth patterns may reflect different elements in the social and economic environments of twentieth-century Viennese working-class women. But given what little we know about these patients, as well as the limits of present knowledge about the processes of human growth, the explanation for these differing growth patterns remains elusive.

Nutrition and the disease environment

At this point we should also note some evidence from other sources bearing on the question at hand. Roman Sandgruber's reports on food consumption in Vienna during the late nineteenth and early twentieth centuries indicate significant alterations in basic dietary patterns, especially before 1914.[31] The primary changes Sandgruber identifies were the rising consumption of milk and beer and the falling consumption of wine, meat (especially during the 1920s), and bread, the decline of the latter two, at least, being signs of deteriorating diet.

Additional evidence on dietary patterns comes from an Austrian government study of incomes and living conditions among Viennese working-class families between 1912 and 1914, also reported by Sandgruber.[32] The study revealed great variation in diet according to household income. Families with annual incomes over 1200 kronen ate more than twice the meat, fish, eggs, fruit, and preserves than did those earning less than 800 kronen. They also drank twice the beer and four times the wine, and consumed 10 to 20 percent more milk and fat (butter, margarine, cheese, etc.) than did those in the least favored group. The poor, however, consumed 30 to 50 percent more bread, cereals, and potatoes than those in the highest income category. While these data do not permit us to quantify the differences in nutritional value linked with these dietary practices, they nevertheless reveal the wide divergence in food consumption patterns of income groups within the Viennese working class, and the apparent disadvantage of those with lower incomes. We cannot determine whether these patterns were typical of all or large parts of the period from 1865 to 1930, or simply were unique to the years covered by the Austrian government inquiry. But despite its limitations, Sandgruber's evidence leads to two conclusions: first, that the quality of diet in Vienna declined during the later nineteenth and early twentieth centuries and, second, that lower income laborers' families had diets far inferior to those with higher incomes.

There is also ample independent evidence of grave food shortages during the war and postwar economic crisis. Austrian wheat production fell by 34 percent between 1914 and 1917 (the last war year for which statistics are available), rye by 38 percent, oats by 52 percent, and barley by 60 percent, and the dearth persisted after the war.[33] According to Rothschild, conditions in 1919 were desperate in Vienna. Between August and December, the maximum daily per capita available ration of bread and flour was 100 to 170 grams. Food and financial aid from outside the country provided little relief.[34] Without question, the years during and immediately after the war were ones of growing immiserization for the entire Viennese working class,[35] and supplies remained short until the national economic crisis ended in 1923.

The possibility also remains that the disease environment in Vienna had an independent influence on the birth weight trend. Because the clinical records used in this study seldom noted information on the state of maternal health, statistics on mortality by disease offer the only measures of the incidence of specific diseases in Vienna during this period. The measure most useful for this study is the tuberculosis death rate, for while it declined by almost half during these years,[36] tuberculosis remained the leading cause of death among young and middle-aged Viennese women throughout this period. The available data allow the calculation of the annual tuberculosis mortality rate for women aged fifteen to forty-four between 1891 and 1914. The possible relationship between this mortality rate and the annual birth weight mean for the same period can then be examined by linear regression analysis. In this instance, however, no relationship was detected.[37] The absence of a statistically significant correlation between the birth weight and mortality trends suggests that, here too, disease factors had little effect on the trend in mean weight at birth.

Concerning the relationship of size at birth to the broad course of economic and demographic change in Vienna during these years, three points should be made. First, the half-century of population growth and industrial development before World War I had no strong influence upon birth weight and, at best, slight influence on length. But the gradual rise in the proportion of low birth weight infants points to declining living standards, a conclusion underscored by the simultaneous rise in the urban stillbirth rate. On balance, the evidence indicates that the nutrition and living standards of Viennese working-class women deteriorated somewhat between the *Grunderzeit* and the war. Second, the birth size data reveal a state of serious nutritional deprivation during the economic shocks of the war and its immediate aftermath. And, third, they suggest a new period of well-being during the relative economic stability of the mid and late twenties. The indications are that the young Viennese women of these years enjoyed higher nutritional and living standards than their mothers, their grandmothers, or their great-grandmothers had ever known.

It also is conceivable that long- as well as short-term influences acted on the Viennese birth weight trend. The higher mean weights of the mid and late twenties seem related to the economic recovery of those years. But their unprecedented level also suggests the possibility of cumulative gains passed on from mother to child.[38] The most likely mechanism for this transfer would be a gradual increase in maternal height and weight through general improvements in net nutrition. Assuming nutritional adequacy, taller and heavier mothers bear heavier babies than those who are shorter and lighter. Increasing maternal stature would therefore result in rising birth weight and length means. Admittedly, there is little in this evidence to encourage the view that prenatal nutrition was improving from the 1860s to the early 1920s, and therefore that stature might be growing. But in the absence of information on maternal size, the possibility should not be dismissed out of hand.

4

DUBLIN, 1869–1930

Population and economy

Of the cities considered in this study, Dublin prospered least in the nineteenth and twentieth centuries. The urban population did not grow at all between the 1850s and the 1890s, and when growth then occurred it owed much more to suburban annexation than to any other source. Until well into the twentieth century, mortality levels higher than those of any English or Scottish city off-set high Irish fertility rates, while low levels of in-migration more or less balanced limited migration out of the city. A community of a quarter-million souls in 1851, Dublin was very little larger seventy-five years later.[1]

The fact of the matter was that Dublin's economy stagnated during the half-century after the famine. At a time of massive migration out of the Irish countryside, the city held little allure for those in search of a better life. The great majority of the dispossessed quit their homeland for Great Britain, the United States, or Canada. The Irish historian Mary Daly estimates that internal migration into Dublin was generally less than 10 percent of emigration from Ireland during these years.[2] So immobile was the urban population that, at any time from the mid-nineteenth century until World War I, from 60 to 70 percent of all Dublin residents were born either in the city or in its immediate surrounds.[3] The course of Dublin's economy during and after the war, however, remains obscure at present, for the recent economic history of Ireland remains largely unwritten.[4]

The primary sign of Dublin's weak economic performance was the gradual decay of urban production. Between 1851 and 1911, employment in manufacturing fell from 31 percent to 24 percent of the total labor force. Indeed, on the eve of World War I there were 5600 fewer manufacturing workers employed in the city than there had been just after the famine. According to Daly, many long-established luxury crafts declined during these years, while the clothing industry failed to adopt modern methods of production. Growth occurred in the printing, metal, and engineering trades, as well as the food and drink sector—principally due to the rising fortunes of Guiness's brewery—but it was not enough to offset the general failure of urban manufacturing. Meanwhile the proportion of unskilled laborers rose. In 1911, nearly one-fifth of all Dublin workers were general laborers, most of them employed in transportation, construction, and agriculture as opportunity provided. One of the few factors mitigating this bleak economic picture was the fact that Dublin was a provincial, and after 1922 a national, capital. Like Edinburgh, it possessed a comparatively large and growing population of professionals, whose higher, more regular incomes helped sustain the luxury trades and the urban service sector.[5]

During these years, the economy of Dublin—indeed the Irish economy generally—was extensively integrated into that of Great Britain. Britain was the principal market for Irish exports and the major source of Irish imports as well. British and Irish financial institutions were also highly integrated, with the result that fluctuations in the British economy usually were reflected across the Irish Sea. Daly observes that, with slight variation, prices and wages in Dublin moved in line with those in Britain. Irish artisans were as well paid as skilled English and Scottish workers, although town laborers earned considerably less than their British counterparts.[6] Thus Dublin seems to have shared the broad business cycles of the economy of Great Britain—at least until World War I—although short-term cyclical patterns also reflected local circumstances.[7]

As in other nineteenth-century cities in Europe and North America, women formed a large part of the Dublin labor force. Typically they were most heavily concentrated in domestic service and the textile and clothing sectors (table 4.1). The skilled trades were almost completely closed to women and, while industrialization created some new job opportunities for women, notably in shoemaking and bookbinding, only a small minority labored in factory settings. By and large those who worked for wages were young, single, and transient, since married women seldom took paid employment outside the home. Daly suggests that, by the end of the nineteenth century, an income-earning wife was acceptable only in the lower reaches of the urban working class.[8]

The number of working women in Dublin fell during the early and middle years of this study—by 16 percent between 1871 and 1911—a sign of growing female disadvantage in the city's stagnant labor market. The decline in

Table 4.1   Dublin: occupational categories of female workers, 1871–1926 (Percentage)

	1871	1881	1891	1901	1911	1926
Professional	3.9	7.6	11.3	7.6	11.0	9.2
Domestic service	53.1	48.4	40.5	43.8	38.2	34.0
Commercial	4.2	0.6	1.0	2.3	5.0	15.3
Clothing, textiles	26.1	25.2	26.1	23.8	22.3	12.2
Food, drink, lodging	3.6	5.5	6.5	5.7	5.8	5.4
Other industrial	5.2	12.4	14.4	16.6	17.4	6.4
Other occupations	3.8	0.2	0.2	0.2	0.3	17.5
Tot. female work force	48,501	47,623	44,240	45,392	40,839	44,404
% Tot. employ. female	37.5	37.5	36.1	33.7	30.2	32.1

Sources: Great Britain, Census of Ireland, 1871–1911; Ireland, Census of Ireland, 1926.

domestic service is in some ways surprising, for it occurred in the face of rising wages for servants and diminishing prospects for other work, as well as the fact that household servants usually were better off in many respects than those employed in comparable occupations.[9] The fall in employment in the textile and clothing trades reflected the general decline of these industries in the city, although it was offset to some extent by the growth of new opportunities in the professions and other forms of manufacturing. World War I did not alter this situation appreciably. While women in other countries assumed nontraditional work roles during the war, no such development occurred in Ireland.[10] But after the war the number of working women began to rise slowly, as new opportunities opened in the commercial and service sectors.

The hospital and its patients

The women in the Dublin sample were patients at the Rotunda, one of the oldest and most celebrated of lying-in hospitals in Europe.[11] Founded in 1745, it was the largest of four maternity hospitals in the city during the later nineteenth century.[12] It occupied a central site north of the river Liffey, on the fringes of working-class Dublin and close to one of the city's principal slums. In 1876 the Rotunda also opened an extramural service which attended childbearing women in their homes. During the years under review, between 10 and 20 percent of infants born in Dublin were delivered in the hospital, the proportion gradually increasing over time. A further 6 to 9 percent were delivered in the city's other maternity clinics, while an additional 20 to 30 percent were born at home under the care of an extern service.

From its founding, the Rotunda followed an open admission policy: it accepted any woman who applied for entry regardless of her circumstances. The hospital charged no fee for its services until the 1890s, when two wards were established to accommodate paying patients; yet even then, free patients took priority when the hospital was overcrowded.[13] Established as a charity for poor childbearing women, the Rotunda served this end until well into the twentieth century. At least one critic claimed that many patients could afford the cost of their hospitalization.[14] But according to George Johnston, Master of the Rotunda from 1868 to 1875, "the greater number of poor creatures who seek the shelter of the Institution are persons steeped in poverty and wretchedness, many of them labouring under great distress and anxiety of mind."[15] The introduction of an extern program did not affect demand for the hospital's services; it merely broadened the Rotunda's work among the poor women of Dublin.[16]

The hospital did not admit patients until they were in labor, or at least revealed clear symptoms that their labor was imminent. In the 1850s admission normally was gained by a ticket obtained from the hospital well in advance of the mother's due date. The ticket required the patient to note her name and address and was to be signed by a hospital governor, a clergyman, or other respectable citizen. Once the ticket had been filled in, the patient was to attend the hospital dispensary where she would have it countersigned, undergo a medical inspection, and receive any necessary treatment. These procedures might seem to have favored married women from stable homes, but in practice those who appeared at the hospital in labor were admitted whether they had a ticket or not.[17]

Like maternities elsewhere, the Rotunda's character began to change after the turn of the twentieth century. In 1911 the National Insurance Act provided financial benefits for many women in childbirth, just as it had in Edinburgh.[18] Beginning in 1913, the hospital also administered private maternity benefit programs sponsored by insurance companies, fraternal organizations, friendly societies, and labor unions. The main beneficiary of these developments, at least initially, was the hospital itself, because it now obtained revenue on behalf of patients whom it once would have served for free. In 1920 the Rotunda began to charge fees for all patients, having requested voluntary contributions from patients for at least the previous two years.[19] The hospital also began to offer a wider range of medical services. By 1920, some 18 percent of all patients were admitted well before labor, many of them treated for medical complications or obstetric problems and then discharged. The Rotunda also took a more active interest in prenatal medicine generally, introducing a clinic for parturient women soon after World War I.[20] The combined effect of these various changes may have been to limit the number of indigent women admitted and to increase the proportion of patients from above the bottom ranks of urban society.

But if this was so (and it is by no means clear that it was) the effect was negligible before 1930, as the occupational structure of the patients indicates. Throughout the years considered here, the hospital accommodated the Dublin poor far more often than any others. Three-fourths of all married patients were wedded to unskilled or semiskilled laborers, clerks, petty traders, or servants, while the husbands of just over 20 percent were skilled laborers. Fewer than 1 percent were from the professional and managerial classes. Unfortunately, the occupations of the unmarried were not recorded.

The women of the Rotunda sample differed in one important respect from the patients of other maternities included in this study. Whereas most lying-in hospitals accommodated a largely unmarried clientele, especially before the twentieth century, only 5 percent of the Rotunda's patients were single. This circumstance reflected the low rate of Irish illegitimacy compared with those of England, Scotland, and most European countries, and also the heavy social penalties incurred by Irish women who bore children out of wedlock.[21] As a result, a higher proportion of the Rotunda patients were multiparous. They also were much more likely to have come from rather more advantageous family circumstances, if not more secure sources of income, than were patients in most nineteenth-century maternities.

Compared with the urban population as a whole, Roman Catholics were overrepresented among patients, despite the fact that the hospital's governance was Protestant. This fact reflected the greater concentration of Catholics at the bottom of the urban economic pyramid.[22] The overwhelming number of patients lived in or near Dublin at the time of their delivery. Fewer than 2 percent of them came from other parts of Ireland, and none at all were from abroad. The Rotunda was the only maternity in Dublin on the north bank of the Liffey and this became its primary catchment area. It also drew some 14 percent of its patients from a wretched slum which lay astride the river in the heart of the city.[23] But although the other civic maternity hospitals were located south of the Liffey, some 20 percent of the Rotunda's population also crossed the river in search of care. The remaining patients lived in the city's suburbs or elsewhere in County Dublin.

Over time the character of the hospital's patient population changed in some respects. In occupational terms these changes reflected broader ones occurring in the urban economy at large. The number of women from unskilled and semiskilled laboring backgrounds as well as petty commerce, clerical work, and food handling increased, while those from skilled laboring and the domestic services fell. The proportion of Roman Catholics rose while that of Protestants declined, again a change which mirrored wider urban population trends. At the same time, the proportion of single patients rose slightly and that of married women fell. Perhaps most significant of all, the numbers of patients who lived in the urban poverty core declined, as did those from South Dublin. With passing years the hospital drew more heavily from North Dublin as well as the city's suburbs and neighboring countryside.

Weight at birth

The results of the multiple regression analysis of the Dublin birth weight data are summarized in table 4.2.[24] While broadly consistent with the findings revealed in the other urban samples, they differ in some important respects. As elsewhere, male sex, birth order, and maternal age were related to differences in neonatal weight: maleness, higher parity, and increasing age all conferred advantage. Similarly, serious maternal illness during pregnancy affected fetal growth adversely, reducing newborn weight by 432.6 grams. But unlike the case in other cities, occupational variables in Dublin had no influence upon weight at birth. Whatever differences in well-being may have existed among men of varying occupational ranks, their newborn infants, and thus their wives, did not reflect them.

At first glance the absence of an occupational effect on birth weight is somewhat puzzling. Two explanations likely account for this fact. The first is that these patients formed a relatively homogeneous population, for they came predominantly from the lower ranks of the urban working class. Only a tiny proportion enjoyed significant economic advantages, and the finding in this instance may merely reflect the small number of such cases included in the sample. Furthermore, the occupations were those of the women's husbands rather than those of the women themselves. At this point we know nothing about the distribution of nutritional benefits within Irish working-class families. But it is hard to imagine that they would have differed much from those observed elsewhere in the prewar United Kingdom, where women commonly

TABLE 4.2   Dublin birth weight sample multiple regression analysis

Variable	Coefficient (g)	t
Biological		
Male child	117.5	10.352
Birth order	14.8	5.518
Mother's age	5.9	4.407
Medical		
Mother ill at delivery	−432.6	−5.204
Social and economic		
Birth in winter	−32.8	−2.469
Resided in South Dublin	−39.0	−2.107
Resided in North Dublin	−44.8	−2.919
Resided in Dublin poor core	−67.5	−3.300
Year of birth 1900 to 1913	102.4	7.091
Year of birth 1914 to 1920	64.7	3.432
Year of birth 1921 to 1930	94.6	5.704
(Constant)	3033.2	84.101

$N = 8310$; adjusted $R^2 = .043$; standard error $= 517.0$.

stinted themselves and favored their husbands when food was in short supply.[25]

Two other variables, however, were linked with differences in neonatal weight. Women who lived in North and South Dublin and the city's poverty-stricken core bore lighter infants—by 44.8, 39.0, and 67.5 grams, respectively—than did those who lived elsewhere. In this case the relationship between place of residence and newborn weight was not in itself causal; rather, lower birth weight reflected the greater poverty of those who lived in the city's center. At the same time, birth weight exhibited a strong association with the business cycle.[26] When compared with children born before 1900, newborns delivered between the turn of the century and the eve of World War I enjoyed a 102.4-gram advantage. Those born during the war and immediate postwar years were not so favored, their edge being only 64.7 grams, but the children of the 1920s shared the same superiority, 94.6 grams. Part of the explanation for this improvement may lie in small changes in the composition of the hospital's patient population. The gradual fall in the number of patients from Dublin's poorest quarter brought fewer of the city's most dispossessed women to the hospital after the turn of the century, while the number of comparatively advantaged suburban patients grew. Yet this influence was contradicted by the concurrent increase in the proportion of women whose husbands had menial occupations and the slow increase in the proportion of Roman Catholic patients. On balance, then, distributional changes in the character of the hospital's patients offset one another. The higher birth weight means occurring after the turn of the twentieth century seem evidence of a significant increase in living standards among the poor women of Dublin.

Analysis of the proportion of low birth weight infants reinforces this conclusion. During the first few years for which data is available, the proportion of infants weighing under 2500 grams ranged below 8 percent. Between 1874 and 1899, however, it normally fluctuated between 8 and 12 percent, the annual mean being 9.8 percent (see fig. 4.1). From 1900 to 1930, however, the average declined to earlier levels, the annual mean being 6.8 percent. In other words, the proportion of low birth weight children fell by almost a third after the turn of the century, another sign of improved nutrition and rising living standards among the Dublin poor in the early decades of the twentieth century.

The hospital stillbirth rate, another possible index of maternal well-being, is rather more ambiguous. Throughout the entire period, the three-year running average of still- and aborted births ranged between 6 and 10 percent of all deliveries (see fig. 4.2). No clear long-term trend can be identified, and short-term patterns of change seem unrelated to economic cycles. The gradual rise in stillbirths from the latter years of World War I until the eve of the Great Depression may have reflected the growing proportion of patients who suffered from pregnancy complications, though the records are unfortunately

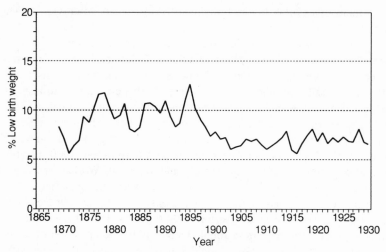

Fig. 4.1   Dublin, 1869–1930: percentage low birth weight (3-year running average)

mute on this point. But given the changes in medical practice occurring in leading maternity hospitals during these years, it seems likely that the rising stillbirth trend at this time was an indication of changing hospital functions rather than a sign of declining living standards.

Birth length

Multiple regression analysis was also performed on the lengths of some of the Dublin newborns. Unfortunately, the routine collection of information on length did not begin until 1900 and therefore we can examine only a thirty-year time span. Nonetheless, the results are instructive (see table 4.3) and they reinforce some of the conclusions drawn from the birth weight analysis.

As was true of weight at birth, newborn length was affected by biological factors. Male children were somewhat longer than female (0.58 centimeter), and maternal age also had a slight influence on length. Unlike the case in Edinburgh, however, maternal illness seems not to have influenced infant length. Nor, with one exception, did the social and economic variables, including occupation and season of birth. The one exception was place of residence. Compared to those who lived in Dublin's suburbs, city women bore slightly stunted children. Mothers who lived in the city's bleakest slums delivered the shortest babies of all, but all Dublin mothers revealed some measure of disadvantage. In addition, birth length varied somewhat with year of birth. Without data from the nineteenth century to serve as a basis of comparison our analysis is somewhat handicapped. But when compared to children born between 1900 and 1913, those delivered during the war and immediate post-

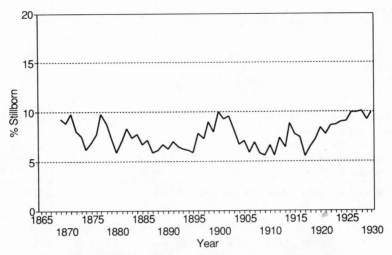

Fig. 4.2   Dublin, 1869–1930: percentage stillborn (3-year running average)

war years were somewhat shorter (0.39 centimeter), while those born in the twenties were not significantly different. Thus the regression on length supports the principal conclusions drawn from that on weight: urban women delivered smaller infants than those from the suburbs, and business cycles were associated with the size of the children they bore. (In the latter instance, the years from 1914 to 1920 seem ones of relative disadvantage, but only when compared to those immediately before and after.)

No quantitative measures of the Irish business cycle exist for the period considered here, making it impossible to ascertain if a statistical relationship might exist between patterns of urban economic growth and mean birth weight. As a result, we must compare annual birth weight means with Mary Daly's descriptive account of economic fluctuations in Dublin. According to Daly, Dublin experienced an economic boom between 1869 and 1873. Thereafter it passed through a deepening recession which persisted, with minor interruptions, until the late 1880s. The 1890s brought a decade of qualified prosperity which persisted into the early twentieth century. From the middle of the first decade of the new century until the eve of the war, however, a growing sense of economic crisis beset the city.[27]

In broad terms, the birth weight mean conformed to the general cycles which Daly has outlined (see fig. 4.3).[28] During the earliest years of the study it fluctuated above 3250 grams. But it fell below that level after 1873 and, with few exceptions, remained there until recovery commenced in 1890. Toward the end of the decade, the mean rose above 3300 grams and the trend continued upward to annual peaks above 3400 grams before declining sharply

TABLE 4.3   Dublin birth length sample multiple regression analysis

Variable	Coefficient (cm)	t
Biological		
Male child	0.58	7.420
Mother's age	0.03	4.436
Social and economic		
Year of birth 1914 to 1920	−0.39	−4.220
Resided in South Dublin	−0.30	−2.354
Resided in North Dublin	−0.30	−3.162
Resided in Dublin poor core	−0.44	−2.889
(Constant)	48.77	223.976

N = 4242; adjusted R^2 = .023; standard error = 2.55.

on the eve of the war. Thus far, it would seem, the birth weight mean followed the known contours of the Dublin business cycle. Unfortunately, rather less is known about the succeeding period. During the war, the Irish "troubles," and their immediate aftermath, mean birth weight tended to move between 3300 and 3350 grams before rising slightly by the end of the 1920s. These changes seem broadly consistent with the general economic decline in wartime Dublin, possibly the only major city in the United Kingdom which did not profit much from the war economy.[29] However, modest economic improvement did occur in the 1920s, more through the resumption of peace than through any substantial growth.

In order to explore this relationship further, linear regression analysis was

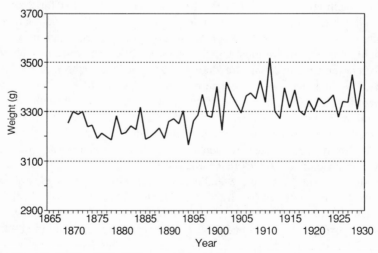

Fig. 4.3   Dublin, 1869–1930: mean birth weight

performed on the annual birth weight mean (as the dependent variable) and the index of British real wages calculated by A. L. Bowley in the later 1930s.[30] Although the reliability of the Bowley index has come into question, it remains a widely used general measure of prices and incomes throughout the British Isles.[31] It masks a good deal of local variation, a serious analytic problem when we consider the distinctiveness of the Irish economy before independence and, perhaps even more so, afterwards. Nevertheless, the high level of economic integration between Ireland and Great Britain suggests that the Bowley index may have some validity for Ireland, too. The regression suggests that 30 percent of the annual variation in mean birth weight can be explained by changes in real wages.[32] Given the uncertainty just noted, it would be wrong to place a great deal of weight on this finding. But it, too, indicates a relationship between mean weight at birth and general economic circumstances.

Nutrition and the disease environment

The qualitative evidence on the state of nutrition in Dublin is scanty and merely suggestive. Few attempts were made to survey Irish diets before the early twentieth century, although observers at that time believed that Irish nutrition had changed for the worse in the half-century after the famine: the older staples of potatoes, oatmeal, and milk had given way to bread, tea, and sugar.[33] In 1904 T. J. Stafford examined the living standards of the Dublin working class in a study patterned on the work of Seebohm Rowntree in York. The survey included the incomes and consumption patterns of twenty-one families whom Stafford considered typical, and it reflected a growing scientific interest in the nutritional value of basic foods. Stafford noted that food costs absorbed almost two-thirds of the family budget, that most families could not afford an adequate standard of nutrition, and that protein deficiency was a serious nutritional problem.[34] Four years later Charles Cameron, Dublin's medical officer of health, reported similar results from another small study of urban working-class diets. He indicated that bread and tea were staples, supplemented largely with condensed skim milk, potatoes, and cabbage. Meat, when available, generally was reserved for the breadwinner of the family.[35]

A further survey undertaken on the eve of World War I offered slightly more optimistic findings, suggesting that meat and fish were found on working-class tables somewhat more often than Stafford and Cameron had observed. Nevertheless, the diet of Dublin's laboring people remained seriously deficient. Some 60 percent of all protein consumed came from bread, while 80 percent of carbohydrate came from bread and sugar. Moreover, the energy values of standard diets were inadequate for working-class families. The sharp rise in food prices after the outbreak of war merely exacerbated an already serious nutritional problem.[36]

Nor did these circumstances change dramatically after the war. In 1939, a study of diets among sixty Rotunda patients attending a prenatal clinic revealed that fewer than 10 percent of women consumed adequate amounts of protein and calories and that the entire sample population was anemic.[37] A survey of the patients' family budgets indicated that, on average, money spent on food was only half the expenditure which the Committee on Nutrition of the British Medical Association considered necessary for an adequate diet. Perhaps nutritional levels had improved during the 1920s only to deteriorate during the depression. Perhaps they remained at their pre–World War I level throughout the interwar years. Without more information on food consumption patterns between 1915 and 1939 we cannot be certain. But the indications are that malnutrition remained widespread amongst the poor women of Dublin until at least the 1940s.

The historians of Irish nutrition L. A. Clarkson and E. M. Crawford confirm these general impressions. They note that the diet of laboring people deteriorated badly in the half-century following the famine. Like the population elsewhere in the United Kingdom, the Irish ate increasing quantities of sugars and fats, and declining amounts of complex carbohydrates. They also took in less iron and calcium over time. Clarkson and Crawford calculate that the caloric value of the Irish laborer's diet fell by perhaps 10 percent during this period.[38] Seemingly, the contributions made by new foods to the energy value of Irish working-class diets did not offset the deficits resulting from the abandonment of traditional food habits.

The possibility exists, in Dublin as elsewhere, that the disease environment independently influenced the birth weight trend. Unfortunately, however, the available sources do not permit calculation of the pathological statistic for Dublin—female age-specific tuberculosis mortality rates—which we have used elsewhere. For this reason the birth weight trend was regressed against the general Dublin tuberculosis mortality rate up to 1920. Again, no statistically significant results were obtained, suggesting that here, too, weight at birth was not directly influenced by the epidemiological history of the city during these years.

But if tuberculosis was not associated with neonatal weight in a measurable way, the course of the disease in Ireland still casts light on the social and economic context of the data on newborn size. The Irish tuberculosis mortality rate was considerably lower than that of England and Scotland in 1850. But while the English and Scottish rates declined from that point onward the Irish rate rose somewhat, reaching its peak in the later 1890s. From that point onward it too declined, but it remained consistently above British rates until the depression.[39] Rates in Dublin were somewhat higher than those for Ireland as a whole, though they followed much the same course.[40] Environmental factors play an important part in the spread of tuberculosis by influencing both the chance of exposure to infection and the individual's resistance to infection. Poverty, malnutrition, crowded housing, and low standards of hygiene all are conducive to tuberculosis infection.[41] Thus the persistence of comparatively high rates of tuberculosis in Ireland generally, and Dublin specifically, is a further sign of poor nutrition and low standards of living, one which reinforces the findings offered by the evidence on size at birth.

The Dublin data thus reveal a strong relationship between the size of newborns and the course of economic activity in the city. When the urban economy was in general decline, mean birth weight was comparatively low and low birth weight rates relatively high; when economic improvement occurred, however, birth weight means rose somewhat. The length of newborns, although gathered over a shorter span of time, also was sensitive to economic cycles. As elsewhere, in Dublin there were important social structural differences in newborn size, although these were most evident in residential patterns rather than occupational categories. Given the close relationship demonstrated elsewhere between standards of nutrition and neonatal size, the Dublin sample provides compelling evidence of improvements in the quality of the diet of the Dublin poor after the turn of the twentieth century. Admittedly, it offers us no reason to question the nutritional surveys of the period, which underscored the poor quality of working-class Dubliners' daily fare. But it does indicate that the poor women of Dublin were rather better nourished after 1900 than their forebears had been since the dark days of the famine.

5

BOSTON, 1872–1900

Population and economy

During the late nineteenth century, Boston was the fourth largest urban center in the United States, as well as by far the most populous city in New England. It had experienced sustained high population growth rates since at least the 1840s, ranging from 30 to 45 percent each decade through the 1870s, and these levels fell only slightly toward the end of the century. Boston's suburbs grew rapidly during these years as well, swelling the metropolitan population to more than double that of the city proper. Close to half a million souls lived in greater Boston in 1870; by the turn of the century it was home to more than 1.3 million.

Here as elsewhere in the contemporary western world, birth and death rates were in decline during these years, births exceeding deaths by between four and ten per thousand annually. Net migration, however, made by far the larger contribution to urban population increase. Eighty-seven percent of growth during the 1870s derived from the excess of immigration over emigration, and while its relative contribution diminished thereafter, migration still accounted for 60 percent of urban growth during the century's last decade. Late nineteenth-century Boston was the prototype of a New-World city, rapidly expanding and teeming with a diverse population. Half were native to Massachusetts, one-third were foreign born (principally in Ireland and Atlantic Canada), and the remainder came from elsewhere in the republic.[1]

Of the five cities considered in this study, Boston was economically by far the most favored. As one of the principal urban places in the nation, it enjoyed the very tangible benefits of America's high rates of economic growth during the post–Civil War era. By 1870 the republic was certainly among the wealthiest of the advanced industrial nations, and the three decades between 1870 and 1900 established its supremacy. These were years of rapid expansion, the American net national product more than trebling during the period.[2] According to the economic historians David and Solar, the cost of living for unskilled laborers, the most disadvantaged group of wage earners in America, fell steadily by one-third in real terms from 1870 to 1900.[3] Even the business cycle had only a minor effect on rates of change in living costs at this time. Boston itself was located in a prosperous corner of the United States, where per capita incomes stood well above the national average.[4] Thus, its citizens enjoyed the blessings of late nineteenth-century American economic growth in generous measure.

During the early part of the century, the economy of the city had rested largely on mercantile foundations. As the major port in New England, Boston had long been a center of shipping, warehousing, and the wholesale trades. After the mid-1830s it also became a railway center of regional importance, confirming its dominant position in the New England economy.[5] Throughout the first half of the century, production remained subordinate to commerce in urban economic life. During the 1840s and 1850s, however, machine fabrication and the factory system began to replace older patterns of craft manufacturing, and by the 1860s Boston had become one of the leading manufacturing cities in America.[6] In the process, the urban economy came to share some important characteristics common to other industrializing urban places, particularly its concentration on the production of consumer goods.

The manufacture of ready-made clothing was the leading industry of the city during the 1850s and 1860s. In Boston, unlike other American cities, clothes were made on a factory basis, most workshops employing between twenty and one-hundred workers. But clothing manufacturing fell off sharply in the city during the final two decades of the century, declining over 50 percent by value in the 1880s alone. Where once its production had stood second only to New York's, by 1900 Boston ranked fifth among American cities in the garment trades. As the industry declined it was also reorganized: the factory system collapsed to be replaced by contract labor and sweatshop production. By the early 1890s almost 90 percent of work in the Boston clothing trades was done on contract, most of it in a household setting and only half performed in the city and its environs, the remainder having been transferred to Maine, New York, or rural New England.[7] Yet, despite their decline, the clothing trades remained a dominant sector of the urban manufacturing economy until after 1900.

Most of the other major industries in the city and suburbs, for example sugar refining, brewing, printing and publishing, furniture and musical instrument manufacturing, and metal founding, also produced consumer goods.[8] As in other industrializing nineteenth-century cities, factory and small-shop forms of production persisted side by side. In 1877, three-fifths of the industrial labor force worked in establishments employing twenty workers or more, but these factories constituted only 10 percent of all manufacturing units. The remaining two-fifths of production workers were dispersed in small, traditional workshops.[9] Thus, as Boston's industrial economy expanded and diversified, the factory system did not dominate urban society as it often did in cities where heavy industries prevailed. Some evidence suggests, in fact, that production became more small scale and decentralized toward the end of the century. According to the historical geographer David Ward, the average number of workers per establishment in Boston in 1900 was half of what it had been some forty years before.[10]

Massachusetts was well integrated into the national economy in most respects, and therefore Boston shared the nation's broad economic cycles during the late nineteenth century. It experienced a major depression between 1873 and 1879 and a second, somewhat less severe one from 1882 to 1885, followed by intermittent, short-term recessions between 1893 and the century's end.[11] Locally, the trades each had their own particular seasonal cycles. The different garment trades, for example, were busiest at various times during the fall, winter, and spring, while the summer months were generally slack.[12]

In 1883 an investigation into the social, economic, and moral condition of working women in Boston noted the great expansion of female wage labor which had occurred during the rise of modern industry in the city.[13] Table 5.1 reveals that these opportunities continued to broaden over the final three decades of the century. The number of employed women almost trebled during this period, and their share of the labor force grew significantly as well. Furthermore, although women remained heavily concentrated in domestic service and the clothing trades, the changing urban economy created new work opportunities for them. Expansion in the commercial, bureaucratic, and public service sectors, in particular, opened many new doors for female workers, including women displaced from declining industries and the growing numbers of those in search of alternatives to household service. The 1883 inquiry revealed that, at best, most working women could expect slight financial reward for their labor.[14] But this did not deter their quest for a place in the labor market.

Hospitals, clinics, and patients

The Boston birth weight data span a shorter time interval than those examined for the four other cities in this study. Unlike the case in the other communities, they also come from three institutional sources rather than one: the New Eng-

Table 5.1   Boston: occupational categories of female workers, 1870–1900 (Percentage)

	1870	1880	1890	1900
Professional	6.3	6.0	6.0	6.8
Domestic & personal service	57.6	51.7	42.2	37.4
Clothing, textiles	27.4	26.0	23.5	18.2
Sales, clerical, office work	3.3	6.5	11.5	18.5
Other occupations	5.4	9.8	16.8	19.1
Total female work force	24,008	38,881	58,252	70,339
% Total employment female	24.2	26.1	28.4	28.0

Sources: United States, Census, 1870–1900; Wright, Working Girls of Boston.

land Hospital for Women and Children and the inpatient and outpatient services of the Boston Lying-in Hospital. The longest run of birth weight statistics was collected at the New England, a general hospital for women and children established in 1862 as an expression of the prevailing separatist tendencies in North American women's professional medical circles.[15] The patient records begin in 1872 when the hospital opened new quarters, including a maternity cottage set apart from the main building to minimize the dangers of puerperal fever. Founded in 1832, the Boston Lying-in had closed its doors for financial reasons between 1856 and 1872. The Lying-in also established an outpatient clinic in 1882. In the 1870s the two hospital inpatient services accommodated between 2 and 3 percent of all births in the city, the proportion rising to 5 percent at the turn of the century.[16] Meanwhile, the outpatient clinic's home birth service expanded rapidly within a short time of its founding. By 1900 it attended double the number of women admitted to both hospitals combined. Together the three institutions accounted for at least 15 percent of all civic births by the close of this period.[17]

The clinics were established in different parts of the city and, to a considerable extent, served different clienteles. In addition, each had its own criteria for accepting patients. As a result, the composition of each patient sample is distinctive. The New England Hospital occupied a wooded acreage in Roxbury on the southern edge of the city. Late nineteenth-century Roxbury was a working-class district with a growing industrial base; it offered expanding job opportunities to unskilled and semiskilled workers and attracted a continuous inflow of upwardly mobile immigrants.[18] The hospital drew its patients largely from among the working-class residents of the central and southern parts of the city, as well as the adjoining suburbs. According to one of its senior physicians, "the class of patients was . . . a much better one, and we have never had any number of the most undesirable cases, which inevitably gravitate to an institution located in the midst of a dense population."[19]

Hospital policies also screened the women admitted to the clinic. The hospital normally charged maternity patients twenty dollars, although the fee might be reduced or canceled altogether for needy cases. While this cost was considerably lower than the thirty to fifty dollars Boston physicians normally charged midwifery patients attended in their homes, it represented four weeks' pay for the average working woman and must therefore have deterred the very poor from seeking admission.[20] Hospital directors also judged prospective patients according to the stern moral calculus of middle-class sexual propriety. They extended charity only to married women and to those among the unmarried whom they deemed worthy: the pious and respectable. The hospital excluded prostitutes and refused unmarried women a second admission.[21] For the most part it served the poor, although according to its directors married women increasingly sought admission because it offered them better care and accommodation than they could enjoy in their homes, to say nothing of a brief respite from the many claims of family life.[22]

The Boston Lying-in Hospital was located in the heart of the West End, just north of Beacon Hill. Once a prosperous working-class community of native-born Americans, during the 1880s and 1890s it was transformed into a low-rent tenement district of foreigners overflowing the North End, Boston's archetypal immigrant slum.[23] A narrow fringe on the southern border of the district housed the service and clerical workers who catered to the wealthy residents of adjoining Beacon Hill and nearby Back Bay, or who labored in the shops and offices of the neighboring urban core. Much of the Lying-in Hospital's clientele thus came from the city's poorest tenement areas.

In theory, at least, the Lying-in also charged its patients a fee, twenty dollars for Boston residents, thirty for those who lived elsewhere.[24] The hospital also accepted a small number of private patients, who paid still higher fees in return for higher standards of privacy and care. But during the period examined here only 30 percent of those admitted paid any fee at all.[25] Whenever possible, the hospital recovered its costs from local overseers of the poor, a fact which placed something of a stigma on those who sought its charity. At least one woman, admitted as a free patient in 1881, paid her fee a month after giving birth in order to avoid being considered a public charge.[26] Nonetheless, fees seem not to have restricted entry to the Boston Lying-in, at least to the extent that they likely did at the New England Hospital.

Like the New England, the Lying-in also barred known prostitutes and even discharged them whey they had been admitted inadvertently.[27] Policy also forbade entry to unmarried women bearing a second or subsequent illegitimate child, but although the hospital professed to scrutinize all applicants carefully, from time to time such patients crop up in clinical records. The hospital reported that its clients fell into two broad categories, "a large and very respectable class, with means sufficient to meet comfortably all the ordinary expenses of living, to whom the interruption and expense of child-bearing is a very serious matter" and "that class whom maternity makes outcasts."[28] In many instances women whom the hospital turned away could be attended free in their own homes by its outpatient service; otherwise they were to be provided for by civic or state funds.

The Boston Lying-in's outpatient service was housed in a single room in the South Boston district, a major industrial suburb with a large immigrant population. Home to much of the city's heavy industry, and close to major railway terminals and docks, South Boston was principally a community of teamsters, factory hands, and general laborers.[29] Although the clinic served the neighborhood in which it was located, because it offered its services to women in their own homes its patients were scattered throughout the city, especially in the tenement districts of the urban core. Unlike both inpatient services, the outpatient clinic charged no fees and drew no moral distinctions among the women whom it served.[30] As a result it was by far the most accessible of Boston's maternity services. The only significant requirement was that a patient have a home in which she could deliver her child. The attendants themselves were Harvard medical students, each assisted by a nurse, who could call on an obstetrician when one was required.[31]

All three clinics, then, shared the nineteenth-century maternity hospital's vocation: they served the needs of poor, vulnerable, and often unmarried women. But because of their varied locations and different admission criteria, their patients also differed from one another in some important respects. The chief distinguishing feature of the New England Hospital's obstetric patients was their residential location. Only 6 percent lived in the city's poorest districts, the North and West ends; the great majority resided elsewhere in Boston or its suburbs. The Lying-in Hospital drew more heavily on its immediate neighborhood, although it also attracted many patients from throughout the metropolitan area. However, it had a much higher proportion of unmarried patients, (43 percent as opposed to 30 percent at the New England and 2 percent at the outpatient clinic), a much higher proportion of mothers in their teens (16 percent as compared with 12 percent and 5 percent, respectively) and a notably high proportion of first births (65 percent, 59 percent, and 19 percent). The outpatients, in contrast, were drawn largely from the tenement zones, virtually all of them were married, and the great majority had had at least one previous child. And unlike those of the Lying-in, where nine patients in ten were American, British, or Canadian born, over half of those in the outpatient service were from continental Europe. One final important difference should be noted here as well. Neither the New England nor the outpatient service accommodated a significant number of blacks. Virtually all black women who sought hospital care for delivery did so at the Boston Lying-in.

Weight at birth

Because of differences in the information available in the clinical records, each institution has been analyzed separately here. In addition, because the information available for black patients was more limited than that for whites and because blacks formed a distinct social and gene pool segment of the city's population, they were treated separately here. Thus, the Boston birth weight analysis consists of four parts, one for the samples of white women and newborns in each of the clinics and one for all black mothers and infants.

Figure 5.1 records the annual birth weight means of these four populations. That of the New England Hospital moved between 3500 and 3600 grams in most years between the early 1870s and the mid-1890s, before dropping somewhat toward the end of the century. The weights of children born under the care of the Boston Lying-in's outpatient service fluctuated in the neighborhood of 3500 grams throughout the entire period. At the Lying-in Hospital the mean usually moved above 3300 grams with a slight upward trend over time. Average birth weight among blacks (who numbered fewer than 400 for the entire period) was considerably lower—a bit over 3100 grams, again with an upward trend. These means accord generally with the few accounts of American birth weights published during the mid-nineteenth century.[32]

Table 5.2 summarizes the results of the multiple regression analysis performed on the New England Hospital patient sample. Here, as elsewhere, ascending birth order, higher age categories, and male sex were positively— and serious maternal illness was negatively—correlated with birth weight differentials. Skilled occupational status was the only socioeconomic variable

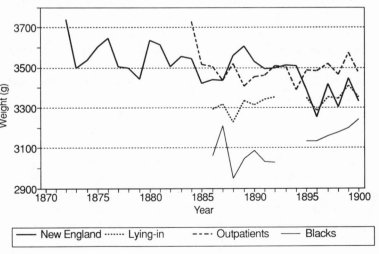

Fig. 5.1   Boston, 1872–1900: mean birth weight

associated with superior birth weight performance (239.7 grams), although in this instance the number of cases was small and the results should be read accordingly. The regression also reveals a curious temporal trend in mean birth weight during the twenty-eight years spanned by the sample.[33] During the final years of the century, a period of intermittent recession, newborns suffered a disadvantage of 154.1 grams when compared to those born during the previous two decades. Indeed, children born at the New England during the mid and late 1890s weighed significantly less than those delivered during the much more serious depression some twenty years earlier. This, however, was the only business cycle associated with significant variation in mean birth weight among newborns at the New England.

Analysis of the inpatient clinic's newborn weights (see table 5.3) once more confirms the salience of birth order, maleness, and perhaps age. It reveals the advantage of Irish-born mothers (95.6 grams), thus suggesting an ethnic differential in neonatal weight. It also demonstrates the disadvantage of women who lived in Boston's slums (42.0 grams), although in this instance the finding is less certain. The outpatient analysis (table 5.4) also reveals the anticipated contributions of infant sex, birth order, age, and maternal illness to birth weight outcomes. It, too, indicates an advantage for Irish-born women (105.1 grams) and a similar one for women who lived in South Boston (93.6 grams). Neither the inpatient nor the outpatient data reveal a time trend, although in both instances the relevant time intervals are somewhat shorter than that for the New England hospital.

Table 5.5 summarizes the results of the regression on the black population. In this instance the numbers of cases and variables were small, there being

Table 5.2   New England Hospital birth weight multiple regression analysis

Variable	Coefficient (g)	t
Biological		
Male child	106.8	4.921
Birth order	55.9	7.742
Mother's age 20 to 34	131.9	3.745
Mother's age 35 or more	115.7	2.140
Medical		
Mother ill at delivery	−124.3[a]	−1.932
Social and economic		
Skilled occupation	239.7	2.907
Year of birth 1893 to 1900	−154.1	−6.788
(Constant)	3261.6	90.852

N = 2716; adjusted R^2 = .057; standard error = 565.3.

[a]Between a critical level of .05 and .06.

Table 5.3   Boston Lying-in Hospital birth weight multiple regression analysis

Variable	Coefficient (g)	t
Biological		
Male child	94.1	4.395
Birth order	47.4	6.371
Mother's age 35 or more	95.7[a]	1.768
Mother's birthplace Ireland	95.6	3.618
Social and economic		
Resided in North End or East		
Boston	−42.0[a]	−1.764
(Constant)	3185.0	149.740

$N = 2256$; adjusted $R^2 = .041$; standard error $= 513.7$.
[a]Between a critical level of .07 and .08.

Table 5.4   Boston Lying-in Outpatient Clinic birth weight multiple regression analysis

Variable	Coefficient (g)	t
Biological		
Male child	144.2	7.436
Birth order	25.4	5.484
Mother's age 20 to 34	113.2	2.502
Mother's age 35 or more	142.3	2.498
Mother's birthplace Ireland	105.1	3.947
Medical		
Mother ill at delivery	−199.5	−4.179
Social and economic		
Resided in South Boston	93.6	2.840
(Constant)	3179.8	71.073

$N = 3163$; adjusted $R^2 = .050$; standard error $= 544.2$.

very little social information available on these patients. Perhaps because of the small sample size, only two variables reveal statistically significant birth weight differentials. Older mothers delivered very much heavier infants (364.9 grams), although the extent of this advantage must be questioned given that only 4 percent of black mothers were aged thirty-five or more. When compared with the period from 1886 to 1892, children born during the last eight years of the century weighed somewhat more as well (111.6 grams). On the whole, multiple regression analysis of the black patient data yielded disappointingly meager results. But as we will see, comparison of birth weight means among the four populations is somewhat more informative.

Taken together, the multiple regression analyses of the four Boston hospital populations reveal the well-known association between newborn weight and three biological variables: newborn sex, birth order, and maternal age. A fourth biological factor, ethnic gene pool influences, may also have contributed to birth weight outcomes, at least in the case of Irish-born women.

As to the relationship between socioeconomic factors and newborn weight, the analysis offers us no clear insights, partly because of missing information and partly because of inconsistencies among the four regressions. With one minor exception, the occupational results show no differential association with weight at birth, a negative finding which seems to imply that the poor women of Boston enjoyed broadly similar levels of well-being whatever their means of support. One regression suggests a disadvantage among North End residents while another indicates that women living in South Boston enjoyed some advantage. But while congruent with our understanding of the character of both districts, these differences may well have been more apparent than real, for the individual regressions show no consistency in their analysis of residential patterns. In any event, place of residence itself has no causal influence on birth weight; it is merely an indicator of social and economic status.

A further ambiguity arises from the fact that two clinical samples reveal clear time trends while two do not, and the two evident trends move in opposite directions. Given the small number of cases in the sample, the trend identified among black women can perhaps be discounted. That found in the New England Hospital patient sample is more difficult to explain. It seems unrelated to changes within the sample population, for the hospital drew its patients from the same segment of urban society throughout the entire period. Nor can it be accounted for by any of the minor distributional changes which occurred in most of the variables over time. In other words, it reflected circumstances outside the hospital itself. The fact that similar time trends were not evident in the remaining samples suggests two possible explanations. The New England may have drawn on a subset of Boston's poor female population which suffered unique disadvantages toward the end of the nineteenth century, a theory which seems improbable given the lack of supporting evidence. Or,

Table 5.5   Boston blacks birth weight multiple regression analysis

Variable	Coefficient (g)	t
Biological		
Mother's age 35 or more	364.9	2.678
Social and economic		
Year of birth 1893 to 1900	111.6	1.960
(Constant)	3038.3	65.795

$N = 339$; adjusted $R^2 = 0.27$; standard error = 499.1.

Table 5.6   Boston birth weight multiple regression analysis

Variable	Coefficient (g)	t
Biological		
Male child	115.7	9.784
Mother's age	12.0	10.636
Mother black	−217.3	−3.548
Social and economic		
Mother married	33.9	2.186
Resided in North End or East Boston	−35.9	−2.789
Boston Lying-in inpatient	−125.3	−8.814
(Constant)	3312.6	45.114

Note: This analysis was performed with data from the three clinics and includes all black patients.

$N = 8398$; adjusted $R^2 = .052$; standard error $= 541.8$.

as seems more likely, the Boston Lying-in's two clinics may more accurately have reflected the circumstances of Boston's poor mothers during these years.

A final multiple regression, performed on the combined samples, reveals three further features of the Boston birth weights (table 5.6).[34] First, the children of married women enjoyed a slight advantage (33.9 grams) over those of single mothers, a finding noted in other urban samples in this study but not apparent in the analyses of the individual Boston clinics. On balance, married patients likely enjoyed somewhat more secure livelihoods than did single pregnant women who, at least when employed in domestic service, often lost their jobs when their illicit pregnancies became known.

Second (and rather more important), the infants borne by black women were substantially lighter than those of white women; the average difference was 217.3 grams, between 6 and 7 percent less than the mean weight of newborn whites. Given the very limited information about black patients in the clinical records, the explanation for this difference cannot be precise. But part of it surely lies in the fact that, as the historian Elizabeth Pleck has noted, the blacks of Boston were a small and deeply impoverished minority.[35] They stood on the bottom rung of the urban social ladder, virtually all of them denied those prospects for economic security and advancement which most whites considered the promise of American life. The low birth weight means of Boston's black infants reflected the low nutritional and living standards in the urban black community. Some modern birth weight inquiries also indicate that, on average, black newborns are lighter than whites even when social and economic factors are held constant. They conclude that this difference is the result of patterns of fetal development intrinsic to each race. However, other authorities hold that the theory of genetically based racial differences in newborn weight has yet to be proved.[36] The dispute can scarcely be resolved here.

But the possibility remains that both genetic and socioeconomic influences may have lowered the newborn weights of infant Boston blacks.

Third, the average weight of white infants born in the Boston Lying-in was significantly lower (by 125.3 grams) than that of newborns delivered in the New England Hospital and the outpatient service. The Lying-in inpatient clinic served a rather different clientele than did the other maternities. Close to the tenement district and the urban core, it was the most accessible obstetric service for many of Boston's poorest women. In addition, because the Lying-in charged fees much less systematically than did the New England, its more open admission policies brought it a poorer, more vulnerable clientele. Like all nineteenth-century maternity hospitals, it also served as a temporary refuge for homeless women both before and after their delivery (though in this respect it differed little from the New England). While the hospital discouraged early admissions, it sometimes accommodated women several weeks before their due dates if room was available.[37] And even when it did not, patients normally were hospitalized for a considerable period after their delivery. During the 1880s and 1890s the average length of stay for patients was more than two weeks, a decline from even longer durations during the 1870s.[38] Thus, because it served as a haven for women in need of shelter, the Lying-in also attracted some of the most impoverished of Boston's maternity cases.

Figure 5.2 charts the low birth weight curve for the three primary patient samples. (The number of black patients was too small to calculate a reliable annual trend.) The year-to-year variation was wide among the New England's patients during the 1870s, largely because of the small numbers of patients. But over the rest of the century the annual proportion of low-weight births within the three samples usually ranged between 4 and 8 percent. The mean proportion of low-weight live births was as follows: New England Hospital, 6.5 percent; Boston Lying-in inpatients, 6.9 percent; outpatients, 4.7 percent. (The proportion of low birth weight infants among blacks, however, was rather higher—12.3 percent.) The trend moved upward for patients at both the Boston Lying-in and the New England, while it sloped downward for those accommodated by the outpatient service. The differences among the three clinics are consistent with the distinctive characters of each institution. The superior performance of the outpatient service, in particular, was due in large part to the preponderance of older, married, multiparous women—who had a much lower propensity to deliver small for dates infants—among its clientele. Rather more important, however, is the fact that the proportion of low birth weight infants in all three services was comparable to that found in the most advanced of late twentieth-century societies. They offer no evidence of nutritional deprivation among the poor white women of Boston, although the same is not true of blacks.

The trends in the proportion of stillborn infants delivered in each clinic,

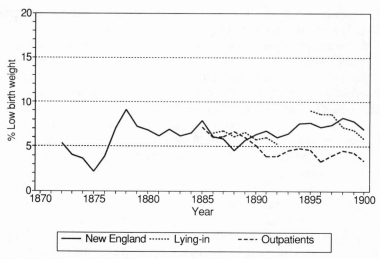

Fig. 5.2   Boston, 1872–1900: percentage low birth weight (3-year running average)

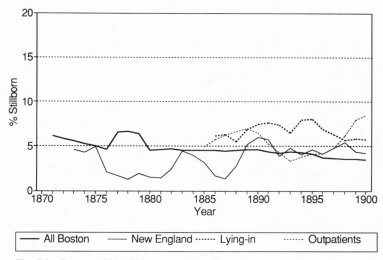

Fig. 5.3   Boston, 1872–1900: percentage stillborn (3 year running average)

another measure of maternal welfare, are noted in figure 5.3. In this case they are plotted against the annual stillbirth rate for all Boston. The trends rose in the New England and outpatient samples, and fell among the Lying-in inpatients as well as the general population. The explanation for these tendencies is far from clear, for the clinical records offer virtually no insight into the complex origins of *in utero* death. The one obvious fact is that, by the 1890s, all three clinics had stillbirth rates at or above the urban average, a sign that. these institutions probably accommodated a disproportionate number of women with problematic pregnancies and deliveries. This circumstance reflected the social and economic condition of the patients themselves, coming as they did from the most disadvantaged strata of urban society. It was not a sign that, because of their superior facilities and services, the clinics were attracting increasing numbers of patients with obstetric difficulties. The women of Boston did not demonstrate much faith in the presumed advantages of scientific obstetrics and hospital childbirth until well into the twentieth century.

In an attempt to explore further the relationship between birth weight and other indices of American economic growth, linear regression analysis was performed on the annual birth weight mean of each hospital (the dependent variable) and indices of economic performance reported by David and Solar.[39] The indices were measures of prices, wages, and living costs at the national level and therefore do not apply specifically to Massachusetts, let alone Boston. But given the advanced position of Massachusetts in the American economy, they serve as acceptable substitutes for unavailable local indices.

In the case of the Lying-in inpatients and the black sample, a relationship was detected between annual birth weight averages and David and Solar's American cost of living index.[40] The regressions suggest that in the first instance 28 percent, and in the second 35 percent, of the annual variation in mean birth weight may be attributed to changing living costs. Generally speaking, as the cost of living fell during the later 1880s and 1890s, the average weights of newborns delivered in this hospital rose. No statistically significant relationship could be detected, however, between the annual birth weight means of the New England Hospital or the outpatient clinic and national economic trends. Linear regression analysis thus suggests a relationship between declining living costs and improved birth weight performance among the very poorest groups of Boston's maternity patients, though not among the ranks of the ordinary laboring poor.

Nutrition and the disease environment

In Boston, unlike Dublin, Edinburgh, and Vienna, the birth weight evidence offers relatively little insight into the relationship between nutrition and economic welfare among the city's female poor. No obvious pattern of difference in newborn weights can be detected among major occupational groups, and time trend analysis is also far from conclusive. The relationship between place of residence and hospital preference on one hand, and newborn weight on the other, is an index of general social-spatial segregation in the city much more than one of well-being. And while the much lower birth weight means among blacks are a sign of their relative deprivation, they only offer us insight into the bleak circumstances confronting an uniquely disadvantaged minority in nineteenth-century American life.

The absence of a strong statistical relationship between weight at birth and most of the nutritionally sensitive social and economic variables in the Boston data, however, is in itself revealing. It may well have been that the working-class women of Boston enjoyed broadly similar nutritional standards whatever their background and circumstances, blacks and the poorest of whites excepted. If this were true then late nineteenth-century Boston provided a greater abundance of food, and a more even distribution of its nutritional benefits, than did the European cities considered in this study.[41] The few contemporary studies of diet in nineteenth-century America bear out this conclusion. In 1895, W. O. Atwater, a chemist at Wesleyan University and one of the first scientific investigators of American food habits, published a summary of late nineteenth-century dietary inquiries conducted in America and abroad.[42] Most of the American studies which he noted were undertaken in Massachusetts, some in Boston, some in smaller industrial towns, all among laboring men and their families.

On the basis of his survey Atwater concluded that American working-class diets were superior to those in Europe, and he produced impressive statistical tables to prove that the caloric and nutritive values of the foods eaten by ordinary Americans were substantially higher than those found on other national tables. "Considering the body as a machine," he remarked, "the American workingman has a more strongly-built machine and more fuel to run it than has his European brother."[43] Atwater believed that if Americans suffered from nutritional troubles, they were largely the problems of abundance rather than those of dearth. He argued that they commonly purchased needlessly expensive and unnecessarily large quantities of food, which led to unhealthy overeating and unconscionable waste.[44] He also held that Americans ate too much fat and carbohydrate and too little protein.

The most recent historian of the American diet, Harvey Levenstein, supports Atwater's findings. He concludes that late nineteenth-century American workers were—in a happy turn of phrase—"committed carnivores."[45] According to Levenstein, the first survey of workers' living standards, conducted among 397 families in Massachusetts in 1874, revealed that over half ate fresh meat at least twice a day. More than 40 percent consumed pies, cakes, or other sweets at all three meals while another 20 percent ate them twice daily. Potatoes and cabbage apart, however, vegetables graced the American dinner table far less often. As to abundance, Levenstein refers us to the rich travel literature of the nineteenth century in which foreigners recorded their impressions of American life. "Virtually every foreign visitor who wrote about American eating habits expressed amazement, shock, and even disgust at the quantity of food consumed."[46] In this respect, as in so many others, the United States was the land of abundance. Most American workers, Levenstein tells us, believed that they dined better than their counterparts in any other country, and they were right.[47]

To explore the possibility that the disease environment influenced the birth weight trend, the annual birth weight mean of the four Boston samples was also regressed against the annual tuberculosis mortality rate between 1880 and 1900 for Boston women aged twenty to fifty-four. No pattern was detected, suggesting again that here, as elsewhere, the birth weight trend was not affected by the prevailing disease environment in the city.

By 1870 Boston's growth rate had already passed its peak, but the urban economy and population continued to grow dramatically for the next thirty years. The city and its region shared substantially in the great expansion of American wealth during the last third of the century. Working women also benefited from these developments, for while they made no dramatic wage gains during these decades, their economic opportunities widened considerably. Contemporary and retrospective accounts of late nineteenth-century American diets indicate that American workers were not only well-nourished but, if anything, fed to excess. The Boston birth weight data thus accord with the high levels of well-being characteristic of all but the poorest of women in the city. Even on the lower levels of the urban social structure, mean birth weight in late nineteenth-century Boston approached modern American levels, and low birth weight ratios were not appreciably higher than those of a hundred years later.

6

MONTREAL, 1851–1904

Population and economy

Montreal was much the smallest of the cities included in this study, at least during the mid-nineteenth century. Although the major population center in Britain's scattered North American colonies, it occupied a peripheral place in the urban network of the western world. Home to some 58,000 in 1851, its population more than quadrupled over the next half-century, until Montreal approached the size of Dublin and Edinburgh. By 1900 it had become the largest urban community in a new transcontinental nation—Canada—and the major economic center of the country. It had also assumed a somewhat larger role in the ranks of European and American cities.

Approximately half of its population growth during these years was generated internally through natural increase, sustained particularly by the well-known high fertility of its French Canadian population. Net migration accounted for another third and suburban annexation the remainder.[1] As the changing ethnic composition of the city reveals, both internal and international migration were important components of population growth. At mid-century, 54 percent of Montreal residents were of British origin while all but 1 percent of the rest were French. But by 1900 French Canadians constituted a clear majority of the civic population while those of British background formed but 37 percent of the total. Meanwhile, substantial European migration had established several large minorities in the city, notably of Germans and east European Jews.[2] The growth of the French-speaking community was particularly striking. In 1901 almost six times as many French lived in Montreal as had fifty years earlier; the English-speaking population had grown by only half as much.

Yet by itself the fact of population increase does not offer a full measure of the city's drawing power. In fact, some of this growth derived from forces which propelled newcomers to the city whatever its attractions. Most of Montreal's internal migrants came from rural communities in the St. Lawrence Valley, where overpopulation was gradually displacing men and women whose language and culture left them few other acceptable destinations within Quebec or Canada.[3] They formed part of the much larger emigration of French Canadians out of the St. Lawrence Valley, most of whom moved on to frontier regions within the province or across the border into the northern New England states. Despite its continued growth, mid and late nineteenth-century Montreal could not absorb more than a small part of Quebec's surplus rural population, and even then, one suspects, its cultural familiarity beckoned as many *Canadiens* as did its economic allure.

In 1850 Montreal was principally a commercial center with a modest craft manufacturing sector. Its internal markets were regional, confined almost entirely to Quebec and Ontario, whose economies rested largely on agriculture and resource extraction. By the later 1840s, however, the first stirrings of industrial manufacturing in the city could be sensed, and over the next half-century the growth and integration of Canadian markets provided new incentives for expanded local production. Montreal offered an abundant source of water power for heavy industrial projects and therefore attracted an array of grist mills, metal works, and engine foundries. The Grand Trunk Railway, the largest industrial enterprise in mid-Victorian Canada, established its machine shops in the city. In the consumer goods sector, clothing and footwear production developed quickly as well. Throughout the second half of the century, the industrial base of the urban economy broadened considerably. The manufacture of food and tobacco products, textiles, rubber wear, transportation equipment, paper goods, chemicals, printed and published materials, and electrical appliances all increased, although the garment trades retained their preeminence. By the 1890s Montreal accounted for one-third of all secondary manufacturing value added in Ontario and Quebec, the industrial heartland of Canada.[4]

Industrial employment in nineteenth-century Montreal was concentrated in manufacturing which produced consumer goods for the relatively small Canadian market, the clothing, tobacco, and footwear trades in particular. Together these industries accounted for a disproportionately small fraction of the value added per urban worker, one that declined substantially as the century progressed.[5] Piece work and the putting out system, traditional devices for reducing labor costs, were used extensively in the garment trades throughout this period and, to a lesser extent, in the boot and shoe trades before the introduction of machines. Thus, a large proportion of the Montreal work force labored in low-wage secondary manufacturing sectors.

In some respects the development of Montreal resembled that of nineteenth-century Boston. But Montreal could not duplicate the higher economic growth rates of the northeastern American city. Its region and nation lacked the far larger population base of the American republic, and despite government attempts to stimulate economic development industrialization and territorial growth in Canada lagged well behind the United States. From the 1850s onward Montreal's economy expanded gradually behind a wall of tariff protection; it served small, slowly growing, and often far flung regional and national markets.

For all its dependence upon internal markets, however, Montreal shared the broad business cycles of the international economy. Close trade and financial ties linked the Canadian and British economies, and the Canadian and American economies as well. In particular, the international financial crash of 1873 ushered in more than two decades of depression, and although it centered upon the agricultural sector the dominant role of farm products in the Canadian economy distributed its effects widely. The late nineteenth century was a period of modest economic expansion, slow population increase, and substantial out-migration for most parts of Canada, Montreal included.[6] Shorter business cycles and the pronounced seasonal economic fluctuations characteristic of Canadian cities also influenced incomes. Winter was invariably a time of reduced hours, lower wages, and higher unemployment for most Montreal workers regardless of their calling.[7]

Unfortunately, the available census information on women and work in nineteenth-century Montreal does not permit systematic comparisons over the full period considered here. Table 6.1 summarizes what is known. As it indicates, the major manufacturing industries in Montreal made extensive use of female labor. During the last three decades of the century, women constituted at least three-fourths of the labor force in the clothing industry, almost half of those employed in tobacco production, and a third or more of those who worked in the boot and shoe trades. One out of three adult women, and one girl in five aged ten to fifteen, were listed as wage earners in the censuses of 1871 and 1881.

But women's economic opportunities deteriorated badly thereafter. Female employment seems to have peaked in the early 1880s, and although the numbers of working women continued to grow, they constituted a sharply declining proportion of the work force toward the end of the century. By the mid-1890s the urban reformer Herbert Ames—the Seebohm Rowntree of Montreal—noted that in the city's working-class districts women made up only 20

Table 6.1   Montreal: occupational categories of female workers, 1871–1911 (Percentage)

	1871	1881	1911[a]
Professional	8.1	6.9	9.3
Domestic & personal service	33.5	33.0	32.6
Clothing, textiles	24.8	36.0	25.9
Boots, shoes	18.3	10.0	1.8
Food, drink, tobacco	5.1	6.2	4.0
Other manufacturing	10.3	7.9	9.1
Commercial	—	—	13.9
Other occupations	—	—	3.3
Total female work force	12,502	19,801	39,810
% Total employment female	32.8	37.7	21.6

Source: Canada, *Census of Canada,* 1871, 1881, 1911.

[a]Occupational categories for the 1911 census are not wholly consistent with those of earlier years.

percent of the city's manufacturing labor force.[8] Some fifteen years later, female job prospects in Montreal had not improved. One marked change was the severe decline in openings in the boot and shoe trades, formerly the third most important source of work for city women. The strong persistence of domestic service, a far from preferred occupation, was another sign of the narrow work horizons open to women. Thus, in an age when the division of wage labor was marked by clear sexual boundaries, the Montreal economy created far more male work than female. For a growing proportion of Montreal working-class women, the only alternative to low pay was no pay at all.

The size of the female labor supply also affected the economic fortunes of Montreal women. Table 6.2 compares the ratio of women to men aged fifteen to twenty-nine in the five cities under study. Women in this age group constituted the great majority of female wage earners, real and potential, in each of these communities. Edinburgh and Montreal had persistently higher ratios of women to men, and therefore proportionately higher available supplies of working women, than did the three remaining cities. But because Edinburgh was an important administrative, financial, and educational center its economy had a large service sector and, therefore, a continuing high demand for female labor. In Montreal, by contrast, the service sector was somewhat smaller and the manufacturing sector rather larger. The demand for women's labor was more volatile and it only increased slowly with the passage of time. In fact, it grew rather less rapidly than did the potential labor supply. The result placed downward pressure on the wages of working women, a fact which further exacerbated their economic plight.

Table 6.2   Ratios of women to men (Females per one hundred males)

	Census Decade							
	1850s	1860s	1870s	1880s	1890s	1900s	1910s	1920s
Boston	—	—	—	118.8	110.3	111.7	—	—
Dublin	—	—	113.6	103.3	107.5	105.6	106.6	111.9
Edinburgh	127.1	129.9	123.9	121.6	123.9	125.9	132.2	123.2
Montreal[a]	121.4	117.4	132.5	133.2	121.2	119.1	—	—
Vienna[b]	—	93.5	—	98.9	105.8	103.2	107.7	117.3

Sources: United States, Census, 1870–1900; Wright, Working Girls of Boston, 6–15; Great Britain, Census of Ireland, 1871–1911; Ireland, Census of Ireland, 1926; Great Britain, Census of Scotland, 1861–1921; Canada, Census of Canada, 1871, 1881, 1911; Austria, Die Bevölkerung der im Reichsrathe vertretenen Königreiche und Länder nach Beruf und Erweb 1880; Austria, Berufsstastistik nach den Ergebnissen der Volkszählung von 31. December 1890; Austria, Berufsstastistik nach den Ergebnissen der Volkszählung von 31. December 1900; Austria, Berufsstastistik nach den Ergebnissen der Volkszählung von 31. December 1910; Olegnik, Historisch-Statistische Übersichten von Wien, vol. 1, 81.

Note: Women between the ages of fifteen and twenty-nine.

[a] Ages sixteen to thirty in 1871.

[b] Ages fifteen to sixty in 1890.

The hospital and its patients

The Montreal birth weights come from the clinical records of the University Lying-in Hospital, founded in 1843 by several members of the McGill medical faculty and a group of English-speaking female philanthropists from the city.[9] Like the other hospitals in this study, it served two complementary purposes, providing training in obstetrics for medical students at the university and sheltering expectant women in need of charitable medical care. Between 1843, when it opened, and 1905, when the records cease, it admitted some 8200 women. The number of births ranged from eighty to 200 annually, 2 to 3 percent of all children born in the city each year. The hospital moved more than once during this period, but always within the central part of the city. Thus it was easily accessible to most city residents. The Lying-in also followed an open admission policy. It accepted patients free of charge, although it normally requested them to pay a modest fee if they could. Few did.

A cluster of economic, social, and cultural determinants shaped the composition of the hospital's patient body. Like other nineteenth-century maternities, the University Lying-in was a refuge for the poor: married women who could not afford medical attendance in their homes, unmarried women who had no other place of resort or who wished to conceal their pregnancies from families and friends. Single women constituted three-fifths of its patients. But the hospital's population had a pronounced ethnic bias. In keeping with the structure of Montreal's social institutions—almost invariably divided along religious and cultural lines—the University Lying-in drew most of its patients from the English-speaking community. Ste. Pélagie, a Roman Catholic refuge for unmarried mothers founded in 1845, served the French Canadian population. It admitted more than twice as many patients in this period as did the McGill affiliate.[10] The only other institutional care available for parturient women could be had in one of the private lying-in hospitals which catered to the clandestine obstetric trade in Montreal, as in most large cities.[11] Nothing else is known about the social background of the Lying-in's patients. But the occupations of the unmarried mothers, at least, probably differed little from those delivered at Ste. Pélagie during these years: 60 percent of them were servants, 26 percent resided at home, and the remaining 14 percent followed miscellaneous callings.[12]

Within this general framework several changes occurred in the social composition of the patients in the hospital during these years. In particular, the ethnic and religious character of the group shifted. In the 1850s, Irish immigrants (Roman Catholics in particular) constituted three-quarters of all patients. Thereafter their numbers declined steadily, a reflection of the sharp drop in immigration from Ireland to Canada from the late 1860s onward. Canadian-born patients, no doubt many of whom were of Irish descent, predominated after the 1860s. The numbers of English and Scottish immigrant patients also increased at this time. Simultaneously, the proportion of Catholic patients declined while that of Protestants grew. In the early 1850s two-thirds of all women in the hospital were Roman Catholic, most of them Irish, but by the later 1880s three-quarters were Protestant. The numbers of married patients also declined. Married and unmarried women attended the hospital in more or less equal proportion during the early 1850s, but from that time onward the unmarried constituted two-thirds to three-quarters of all patients, until the turn of the century, when their numbers fell off sharply. These changes apart, the social and cultural characteristics of hospital patients varied little over time.

Weight at birth

Figure 6.1 depicts the annual birth weight means of all live singleton infants weighing 1500 grams or more delivered at the University Lying-in between 1851 and 1904, a total of 4877 in all. It indicates that, for the most part, the average weight of newborns fluctuated above 3500 grams between the early 1850s and the mid-1870s. From that time onward, however, the birth weight trend fell steadily and sharply until the early twentieth century, by which time it ranged around 3100 grams. The reduction in mean birth weight amounted to about 400 grams. The only other well-documented declines of this magnitude occurred during the siege of Leningrad from 1941 to 1943 (which ap-

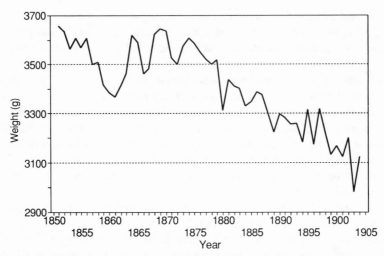

Fig. 6.1   Montreal, 1851–1904: mean birth weight

proached 600 grams) and the famine in western Holland in 1944–45 (300 grams), both of which resulted from acute deprivation. But in both European instances the absolute drop in weight reduced means to below the lowest Montreal level.[13] Nonetheless, the parallels between the two wartime declines in newborn size and that in late nineteenth-century Montreal imply a protracted decrease in the nutritional welfare of working-class women in the city.

Two multiple regression analyses were performed on the Montreal data, one on all patients and one on those hospitalized for seven days or less before giving birth. The results are summarized in table 6.3. The biological characteristics vary in what by this point are quite predictable ways. Male infants weighed 101.5 grams more than female, ascending birth order added 40.1 grams for each increment, and advancing maternal age 4.0 grams for each year. In this instance, however, maternal illness bore no statistically significant relationship to newborn weight, perhaps because the number of such cases noted in the patient records was very small.

Among the ethnocultural groups only one—Irish Protestants—delivered newborns with significantly different weights, an average of 80.9 grams more than other mothers. While this fact seems to point to cultural or genetic influences on newborn size, the explanation in this instance lies with the composition of the sample. The Irish Protestant patients in the hospital were slightly older on average than others. For these reasons a somewhat higher proportion were married and therefore a larger proportion of them were multiparous mothers. They also were clustered in the first twenty years of the period under consideration, at a time when birth weight means were particularly high. The small number of patients in this category perhaps contributed further to this

Table 6.3 Montreal birth weight sample multiple regression analysis

Variable	All patients[a]		Patients 0–7 days[b]	
	Coefficient (g)	t	Coefficient (g)	t
Biological				
Male child	101.5	6.590	111.5	5.567
Birth order	40.1	6.389	38.0	4.901
Mother's age	4.0	2.289	3.4[c]	1.542
Mother Irish-born Protestant	80.9	2.640	109.2	2.810
Social and economic				
Days in hospital before delivery	2.4	8.099	—	—
Year of birth 1860 to 1862	− 144.9	− 4.192	− 136.7	− 3.289
Year of birth 1880 to 1882	− 197.0	− 5.220	− 226.9	− 4.052
Year of birth 1883 to 1885	− 213.1	− 5.413	− 196.3	− 3.628
Year of birth 1886 to 1892	− 277.8	− 10.733	− 249.0	− 6.735
Year of birth 1893 to 1904	− 352.9	− 17.315	− 342.5	− 13.393
(Constant)	3296.2	81.595	3295.0	63.910

[a]N = 4580; adjusted R^2 = .106; standard error = 520.3.
[b]N = 2776; adjusted R^2 = .096; standard error = 526.4.
[c]Not statistically significant.

effect. Consequently, the superior birth weight performance of Irish Protestant mothers was the result of distributional factors, not cultural patterns or gene pool effects.

Few social and economic variables were entered into the regressions because the case records of the hospital provided little information about the social characteristics of the patients. The most serious deficiency is the lack of information about the occupations of the mothers or, for those who were married, their husbands. As a result we cannot determine what influence, if any, social structural differences had upon newborn size in Montreal in the way that this was possible in the other four cities. Still, the records include information on three socioeconomic factors which bore a clear relationship to variation in weight at birth.

Prolonged hospitalization before delivery increased the weight of a woman's child, in this instance by 2.4 grams for each day of institutional care. The effect was not significant for women who delivered within a week of their admission. (Half of all patients gave birth within a day of entry, another 10 percent during the next six days.) But longer-staying patients bore heavier children and the longer they stayed, the heavier their newborns were likely to be. In the Montreal case this factor was of considerable significance. Unlike the other hospitals examined here, the University Lying-in did not restrict predelivery admission systematically. As a result, almost 40 percent of the patients in the sample were hospitalized for at least a week before giving birth and 27 percent enjoyed at least three weeks of prenatal care. Thus, the benefits of hospitalization were spread particularly widely among the mothers in the Montreal sample.

No clear relationship was detected here between birth weight and periodic fluctuations of the business cycle.[14] In this instance the regression explored variation in newborn weight among a series of business cycles. Table 6.3 indicates significant variation among five intervals. One is difficult to explain: the children delivered between 1860 and 1862, a period when the business cycle was on the rise, weighed 144.9 grams *less* on average than those born during the remaining years between 1851 and 1879. Here, too, unusual sample characteristics seem the most likely explanation for the anomaly. The number of births occurring in these years was small, of whom an unusually large proportion of them were female. In addition, the proportion of patients hospitalized more than a week before delivery was rather lower than that during most other periods. Together, both factors reduced birth weight means during these years.

As to the four remaining intervals, which together encompass the years 1880 to 1905, mean weight at birth was in continuous decline throughout this period regardless of the state of the business cycle. In this case the statistical relationship detected by the regression was one between birth weight and broader changes in the economic circumstances confronting working-class women rather than between newborn size and specific short-term phases of economic activity.

When analysis was restricted only to patients who bore children during their first week of hospital care the results were similar. All the statistically significant variables included in the first regression equation were significant in the second as well, apart from hospitalization itself and with the exception of maternal age. From this we may conclude that the significant variations in birth weight isolated by regression analysis were the product of factors acting outside the hospital environment, not the results of institutional care.

As figure 6.2 indicates, the low birth weight rate fluctuated erratically during the 1850s and 1860s, generally at levels below 5 percent. From the mid-1870s onward, however, the overall trend moved upward until, by the turn of the century, it ranged around 10 percent. Given the comparatively small numbers of patients in most years, annual changes are somewhat more extreme than those, for example, in Boston or in Dublin. But the low birth weight trend is consistent with that of the birth weight mean, and with the exception of the final few years (when average birth weight reached its nadir) it lies within the range commonly found in developed societies today (under 8 percent).

The proportion of stillbirths in the hospital is another measure of maternal well-being. The trend is revealed in figure 6.3. It, too, reinforces the conclu-

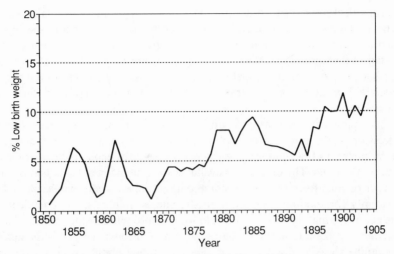

Fig. 6.2   Montreal, 1851–1904: percentage low birth weight (3-year running average)

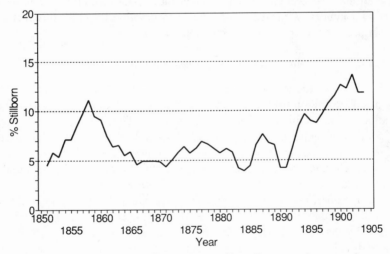

Fig. 6.3   Montreal, 1851–1904: percentage stillborn (3-year running average)

sions drawn from the birth weight analysis, at least in part. During most years the ratio of stillbirths to all deliveries in the University Lying-in varied between 4 and 8 percent. Two peaks occurred, one in the late 1850s and one—more a trend than a peak—between the mid-1890s and the end of the period covered by the patient records. The limits of the information gleaned from the case files leave the explanation of the first peak in doubt. The second, however, coincided with a continuing rise in the incidence of low birth weight and a further decline in the birth weight mean. Without similar information on all births in the city, we cannot entirely rule out the possibility that this stillbirth trend was distinctive to the hospital and its patients. But as the evidence from Boston, Edinburgh, and Vienna indicates, stillbirth and low birth weight trends tended to move in sympathy with one another during most of the period under review, quite likely in response to similar underlying environmental influences.

In keeping with the birth weight analyses of the other four cities, linear regression analysis was also employed to examine the relationship between the Montreal birth weight trend and other measures of economic performance in the community. The only series available were an index of Canadian wholesale prices for fifteen basic food commodities and a broader wholesale index of seventy commodities, including foods, metals, minerals, and chemicals.[15] It is not likely that these indices would bear a close relationship to living costs for neither of them represents a basket of common consumer goods. Nonetheless, in the absence of any superior measures of household wages or expenditures, these were used. No statistically significant association was discovered between the birth weight mean and either index. But given the limitations of these two indices as measures of urban consumption patterns, this fact can neither prove nor disprove that such a relationship existed.

Nutrition and the disease environment

We know very little about diet in nineteenth-century Montreal. The city did not stimulate even a primitive dietary survey such as those which described conditions in contemporary Dublin or Edinburgh. Thus we are left with nothing but a few fragments of impressionistic evidence from which to draw inferences. In Montreal, as in most nineteenth-century cities, indigence and hunger were chronic social problems, particularly during the winter months. Several charitable orders of the Catholic church assumed responsibility for feeding the poor, and their soup kitchens became a permanent part of the urban social welfare infrastructure.[16] The Montreal Diet Dispensary, established in 1879 by the YWCA, also delivered food to poor families with serious illness in their homes.[17] Although there is no way of estimating what proportion of the city's population relied on such assistance, the continued existence of these organizations and the ongoing demand for their services point to chronic malnutrition within the ranks of the urban poor.

As to the quality of diets, two points can be made. Impure foodstuffs posed a serious problem in the city, or so it seemed to public health officials at the time. They repeatedly claimed that the adulteration of food was widespread, that of drinks in particular. Meat was the only commodity inspected at all and the inspection process was far from thorough. In 1892 the city's yearly sanitary report claimed that at least half of all meat sold in Montreal came from filthy, uninspected abattoirs.[18] In addition, the poor ate a very limited range of foods. One city doctor noted that working-class diets consisted of beef, lard, potatoes, and milk. The most explicit contemporary statement we have on the subject comes from a physician who observed in 1887: "Nourishment is so expensive and the capacities of the worker are so limited that the poor family buys inferior and tainted foods"[19] (my translation). Such comments tell us little, to be sure, but when we compare them with similar observations about the meat-laden dinner plates of American working-class families, the contrast seems clear. The poor of Montreal did not dine as well as their neighbors to the south.

As elsewhere, the influence of the disease environment on weight at birth in Montreal was explored by comparing birth weight means with tuberculosis mortality rates. In this instance no information on tuberculosis deaths was available for the first twenty-five years of the period, and no age- and sex-specific mortality rates could be calculated for the remainder. Therefore, the annual birth weight mean was regressed against the annual urban tuberculosis mortality rate from 1876 to 1905. No statistically significant association could be detected, suggesting that, here too, the general disease climate had no appreciable influence on weight at birth.

In the absence of information on the backgrounds of these maternity patients we cannot explore the relationship between socioeconomic factors and size at birth in Montreal. It is likely that the substantial decline in newborn weight after the mid-1870s was associated with growing malnutrition among poor women in the city, but the hypothesis cannot be proved. The qualitative evidence indicates, however, that the economic circumstances of most Montreal working women were limited at best, and they deteriorated sharply after the early 1880s. By the turn of the century Montreal offered few more jobs for women than it had two decades earlier, domestic service apart, even though the civic population had swollen by 70 percent in the interval. Urban growth failed to create employment in those manufacturing sectors which had long been open to women. Nor had the bureaucratic and clerical revolutions—which soon were to broaden the range of women's work—made much impact on the Montreal economy by the end of the century. The supply of female labor remained abundant in the face of weakening demand, undermining women's earnings. Thus the parallel between the declining economic status of women and the simultaneous drop in weight at birth seems to have been more than a coincidence. The dramatic fall in the Montreal birth weight mean was consistent with a broad decline in the economic circumstances of urban working-class women and, most likely, of their nutritional standards and general well-being.

7

SIZE AT BIRTH, NUTRITION, AND
ECONOMIC DEVELOPMENT

The patient records examined here tell us less than we would like to know about the thousands of women included in these five case studies. They were gathered by physicians, midwives, and nurses whose understanding of fetal development was slight by present standards and whose purposes differed markedly from those of this inquiry. Without the necessary data, we cannot determine the influence of several leading factors upon newborn size in the past which we now know to affect *in utero* growth. Most important of all, the available information concerning the characteristics of these maternity patients—about their physical stature, their medical condition, and their socio-economic circumstances in particular—is rudimentary at best, and this problem imposes limits on the findings of this study. In the absence of information on maternal height and weight, for example, we cannot assess the influence of any changing patterns of maternal stature on newborn weight. Nor can we account for the effects of alcohol and drug abuse knowing nothing of consumption patterns among the women in these samples (although in this case the possible impact of smoking can be largely discounted, as cigarette use among women did not become common until the interwar years). In Montreal we must even do without the most elementary measure of a patient's social and economic position: occupation.

Yet whatever their limitations these records are richly informative in themselves, and an understanding of the circumstances surrounding their collection greatly mitigates their deficiencies. By far the most important circumstance is the fact that the vast majority of women admitted to these hospitals came from the ranks of the wage-earning poor. Married or single, young or old, most of them were members of the urban proletariat. Some of the patients were indigent, a few were well off—increasingly so after the first decade of the new century. But throughout the years considered here the maternity hospital was preeminently a working-class institution everywhere in the western world. Thus this study reflects the experiences and conditions of some of the least advantaged women in their respective societies.

Genetic, maternal, and medical factors

Among the influences on newborn size detected in these five case studies, most of those falling into the genetic, maternal, or medical categories identified in chapter 1 are predictable and serve merely to confirm the general reliability of the original records. As similar studies have shown for the better part of the past two centuries, male infants and children of higher parity enjoyed an advantage in weight and, in most instances, length. In contrast, the children of multiple births—excluded from analysis here—were considerably smaller than normal. The findings concerning the independent effect of maternal age are less consistent, but on balance they seem to support the theory that older women bear larger children, a proposition widely accepted in late nineteenth-century medical circles but now generally denied.

The newborns of women who suffered from serious illness were lighter and shorter than those of healthy mothers. In such cases, it would appear, infection made additional claims on maternal nutritional resources, thus reducing the nutrients available to support fetal growth. But the interaction between disease and nutrition during gestation and their effects on neonatal size are not so clear in this instance as they are during subsequent childhood growth.[1] In the course of childhood illnesses, even those which are mild, growth tends to slow. But the influence of minor maternal illness on fetal growth is not apparent in these case studies. It may well be that the mother buffers her unborn child from the insults of lesser infections and only transmits the effects of more serious debilities. In a more general sense, as well, no association could be detected between the disease environment of these years—a crucial period during the epidemiologic transition—and the trend in birth weight means.

The evidence concerning ethnic or racial gene pool influences on neonatal size is rather more ambiguous. The ethnically diverse sample in Vienna displayed no variation in infant weight or length according to ethnic origins. Whatever genetic differences may have characterized its various national and cultural groups, they seem to have had no bearing on newborn proportions. Nor, with two exceptions, can any ethnic or racial group be distinguished from the sample populations in the remaining case studies.

One exception is the Irish, who stood apart from the norms of western society in so many ways during the nineteenth and twentieth centuries. In Boston the children of Irish mothers weighed somewhat more than all others, the differences being small but significant. In Montreal, Irish Protestant (though not Irish Catholic) women delivered heavier than normal children, though this finding appears to have been the result of distributional characteristics within the sample population. In Edinburgh, however, no significant differences in birth weight distinguished the Irish from other ethnic groups. These results seem to rule out a gene pool effect, for if Irish women had a hereditary disposition to bear larger infants than those of other ethnic groups, similar differences should be expected in all populations.

But an environmental explanation seems equally problematic. Superior Irish birth weights generally accord with the view that, before the great famine of the later 1840s, the Irish were very well nourished by nineteenth-century standards, and by those of recent times for that matter.[2] This circumstance, however, cannot explain why poor Irish immigrant women in America one or two generations later would fare better than their equally poor urban contemporaries, especially when their countrywomen in Edinburgh shared no such comparative advantage. There is no reason to suspect that Irish immigrants possessed superior cultural or economic defences against the insults of poverty when compared with other residents of the nineteenth-century city.

Boston's blacks are the other exception. During the fifteen-year period for which data are available, black newborns weighed 6 to 7 percent less than did white. Once again, however, the reasons for this discrepancy are not wholly clear. The city's small black population was an uniquely impoverished minority during the late nineteenth century, a condition which must certainly have accounted for most of the difference. But whether it provides a full explanation is uncertain. The modern medical literature is divided on the issue of inherited ethnic and racial differences in newborn size. It offers no clear guidance about whether or not some characteristic intrinsic to blacks lowered the average birth weights of black Bostonians' children. Concerning the broader question of gene pool effects upon fetal growth, therefore, the most that can be said is that these five case studies offer no convincing proof of ethnically or racially based genetic influences upon size at birth. Quite the contrary, the weight of the evidence seems to lie on the other side, indicating that mean differences in newborn size did not depend on differences in the respective gene pools of the ethnic and racial groups included in these five case studies.

Intergenerational, nongenetic factors

The possibility also exists that nongenetic influences on newborn weight may be transmitted from one generation to the next. In this case we may turn for evidence to the Irish famine and the possibility that it had long-term intergenerational effects on Irish women and their offspring. Between 1845 and 1849

Ireland passed through the last great peacetime subsistence crisis in the western world. The questions posed here are these: did the famine bequeath the legacy of a stunted generation? Did it leave its mark on a second generation, the children of Irish women who themselves were born during the crisis? Two of the five case studies—those of Dublin and Montreal—provide us with an answer.

For analytic purposes, only patients born in Ireland between 1825 and 1874 were examined at this point. In the case of the Rotunda in Dublin, this was considered to be all patients attending the hospital (lacking any information about patients' birthplaces, this assumption seemed reasonable considering the limited immigration to, and massive emigration from, Ireland during these years). At the University Lying-in in Montreal, the Irish formed a large subset of the patients.

Multiple regression analysis was performed on the data set for each of the two hospitals in order to determine the variables associated with differences in birth weight means. Both populations were divided into six cohorts by maternal birth date (1825–34, 1835–44, 1845–49, 1850–54, 1855–64, and 1865–74) and these were entered into the regression as separate variables, with the exception of the famine cohort which was represented by the constant. The analysis thus tested whether or not the remaining maternal birth cohorts delivered children whose birth weights differed statistically from those born during the famine. Because, as we have seen, a large number of variables in both sets of data had no influence on birth weight, the regression was performed on a limited number of variables, those of the birth cohorts included. The results of these regressions are found in tables 7.1 and 7.2.

Table 7.1   Dublin birth weight sample multiple regression analysis (by birth cohort)

Variable	Coefficient (g)	t
Birth cohort		
1825 to 1834	−98.3[a]	−1.330
1835 to 1844	29.4[a]	0.926
1850 to 1854	6.9[a]	0.248
1855 to 1864	−5.6[a]	−0.229
1865 to 1874	39.7[a]	1.498
Biological		
Male child	124.0	8.165
Birth order	16.3	4.579
Mother's age	7.5	3.799
Medical		
Mother ill at delivery	−357.0	−4.495
(Constant)	2923.6	53.817

$N = 4542$; adjusted $R^2 = .040$; standard error $= 511.4$.
[a]Not statistically significant.

Table 7.2   Montreal birth weight sample (Irish born) multiple regression analysis
(by birth cohort)

Variable	Coefficient (g)	t
Birth cohort		
1825 to 1834	−25.7[a]	−0.519
1835 to 1844	−36.8[a]	−0.729
1850 to 1854	−68.2[a]	−0.858
1855 to 1864	−154.3	−2.102
1865 to 1874	−290.3	−3.512
Biological		
Birth order	51.8	5.104
Male child	144.5	5.073
(Constant)	3412.9	69.165

$N = 1276$; adjusted $R^2 = .045$; standard error $= 507.6$.
[a]Not statistically significant.

The Dublin regression indicates that none of the maternal birth cohorts yielded average birth weights with a statistically significant difference from those of women born during the famine years. The University Lying-in regression singles out only the birth cohorts of 1855 to 1864 and 1865 to 1874 as significantly different from that of the famine born, a fact which requires explanation. The regression indicates that women in these age groups delivered children weighing well *below* those of the famine cohort, quite the opposite of what would be expected if the famine created long-term deficits for its newborn victims. In this case the explanation has nothing to do with the timing of the mother's birth. Instead it is related to the general fall in mean birth weight in Montreal toward the end of the century. Those born from the late 1850s onward were more fully exposed to the progressive birth weight decline which occurred in the city after 1880 than were any earlier age groups.

Thus, neither regression provides any sign that the food crisis imposed enduring physical debilities either on the famine generation or on that which succeeded it. However catastrophic the famine may have been, it seems to have been a short-term event when viewed from the perspective of human biology. Women born during the famine delivered infants no different in size from those born before and after the crisis. And their children—the famine's second generation—began life with no sign that they suffered from its imprint.

Social and economic factors

The social and economic influences on variations in newborn size observed in these case studies are rather more informative. They can be grouped into two broad categories: social structural determinants and general economic determinants. Several kinds of information contained in the patient records noted factors which either influenced directly, or reflected indirectly, the social distribution of economic benefits in each city. By far the most important among them is occupation, in the case of a married woman normally that of her husband, in the case of an unmarried woman invariably her own.

Occupation influenced birth weight variation in three of the four communities for which employment information was available in the patient records. In Boston this influence was confined to a single group, the wives of skilled workers. (The Boston results are tenuous, however, for they come from a small number of cases and from only one of the three clinics examined for this study.) But in Edinburgh and Vienna, domestics and women who worked in food-related jobs bore somewhat heavier infants, as the wives of professionals and managerial employees also did in Vienna. In addition, the children of Viennese women in these same occupational categories were slightly longer than the others. Broadly speaking, where occupational differences in newborn size existed, two groups of women enjoyed a significant advantage: those with superior incomes and those employed in household service and food handling, whose work conferred special nutritional benefits. Indeed, one of the most significant of this study's findings is the differential effect of occupational status within working-class communities, an outcome all the more striking because these hospital populations were relatively homogeneous in terms of social class.

The fact that size at birth was more sensitive to occupational differences in Edinburgh and Vienna than in Boston and Dublin is also revealing. Throughout most of the period under consideration, mean birth weight was substantially lower in the former cities than in the latter (fig. 7.1). The strong possibility thus exists that the socioeconomic factors which influence weight at birth had differential effects in these varied settings. In Boston, particularly, all occupational groups seem generally to have shared the same basic nutritional benefits, while in less prosperous Edinburgh and Vienna some occupations were rather more advantageous to maternal welfare and fetal growth than others. It would seem that, at least in Boston, the general level of working-class well-being was high enough to eliminate sharp differentials among laboring people.

Place of residence was another factor which reflected the social gradient. Dublin offers clear evidence of the association between patterns of residence and newborn size. Women who lived in the city's poorer central districts bore smaller, lighter children than those who lived in its more prosperous surrounds. The role of residential patterns can also be seen in Boston although, in this instance, social differences were associated with the location of each

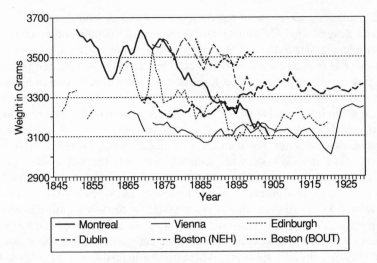

Fig. 7.1   Mean birth weight, 1847–1930: five cities (3-year running average)

clinic and the areas of the city occupied by their respective clienteles. Invariably, however, a woman's address was an index of her economic standing, not an independent influence on fetal development.

In some circumstances marital status also had an independent effect upon newborn weight. Married women in Edinburgh and Boston delivered somewhat heavier babies (although no differences were evident in neonatal length). The likely reason is that these married women enjoyed somewhat greater economic security than did unmarried mothers, and their newborns reflected this advantage. What then requires explanation is the absence of a marital effect in the remaining populations. One possible cause in Vienna was the high proportion of domestics among single mothers, who in turn constituted a substantial majority of the sample. In this case the occupational advantages of service for fetal development, which have already been noted, may well have offset the possible economic disadvantages of pregnancy outside marriage. Unfortunately, however, this hypothesis cannot be tested either for Dublin or Montreal because their clinical records lack information on the occupations of single women.

General economic factors

General economic determinants form the second broad category of socioeconomic influences on newborn size. Here the evidence on annual seasonal fluctuations in birth weight, as well as long-term variations associated with economic cycles, is relevant. Birth weight varied by season in all three European cities, but not in Boston or Montreal. In Edinburgh and Vienna newborn weight rose in autumn while, in Dublin, winter was a time of depressed birth weight means. The Edinburgh and Viennese samples also revealed similar seasonal patterns of variation in birth length. In every instance these differences seem related to seasonal variations in the abundance of food as well as its cost relative to the rest of the household budget. Autumn was a time of relative plenty, when food was comparatively inexpensive and other items in the normal basket of consumer goods were not especially dear, but the winter months were hard. Underemployment and unemployment reduced already modest incomes at a time when fuel, clothing, and food costs were at their annual peak.[3] Smaller newborns were one result. In Boston, however, not a hint of seasonal variation in birth size can be detected. Evidently the greater wealth and abundance of American life, and perhaps the less rigorous winters of New England, eliminated the worst effects of these seasonal cycles, even among the poor. Montreal also seems to have experienced no seasonal variation in the size of its newborns, though its winters were colder and its economy less dynamic.

For a number of reasons the relationship between size at birth and general economic trends is rather more difficult to assess. One problem lies in the inherent limitations of any statistical index of economic behavior with which birth weights and lengths might be compared. The range of indices available is broad, covering the spectrum from measures of income and expenditure at the individual or household level, through more general series on earnings and costs in specific communities or economic sectors, to indicators of national accounts. These measures invariably establish averages and trends, but they seldom describe the range of variation about the mean, and therefore they often cannot capture the experience of large and important subgroups within a population.

The reliability of such indices raises another problem. It largely depends on the comprehensiveness of statistical information from the past, as well as the care with which it was first gathered. Not surprisingly, the quality of such data varies considerably from one community to the next, particularly during the years before modern bureaucracies began routinely to collect information on economic activity. As a result, some economic indices are a good deal more reliable than others as guides to past circumstances, and even the best of them is of limited value, especially when the condition of distinctive subpopulations is in question.

The sampling procedure used to create the data bases for this study also complicates the analysis of links between economic trends and newborn size. The infants delivered in these institutions were, of course, samples of all children born in the five cities during these years, samples whose character and biases can be clearly identified. In most instances the data bases were constructed by further sampling these clinical populations on a random basis, a process which introduced a limited range of error for each sample in every year of the study. As a result, the birth weight means for each city fluctuate from year to year far more than do contemporary national data, based as they are on very large populations. The small year-to-year fluctuations observed in mean birth weight and length are in part a product of the sampling process itself, an effect which cannot wholly be distinguished from the influence of cyclical economic factors.

Two approaches were used to explore the relationship between newborn size and economic trends. Distinctive periods of economic activity, based on quantitative and descriptive indicators of business cycles, were identified in every city, and these intervals were introduced as variables into multiple regression analyses which compared the birth weight and length means for these time periods with one another. Then the yearly birth weight means for each city were compared with other annual statistical indices available for these communities using linear regression analysis. The first technique identified significant differences between broad time intervals while the second examined the relationship between trends in several measures of economic activity and in size at birth.

Of the two, the first proved the more revealing. In Dublin, Edinburgh, and Vienna, newborn weight and length varied significantly—and in some cases substantially—according to the business cycle. Birth weight proved particularly sensitive to these broad swings in economic activity, declining in times of recession or slow economic growth and rising in periods of more rapid expansion. The effects were seen most clearly in Vienna, the only community in the study which experienced a severe and protracted economic crisis, but they were apparent in the two other European cities as well.

In Boston and Montreal, by contrast, no such relationship could be detected. Most of the Boston data span a short time period, thus limiting the definition of broad intervals in the business cycle. But rather more significant, the absence of a cyclical pattern in birth weight means is consistent with other findings which indicate relatively little social differentiation in birth weight means among the poor women of Boston, blacks excepted. It suggests that the socioeconomic factors supporting fetal growth were distributed surprisingly evenly within the city's lower ranks. Montreal reveals yet another pattern of change. Here some association between short-term business cycles and mean birth weight can be identified during the early years of the study, but from the 1880s onward no such links seem to exist. The city's female poor, or at least those patients in the maternity hospital, suffered from growing deprivation whatever the course of the urban economy.

The results of the second method used to analyze the effect of economic change on newborn size inspire rather less confidence. A statistical relationship was established between the annual birth weight mean and an available index of urban economic activity in four of the five cities, the cost of living in

Boston and Vienna, real wages in Dublin, and wage earnings in Edinburgh. But in two instances the relationship was one between yearly mean weight and the annual series themselves, while in the remaining two it existed between weight and rates of change in the annual indicators. Moreover, none of these indices are strictly comparable with the others: they all measure somewhat different facets of economic activity and no two were constructed in precisely the same way.

In fact, many of the price and real wage series on which historians have relied for many years are now being seriously challenged, notably those which A. L. Bowley published for the United Kingdom in the later 1930s. More specifically, there is increasing doubt about the extent to which real wage indices, in particular, reflect the living standards of working people in earlier times.[4] As noted above, the sampling process also introduces a degree of possible error in annual birth weight means, and by virtue of its particular composition each index possesses a limited descriptive value. Add to this the fact that a considerable amount of unexplained variation exists in size at birth and the limits of linear regression analysis in this case become clear.

The relationships detected between trends in mean birth weight and those of the economic indicators used here thus seem tenuous at best. We should not expect especially strong correlations between common measures of annual economic performance and yearly weight and length means. In fact, weight at birth is an independent measure of women's living standards, one which largely reflects their nutritional welfare. It is influenced by other factors than those expressed in wage and price series, and therefore its trends should not be expected to correspond too closely with independent measures of economic activity.

Institutional influences

An institutional effect was also linked with variations in fetal growth. Women hospitalized for some time in advance of delivery bore larger infants than those admitted just before giving birth, and the longer they remained under hospital care the larger their children were likely to be. The case records yielded information on the duration of predelivery care in Edinburgh, Montreal, Vienna, and Dublin, and newborn size varied with length of hospitalization in the first three instances. Despite administrative policies which generally discouraged early admission, some 22 percent of patients at the Allgemeines Krankenhaus Geburtskliniken stayed more than a week before giving birth, while 11 percent were hospitalized for more than three weeks. At the University Lying-in the proportions were even higher: 39 percent and 27 percent, respectively. Information on length of predelivery care at the Royal Maternity in Edinburgh is only available between 1847 and 1876. During this period, again despite hospital policies discouraging the practice, 24 percent of patients remained for at least a week before giving birth, 13 percent for more than three weeks. (In Dublin, by contrast, the Rotunda Hospital rigorously excluded patients unless their delivery was imminent; only 0.5 percent of the sample spent more than a week in hospital before delivery—too small a number to yield statistically reliable results.)

The duration of institutional care before delivery is particularly significant because, while the rate of fetal weight gain is greatest during the last third of pregnancy, it diminishes toward the end of gestation. Thus, the fetus of a woman in hospital for the last few days of a normal pregnancy would not likely be much affected by the institutional environment, in part because the period was short, in part because the rate of fetal growth had slowed by this time. But the longer a woman remained under hospital care, the longer she was exposed to institutional influences, and the greater the exposure at that time when her unborn child was gaining weight most rapidly. As a result, a woman hospitalized for more than three weeks in advance of delivery would experience these effects for a substantial part of her unborn child's stage of most rapid growth.

As table 7.3 indicates, birth weight increased with the duration of hospitalization in Edinburgh and Montreal, and both weight and length increased similarly in Vienna. Stays of two to three weeks added 142, 52, and 81 grams respectively to birth weight in the three city samples, while sojourns of more than three weeks contributed 166, 127, and 134 grams. In Vienna extended hospitalization also added 0.4 or 0.7 centimeters to birth length depending on the duration of stay.[5]

The clinical records offer no indication that medical problems brought these patients to hospital well in advance of their due dates. On the contrary, in the Edinburgh Royal Maternity—the one clinic which gathered information on the patients' pregnancy histories—no significant difference was detected between the length of predelivery hospital care of women with a history of miscarriages and that of women who had none.[6] In all three instances hospitalization varied with the mother's age, marital status, and parity. Younger

Table 7.3   Size at birth by duration of predelivery hospital care

	Edinburgh			Montreal			Vienna			Vienna		
Days	Wt.[a] (g)	S.D.[b] (g)	N	Wt. (g)	S.D. (g)	N	Wt. (g)	S.D. (g)	N	L.[c] (cm)	S.D. (cm)	N
0–7	3285	532	1480	3382	563	2979	3114	486	7819	49.8	2.6	7758
8–21	3427	530	212	3434	552	592	3195	469	1149	50.2	2.3	1140
22+	3451	461	244	3509	536	1306	3248	447	1084	50.5	2.2	1073
Total	3322	527	1936	3423	557	4877	3137	482	10,052	49.9	2.5	9971

[a]Wt. = weight; [b]S.D. = standard deviation; [c]L. = length.

women enjoyed longer care than did older, the unmarried longer than the married, and the primiparous longer than the multiparous. Season of birth and place of residence also had an effect upon the duration of hospitalization. Patients who lived in Montreal and Vienna stayed somewhat longer in the colder months than the warmer. Those who lived outside Edinburgh and Vienna were hospitalized considerably longer than were civic residents. Among Viennese mothers, occupation also was strongly correlated with the length of hospital sojourn. Domestic servants and unemployed women, in particular, stayed much longer than did those in other categories.[7]

Thus, the duration of predelivery hospital care seems linked much more closely to the welfare needs of patients than to their medical condition. The young, the unmarried, the previously childless and the stranger to the city were most likely to spend an extended period in hospital before giving birth. So too were those who worked in domestic service, where the shame and censure of pregnancy outside marriage commonly led to dismissal, as well as the unemployed, so often in great need of charity. By contrast, older women with children and comparatively stable home lives were much less likely to seek out a refuge before delivery. This should come as no surprise, for their labor was so important to the household that their clamoring families could ill begrudge them even a few brief days from home.

If the explanation for longer hospital sojourns was therefore not medical, and if those who remained in care longest tended to be economically and socially the most vulnerable, the greater size of the newborns of early admitted mothers must have been due to the care which these women received while in hospital. The care itself was simple. In essence it consisted of rest and regular meals. Until well into the twentieth century, maternity hospital patients generally came from working-class backgrounds and thus were accustomed to hard physical work. By relieving them of the burden of work, hospitalization reduced their everyday nutritional requirements. At the same time, patients normally received regular meals, freeing at least the destitute—and perhaps others who were considerably better off—from the haphazard diets which must surely have been their lot. The ultimate effect was to increase their nutritional intake at a time when they were at relative ease, a benefit to themselves and to their unborn children as well. These results and their interpretation accord closely with the late nineteenth-century findings of Pinard and others about relationships between institutional care and fetal development, as well as more recent investigations into the influence of heavy work on newborn size.[8]

The role of nutrition

The contribution of maternal nutrition to fetal development in these populations is especially clear. Its most obvious signs are the larger infants born to servants, who shared some of the benefits of domestic life enjoyed by their more prosperous employers, as well as to women whose work gave them access to food. Nutritionally speaking, these were privileged occupations. The superior birth weights and lengths of infants delivered by higher-income mothers, as well as those of children born during upswings in the business cycle, almost certainly were related to better maternal diets too.

The influence of extended institutional care on newborn size underscores the importance of dietary factors. The effect was particularly visible in Vienna during the deepening economic crisis of 1915 to 1922. Food shortages grew increasingly serious during these years, as the Austrian economy slowly collapsed under the cumulative burdens of warfare, disintegration of the empire, and hyperinflation.[9] Figure 7.2 indicates that the women who delivered soon after their admission absorbed the brunt of the crisis. Within this group newborn weight fell lower than it had been at any time since the late 1860s. The weights of infants whose mothers spent more than a week in hospital before giving birth, however, declined much less, and these declines occurred only in 1918, 1921, and 1922, the years of most serious crisis. For them the institution served as a nutritional buffer, shielding both mother and child from the worst insults of the dearth.

When the qualitative evidence on working-class diets is examined, it reveals that the poor of Dublin, Edinburgh, and Vienna were ill-nourished by late nineteenth-century North American standards. Despite their many cultural differences, the working classes of these cities shared strikingly similar diets. They seldom ate meat or vegetables, relying heavily instead on bread,

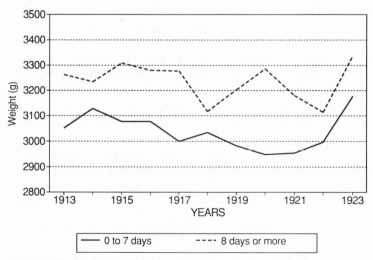

Fig. 7.2   Vienna, 1913–1923: birth weight by length of hospitalization

potatoes, milk, margarine, and sugar, supplemented by beer in Vienna and tea in the Irish and Scottish cities. These diets often provided ample amounts of carbohydrate, but they lacked adequate supplies of protein and the essential vitamins found in fresh fruits and vegetables. In many instances they must also have failed to supply a sufficient number of calories. The meat-centered working-class diets of Boston, by comparison, were much richer in proteins and fats, and richer in carbohydrates as well. On average they must also have had a higher energy value.

These contrasts in staple diets may well hold clues to the differing birth weight means observed in these four cities. As noted in chapter 1, the energy value of diet during pregnancy affects fetal development: inadequate calorie intake causes fetal growth retardation. In addition, iron and folacin deficiencies may also produce fetal abnormalities and reduce newborn weight. The staple working-class diets of the three European cities in this study were clearly deficient in iron and folates, and often in calories too. Meanwhile, Boston's working men and their families enjoyed abundant iron supplies in their daily fare (though perhaps insufficient folacin) and, on average, their daily calorie intake must also have been much higher. The origins of the striking differences between the higher birth weight means of Boston (and perhaps Montreal as well) and the lower means of the three European cities lie almost certainly in these differing dietary patterns and their varying effects upon fetal development.

Two comparative perspectives

While hundreds of studies of size at birth were conducted in Europe and North America between 1850 and 1930, very few examined patterns of change over time (and then only for very short durations). They also defined their population samples in a wide variety of ways, according to the purposes and habits of mind of each investigator. Moreover, only a few of them rested on population samples as large as those employed here. For these several reasons, the many nineteenth- and early twentieth-century inquiries offer no useful bases for close comparison with the evidence presented here. The best they can provide us with is a rough impression of the average weight of children born in a particular community at a given point in time. The French physician Foisy, for example, reported an average birth weight of 3307 grams for 641 full-term newborns of multiparas and 3184 grams for 474 newborns of primiparas delivered in Paris in 1868–69. The German doctor von Sobbe noted an average weight of 3227 grams for 2000 newborns in Marburg between 1850 and 1870, although he excluded all infants weighing 2800 grams or less from his calculations.[10]

Recent historical studies of birth weight in Philadelphia and in three Norwegian cities during the nineteenth and twentieth centuries, however, support the major finding of this investigation. Goldin and Margo examined the weights of 4471 live-born infants delivered at an almshouse hospital in Philadelphia between 1848 and 1873.[11] The children weighed just over 3400 grams on average, with fewer than 10 percent below 2500 grams. In this instance institutionalization had an important effect on the birth weight mean, for two-thirds of all mothers spent at least a month in hospital prior to delivery. But even discounting an institutional effect, the Philadelphia mean lies within the range of those recorded in both Montreal and Boston (its black newborns excepted). As elsewhere weight varied with maternal age and medical condition, and also the infant's gestational age, birth order, and sex. The year of birth also had an effect, mean weight dropping sharply during the second half of the Civil War decade, a period of declining real wages. No significant seasonal pattern of birth weight variation occurred, a finding which parallels that in Boston. Here, too, American abundance seems to have eliminated the seasonal variations in fetal development observed elsewhere. And as in Boston, Irish women delivered slightly heavier children, though whether the difference was due to gene pool, cultural, or economic influences—or some combination among them—is unclear.

Rosenberg's study of the Norwegian birth weight trend rests on data from three cities—Oslo, Bergen, and Trondheim—spanning a century and a quarter beginning in 1860 and employing a sample of 9152 mothers.[12] The annual mean fluctuated between 3200 and 3600 grams, with a tendency to increase over time. Here, too, parity and infant sex affected newborn size, as did the age of menarche, a factor influenced by nutritional and other social conditions in a woman's infancy, childhood, and early adolescence. (Age at first menses generally declines as living standards rise.[13]) In this case birth weight rose slightly as menarcheal age decreased. Married women enjoyed a birth weight advantage over single mothers, as did domestic servants over factory laborers. These results parallel the findings noted here for other European cities. The trend in weight sloped downward until the turn of the century, particularly for unmarried women, the decline being 73 grams. But over the next eighty years it rose gradually by 155 grams. No sharp declines or increases were noted, however, in association with economic fluctuations.

Trends in newborn size

The trends in birth weight and length in these five cities reflected the changing economic and social circumstances of each hospital's body of patients and, more generally, of women in the same social strata from which these patients came. No conclusive evidence suggests that genetic factors affected shifts in infant dimensions over time. Nor are there any indications that variations in the disease environment, or other medical conditions affecting the mothers-to-be, influenced the course of average newborn size. In the absence of any evidence on maternal height and weight, nothing can be said about the effect of changing patterns of female stature on fetal development. But adult size is also heavily influenced by nutrition and living standards, and therefore reflects the same range of socioeconomic factors which contribute to *in utero* growth.

Thus, standards of maternal nutrition during pregnancy had by far the most powerful influence on trends in fetal weight and length. In particular, the variations in newborn dimensions observed by occupation, the cumulative effects of prenatal institutional care, and the dramatic decline in the Viennese birth weight mean between 1915 and 1922 all are signs that diet was the principal factor affecting changing patterns of neonatal size. The birth weight decline in late nineteenth-century Montreal was most likely an indication of increasing malnutrition among the female working poor of that community as well. In effect, the annual means of newborn weight (and to a lesser extent length) are measures of nutritional welfare for the working-class women who lived in these five cities.

Like all indices, these ones have their limits. In particular, their long-term trends are more revealing than their short-term fluctuations. A large amount of individual variation in birth size is noted even in contemporary studies, and the greater meagerness of the information to be gleaned from older clinical records merely exacerbates this problem. Broadly based modern inquiries, especially those involving entire national populations, usually obscure this fact and generally reveal only a limited amount of annual variation in mean size at birth. But compared with such studies, the annual population samples examined here are small and therefore they reveal much more variation from one year to the next. As noted above, the sampling procedures used to create the urban data bases also introduced a small but significant range of error. For these reasons the influence of economic factors on small year-to-year changes in birth weight and length means cannot easily be isolated from fluctuations caused by sample selection.

The exceptions were times of serious economic distress or substantial improvement in living standards. The birth weight decline in Vienna between 1915 and 1922 was severe and prolonged. The trend during these years reflected the gathering nutritional crisis afflicting working-class women and men in particular. On the other hand, the weight trend during the mid and late twenties reveals levels of working-class diet superior to those not just during the previous crisis but for the entire prewar period encompassed by this study. Thus, if nutrition cannot be singled out as the dominant factor in the small, short-term fluctuations observed in average birth size, in the case of more substantial variation it can. The long-term course of birth weight means clearly reflects the changing nutritional value of working-class women's diets.

Any attempt to compare the birth weight trends in all five cities is complicated by intrinsic differences among the patient groups in these samples. Each institution served the obstetric needs of working-class women somewhat differently from the others, and therefore each body of patients was in some ways distinctive, even though most patients came from the same broad social segment of their respective communities. Nor did any of these patient samples share identical patterns of parity, marital status, occupation, and class or social standing. As a result, the comparisons made are between broadly similar populations, not between precisely defined groups sharing a number of common attributes.

Figure 7.1 indicates that, with a partial exception in Boston, the birth weight trend in these five cities either declined (in Edinburgh, Montreal, and in one Boston hospital) or remained flat (in Dublin, Vienna, and a second Boston clinic) during the years before 1900. (The Boston exceptions were the city's small group of black newborns and the infants born at the Boston Lying-in, in the heart of the tenement district, two groups of especially disadvantaged newborns whose mean weights increased somewhat between 1885 and 1900.) After the turn of the century the trend rose in Dublin and Edinburgh but, in Vienna, it did not move upward at all until the early 1920s, after the crisis of war and the postwar economic collapse.

In essence, these curves chart the course of nutritional standards among lower-class women in these five cities. Generally speaking, they reveal a pattern either of decline (in some cases severe) or of no significant rise in the dietary standards of working-class women before 1900, and of only modest betterment thereafter. Clearly, the second half of the nineteenth century conferred few nutritional benefits, and in some cases imposed serious deprivation, on lower-class urban women on both sides of the Atlantic. The first thirty years of the twentieth century, however, brought about some improvement in their dietary condition, at least in western Europe. These patterns are all the more striking for the range of cities in which they occurred, Old World and New, large and small, fast growing and slow, industrial and commercial.

Figure 7.1 also reveals striking and generally persistent differences between the weight means of each of these cities. Most obvious of all is the pattern of high birth weights in North America, Boston from 1872 to 1900, and Montreal from 1851 until the early 1880s. During these periods, newborns in both communities weighed about 10 percent more than they did in the three European cities. The newborns of Dublin and Edinburgh weighed less than those of North America but more than those of Vienna, excepting a brief period around the turn of the century when the Edinburgh weight curve reached its nadir. Viennese newborns weighed less than all others, although when improvement occurred during the mid and late 1920s mean birth weight in the city began to rise toward levels then prevailing elsewhere.

These weight differentials are revealing in themselves, for they provide a comparative yardstick of nutritional health. They indicate that the poor women of Boston and Montreal were considerably better nourished than those in the other cities, although Montreal dietary standards declined to European levels toward the end of the nineteenth century. They also establish that, before the early 1880s, Scottish women were somewhat better fed than the Irish, but by the early 1890s these positions had been reversed.[14] Both, in turn, fared better than their Austrian counterparts, who remained comparatively ill nourished throughout virtually the entire period.

The low birth weight trends in the five cities generally reinforce these impressions—not surprisingly, for the annual proportion of low birth weight infants is itself an important influence on yearly birth weight means (figs. 7.3 and 7.4). At this point we must proceed cautiously, for the small numbers included in some of the samples do not bear heavy analytic weight. Nevertheless, in all five communities low birth weight rates moved in broad sympathy with birth weight means. Declines in the former coincided with rises in the latter, and vice versa. Like the birth weight trend, the incidence of low birth weight also varied with broad economic cycles, although not necessarily with short-term fluctuations. In other words, the low birth weight trend, too, is an independent measure of women's nutritional condition.

But in Vienna, at least, additional factors may also have been at work. In the early twentieth century the incidence of low birth weight rose to new levels—more than 14 percent of all deliveries—and remained above its former range until the close of the period. The reasons for this shift are not entirely clear. The most likely possibility, however, is that, with the growing sophistication of obstetric medicine, the hospital attracted an increasing number of women suffering from serious medical complications of pregnancy, patients who had a greater tendency to deliver abnormally light children.[15] Thereafter the low birth weight trend continued to reflect changing economic and nutritional circumstances in the city, but it did so at rather higher rates than before.[16]

Figures 7.3 and 7.4 also reveal sharp contrasts among the five cities in the relative incidence of low birth weight. From the final decades of the nineteenth century, Edinburgh and Vienna consistently experienced the highest rates, levels which stood well above those characteristic of the modern industrialized world. In late nineteenth-century Dublin, the low birth weight rate approached that of the other European centers, although as the urban economy improved it fell to modern levels. For the most part, rates in the new world differed little from today's patterns as well, even though both ends of the Montreal trend fall outside the normal modern range. (The early rates may well be low because of the small numbers of patients in the sample; the later high rates reflect the general decline in mean birth weight toward the end of the century.) Here, too, we find compelling evidence that working-class women in North

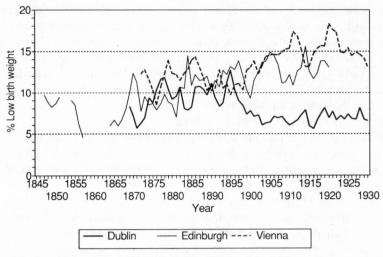

Fig. 7.3   Low birth weight, 1847–1930: Dublin, Edinburgh, and Vienna (3-year running average)

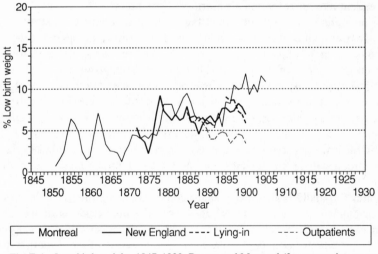

Fig. 7.4   Low birth weight, 1847–1930: Boston and Montreal (3-year running average)

America enjoyed higher living standards than did their western European contemporaries.

One final point should by now be obvious. In none of these cities can we discern a so-called secular trend in size at birth. Economists often use the term to describe a linear pattern of change—either growth or decline—over a long span of time, and the concept has also been deeply embedded in historical accounts of human growth. Our common sense and a considerable body of scientific evidence both tell us that, at least in the western world, human stature has increased substantially since the dawn of the modern era. The assumption that such growth had been steady and continuous was once an implicit part of this understanding. But human biologists now understand that growth characteristics fluctuate according to changes in the physical, social, and economic environment.[17] Recent work in anthropometric history, for example, has revealed complex patterns of change over time in adolescent and adult male stature.[18] Average height has risen during some periods and declined in others. It has also varied considerably from one community to the next, in patterns which themselves have changed markedly over time. This account of newborn weight offers compelling new evidence of the diversity of patterns of human growth in the modern western world.

Birth weight and male height compared

In recent years a number of important studies have examined the height trends of youths and young adults in Europe and North America from the eighteenth century to the late twentieth century. This work has been based largely on data gleaned from military induction records, supplemented in some cases with information originally gathered by philanthropic agencies and military academies. Because an individual's height is powerfully influenced by his or her nutritional condition, aggregate measures of the height of given populations are, in effect, indices of their nutritional status. Thus the purposes of inquiries into the history of stature are broadly similar to those of this study: to learn more about the nutritional condition of communities in the past, and to examine changes in their living standards over time.

Like the birth weight data, that on height derives largely from working-class populations. But because most of the institutions which created these records only admitted men and boys, height studies reflect the condition of males almost exclusively. In addition, because height at any age is the product of influences acting over the entire span of life mean height provides an index of long-term trends in human welfare rather than patterns of short-term variation. Although these indices measure separate populations and somewhat different forms of change over time, mean birth weight and height are complementary measures of human growth and, when possible, should be compared. Thus, three recent studies of height in Austria-Hungary, the United States, and the British Isles provide an opportunity to compare birth weight as a measure of female welfare with a similar one for men.

John Komlos has gathered information on the heights of army recruits in the Habsburg Empire born between the 1730s and the 1920s. While the data are most abundant for the eighteenth century, a considerable number of cases

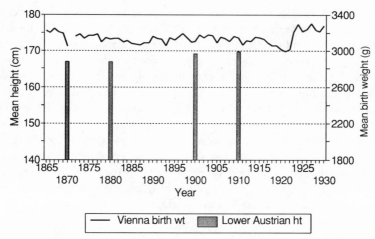

Fig. 7.5   Vienna and Lower Austria, 1865–1930: birth weight and adult height

are also reported for the late nineteenth and early twentieth centuries.[19] These recruits were born in Lower Austria, the province where Vienna was located, and presumably included many young men from the city. In figure 7.5 the height means of decennial recruit birth cohorts are plotted against the Viennese birth weight mean. (The left vertical bar, for example, indicates that the height at age 21 or 22 of Lower Austrian soldiers born during the 1870s was 166.8 centimeters.) The heights of the recruits show an unmistakeable rise at a time when the birth weight mean reveals no sustained trend in either direction.

In a similar inquiry, a group of American historians have examined the heights of native-born American whites since the early years of the eighteenth century. Their most recent findings are reported by Robert Fogel.[20] The height information for the period spanned by the Boston birth weight series was drawn from two sources: a sample of regular American army recruits during the 1870s and one of Ohio National Guard enlistees during the 1880s and 1890s. In figure 7.6 the Boston birth weight means are compared with the average heights of quinquennial (five-year) birth cohorts of men aged twenty-five to forty-nine when measured. In this instance the birth weights recorded at the New England Hospital declined slightly during the 1870s and early 1880s, in sympathy with height means. Thereafter, the birth weights of the other clinical populations either rose or were stable (although those at the New England continued to decline) at a time when average height began to rise once more. It seems that in this instance birth weight and adult male height tended to fall and rise together.

Floud, Wachter, and Gregory have analyzed the height trend in the United

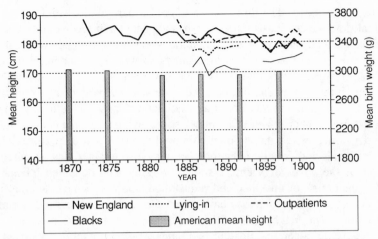

Fig. 7.6   Boston and United States, 1872–1900: birth weight and adult height

Kingdom between 1750 and 1980, and in doing so have examined regional patterns in adult male height. Their analysis of height differentials, however, extends only to the birth cohort circa 1860 (i.e., that which reached maturity in the early 1880s), and therefore their regional height series do not overlap with those of the Dublin and Edinburgh birth weight series to any great extent. They indicate that Irish heights were on the increase during the postfamine years, while by the mid-nineteenth century those of urban Scots were in decline.[21] As to weight at birth, in Dublin it fluctuated within a very narrow range during the 1870s and early 1880s while, owing to gaps in the data, it is difficult to identify a trend in the early years of the Edinburgh series. Unfortunately, therefore, adult male height and birth weight cannot usefully be compared in either city.

Considering the two remaining communities, we are left with a seeming paradox. Height and birth weight averages diverged over time in Vienna while in Boston they moved in tandem. In other words, the nutritional status of Austrian women seems to have differed from that of Austrian men—to the disadvantage of women—while in Boston the two sexes apparently enjoyed much the same nutritional standing. This contradiction, however, is more apparent than real and its likely explanation lies at the very heart of family structures, and living standards, in each of the two cities.

The Viennese working-class family was a deeply patriarchal institution. Father was both the breadwinner and the ultimate source of domestic authority. So entrenched was male preeminence in the family power structure that when the patriarch was removed (a particularly common experience during World War I), another male relation—son, father, or brother-in-law—often replaced him as family head. The dinner table offered a particularly striking sign of paternal dominance. Proletarian husbands expected and received the best of the family's food, and the greatest quantities too, in households where there seldom was enough to feed everyone satisfactorily.[22] In preferring their husbands at mealtime, working-class Viennese women thus deprived themselves and their children. Whether this practice is viewed as a particularly oppressive feature of patriarchal family life or as a rational response to the family's need to invest in the labor power of its major source of income, the consequences were the same. Wives and children commonly were less well nourished than their husbands and fathers. (This practice may also explain why, as noted in chapter 3, the wives of Vienna's skilled working men delivered infants no heavier than those of unskilled and semiskilled laborers. Female deference to male demands at mealtime may have meant that skilled workers appropriated most of the nutritional benefits of their higher incomes for themselves.)[23]

Late nineteenth-century Boston, by comparison, was a city of abundance, even for its laboring community. As we have seen, working men and women in Boston ate well—indeed very well—by contemporary western European standards. As de Tocqueville had observed much earlier in the century, American women also enjoyed much higher status within their families and communities. The most oppressive features of the European patriarchal family had long since disappeared, if they had ever been present, in American social life. Whether this circumstance was due to the more egalitarian character of life in the United States or to the fact that Americans were a people of plenty is immaterial here. The important point to note is that women ate as well as men, at least in working-class Boston. There is no evidence to indicate that women deferred to their husbands at the table, doing without to feed their menfolk properly in order that they might labor hard on the family's behalf.

Finally, we should note an important difference between the living standards of European and North American men as measured by adult heights and those of European and North American women as indicated by their newborn infants' weights. According to Robert Fogel, the gulf between standards of living in the United States and northwestern Europe narrowed considerably after 1800, to the point at which they were broadly similar by the 1890s (although American levels remained significantly above those of southwestern Europe throughout the entire period).[24]

But as we have seen, the same was not true of women's nutritional standing. During the late nineteenth century, working-class women in both European regions experienced significantly lower living standards than did their North American counterparts. The transatlantic gap closed very little before the end of the nineteenth century, and to the extent that it did the principal cause was a dramatic decline in the lot of the Montreal poor, whose living standards dropped sharply to contemporary European levels. Here, too, we can see that the nutritional histories of European women differed from those of their husbands and lovers, a fact which clearly distinguished them from the more privileged women of America.

Birth weight past and present

Table 7.4 includes the historic birth weight means and low birth weight rates for the five cities and recent measures of neonatal size for the same or comparable communities. Unfortunately, precise comparisons are only possible in Dublin because contemporary information on birth dimensions is now normally aggregated to the regional or national level. But despite this limitation, the task of comparing past and present experience remains of considerable value. Here, however, particular care must be taken to insure that the data being compared are defined in precisely the same ways. For this reason the birth weight means and low birth rate ratios from the data bases for each city have been recalculated in conformity with the definitions employed in the studies from which the contemporary statistics have been drawn. In Dublin only live, single births were included, while in Edinburgh all births, live and stillborn, were incorporated. In the three remaining cities calculations included all live births. Given the statistical limitations of the five historic data samples, when comparing the retrospective means and ratios with those from the recent past we should not attach much significance to differences of less than 100 grams or 3 percent.

The most striking finding yielded by these comparisons is the high degree of continuity within these communities over time. Birth weight means and low birth weight rates in late nineteenth-century Boston differ very little from those recorded in the United States during the 1970s and 1980s. The only apparent change was a slight rise in mean birth weight among blacks, and it was not accompanied by improved low birth weight performance. In fact, this seeming increase may well have been largely a product of the sample composition of the California study noted in table 7.4. A diet intervention study of poor black pregnant women in New York City during the 1970s revealed a much lower birth weight mean and supports the hypothesis that the birth weights of American blacks have changed relatively little during the past century.[25] In addition, newborn size in nineteenth-century Montreal differed little from recent levels in Quebec, although as we have seen, dramatic declines occurred in the city from the 1880s onward. Modern Scottish birth weight means are also broadly similar to the comparatively low averages recorded during the second half of the nineteenth century and the early part of the twentieth, although in this instance a major improvement has occurred in low birth weight rates. In Dublin and Vienna, on the other hand, newborns delivered between the mid-1860s and the eve of the Great Depression weighed signifi-

Table 7.4   Mean birth weight and low birth weight, retrospective and contemporary

| | Retrospective | | Contemporary | | |
Place/Period	Mean weight (g)	LBW (%)	Mean weight (g)	LBW (%)	Place/Period
Boston 1872–1900					
Whites	3409	5.9	3480	3.6	California 1974–77[a]
				5.3	USA 1980[b]
Blacks	3094	12.3	3230	7.7	California 1974–77[a]
				11.7	USA 1980[b]
All	3397	6.2	3299	7.4	USA 1977[c]
				6.3	USA 1980[b]
Dublin 1869–1930	3282	8.0	3473	4.4	Dublin 1978–79[d]
Edinburgh 1847–1920	3132	15.2	3062	7.7	Scotland 1974[e]
Montreal 1851–1905	3375	5.7	3303	6.3	Quebec 1988[f]
Vienna 1865–1930	3097	12.9	3320	5.8	Austria 1978[g]

Sources: Shiono, et al., "Birth Weight among Women of Different Ethnic Groups"; Kessel, et al., "The Changing Pattern of Low Birth Weight in the United States"; World Health Organization, "The Incidence of Low Birth Weight"; Dowding, "Distributions of Birth Weight in Seven Dublin Maternity Units"; Canada, Statistics Canada, Canadian Centre for Health Information, *Health Reports.*

[a]This data base comprises 29,415 live singleton births, at gestational age of twenty-eight weeks or more, weighing at least 500 grams, in northern California, 1974–77.

[b]Approximately 80 percent of all live births in the United States in 1980.

[c]Live births in the United States, 1977.

[d]Comprises 19,629 live singleton hospital births in Dublin, 1978–79.

[e]All live and stillbirths in Scotland, 1984.

[f]All live births in Quebec, 1988.

[g]All live births in Austria, 1978.

cantly less than today, and low birth weight rates have fallen substantially as well. The improvement in Vienna, where the historic experience of newborn size was the least favorable among the five cities, has been particularly striking.

Generally speaking, then, neonatal size appears to have attained modern levels in Boston and Montreal by the mid-nineteenth century, and despite some significant fluctuations has changed very little since that time. It also seems clear that in the past, Edinburgh newborns were small compared to North American infants, and that little improvement in average birth size has occurred in Scotland since the 1920s. The only substantial changes have occurred in Austria and Dublin, where North American standards of birth weight have now been achieved, reflecting major improvements in nutrition and the quality of life for mothers and infants alike.

When we attempt to compare the neonatal weight means and rates of low birth weight from each of the five cities with similar measures of newborn size from other contemporary communities, problems of definition immediately present themselves. To choose two important examples, low birth weight is not consistently defined in the same way in modern reports, nor is the concept of a live birth.[26] Consequently, minor inconsistencies inevitably occur when comparisons are made, and therefore small differences in birth weight means or low birth weight rates between communities should not normally be considered too significant.

Nonetheless, striking contrasts are usually evident in newborn size and the proportion of infants born at high risk when developed and underdeveloped nations are compared. Low birth weight rates are considerably higher, and birth weight means somewhat lower, in poor countries than in the industrialized world. According to a World Health Organization report in 1980, mean birth weight in Asia during the previous two decades was about 2900 grams, while the overall incidence of low birth weight varied widely, averaging 20 percent; comparable figures for black Africa were 3000 grams and variation between 13 and 17 percent. In Europe and North America, by contrast, means were about 3200 grams and rates were 7 percent.[27] A low birth weight rate of 10 percent or more is generally considered a characteristic of underdeveloped societies.[28]

Judged by these standards, the birth weight histories of Boston and Montreal, and twentieth-century Dublin as well, reflect the relative economic advantages of developed societies, whatever their patterns of short- and intermediate-term change over time. But Edinburgh and Vienna, as well as nineteenth-century Dublin, shared fetal growth characteristics with the least impoverished parts of the late twentieth-century developing world. Their lower average birth weights and higher low birth weight rates mark them in our eyes as historic developing societies. Only once, and then only briefly during a profound economic crisis, did one of these western cities—Vienna—know conditions which are the common experience of most of Africa, Asia, and South America today. Thus, by the standards of the truly poor societies with which we now are familiar, even the most vulnerable subjects of this study—the black mothers of Boston and the working-class women of Vienna—seem comparatively well off.

Birth weight and economic development

At one level the economic history of each of these five cities during the years under review was unique. Each was a dominant economic power in its region or nation and each therefore prospered according to the economic growth of its hinterland as well as the capacity each possessed to profit from its markets. The size and wealth of these regions differed markedly, however, and as a result, the five patterns of urban economic and population growth also contrasted, in some cases sharply, with one another. In the absence of common statistical measures of economic development for most of these communities, we must compare them largely by descriptive means.

Late nineteenth-century Boston was the premier city in New England, ranking second only to New York as the leading urban center on the American Atlantic seaboard. It was well placed to profit from the rapid growth of the American economy during the post–Civil War era and profit it did. The city successfully exploited both regional and national markets for its goods and services, as well as its entrepôt functions in international trade. Its population more than doubled during the last thirty years of the century, predominantly because it attracted a continuing flow of migrants. To the extent that population growth rates are a measure of urban economic success, late nineteenth-century Boston succeeded triumphantly.

Although a small city by contemporary standards, Montreal was the dominant urban center in both its region and its nation during the second half of the nineteenth century. It became the major industrial center in Canada and claimed most of the new Canadian nation as its economic sphere. But while its growth patterns were in many respects similar to those of Boston, the contrasts between them are ultimately more important. Its economy and population grew more slowly, dependent as they were on far smaller, slower growing, and often more remote markets. The best the city's economic hinterland could offer was the prospect of modest prosperity, not the promise of great wealth.

Dublin was the least industrialized of the cities considered here. An administrative and commercial center of historic importance in Ireland, its manufacturing economy stagnated during the half-century following the famine, when massive emigration and economic reorganization characterized the Irish countryside, and growing economic integration between Great Britain and Ireland increased competitive pressures on Irish production. The twentieth century brought modest economic growth to the city, but both before and after Irish independence, Dublin remained the prisoner of its setting as the major urban place on an island with a small population, a narrow range of resources, and a limited ability to compete with the industrial potential of its nearest neighbor. The population history of Dublin was an index of these limitations. The city did not expand at all during the second half of the century and thereafter its growth was slight.

Edinburgh shared much in common with the Irish capital: important administrative functions, a low population growth rate, a narrow manufacturing sector, and integration into the larger economy of the British Isles. Much of its economic life centered upon the city itself, the leading consumer of most of its services as well as many of its manufactures. With few productive activities commanding national, let alone international, markets, Edinburgh was at best the second city in its region, overshadowed in wealth and population by neighboring Glasgow. In the Victorian and Edwardian constellation of British provincial cities Edinburgh was not particularly favored, as its population history reveals. After half a century of modest growth following 1850, it ceased to expand at all. Stagnation beset Edinburgh during the early twentieth century as it once had done to Dublin. Not only did the city attract few newcomers but it failed to retain most of the daughters and sons whom it bred.

Vienna stands in contrast to the other four cities by virtue of its location, functions, and cultural history, if for no other reasons. It was a proud imperial capital, a magnificent urban stage for a glittering court and an ambitious bourgeoisie, and the major center of industry, finance, and administration for the entire Habsburg Empire. It also was home to one of the largest and most impoverished industrial proletariats in central and western Europe. Throughout most of the nineteenth century, economic development within the Habsburg domains had been uneven. By 1900, however, the Vienna basin was one of the most advanced regions within the empire, even though it continued to lag somewhat behind northwestern Europe. As a result, the city's allure attracted migrants from every corner of Franz Josef's lands and its population grew steadily until the final years of World War I, when military, economic, and political collapse brought down the House of Habsburg and with it Vienna's imperial role. From that point on it became the diminished capital of a much diminished nation, shorn of most of its former economic and political power.

But while their forms and rates of growth offer a study in contrasts, these five cities also shared important economic characteristics. In particular, some leading elements of their economies were common to them all, and they all experienced structural economic changes which held major implications for women. The clothing and textile industries and domestic service, the two largest employers of female labor, were especially important in this respect. The cloth and garment trades were major sectors in each urban economy during the mid and late nineteenth century. In all five cities, however, their importance shrank with passing time, and by the early twentieth century they all occupied a considerably smaller proportion of the urban work force. In some instances an absolute fall occurred in production and employment, in others the decline was merely relative to other industries. In either case these industries lagged well behind the leading sectors of all five urban economies.

The transformation of the service sector was even more striking. Domestic service was the largest employer of female labor in most nineteenth-century European and North American cities, often including more than half of all gainfully employed women. But domestic service waned dramatically with the approach of the new century, and it continued to contract well after 1900.

In this case, too, the declines were absolute in some cities and relative in others, but the central fact remains that the principal older sources of work for urban women diminished sharply over time.

Instead, many women sought and found new kinds of work during these years. Some growth occurred in the minor professions, rather more in commercial and bureaucratic tasks. In some circumstances women also entered the manufacturing labor force, the Edinburgh printing trades for example, or the new electrical and machine construction industries in prewar Vienna. Industrial labor shortages during World War I drew growing numbers of women into the paid labor force, especially in Europe, although in the postwar era earlier gendered patterns of work often reasserted themselves. Inevitably, the new job opportunities open to women varied from one urban center to the next, according to the structure of each city's economy and to its rate of growth.

Table 7.5 provides a comparative overview of changes in the patterns of women's labor force participation in the five cities. In Dublin and Edinburgh, the two cities with the least dynamic economies and correspondingly low rates of population growth, a clear downward trend is evident. Women formed a smaller proportion of the total labor force over time, and the proportion of adult women engaged in gainful labor similarly declined. Montreal seems to have shared the same experience, although this conclusion rests upon more fragmentary information. Vienna's working women maintained their relative place in the urban labor force, but the proportion of adult women who worked fell after the turn of the century. In Boston, by contrast, an upward trend is evident. The city enjoyed significant economic and population growth during this period, and with them an expanded role for female labor.

What, then, can we conclude about the relationship between mean weight at birth and economic change? In both Dublin and Edinburgh, where women's economic opportunities contracted gradually but persistently throughout most of this period, birth weight means were lowest when population and economic growth were stagnant—the later nineteenth century in the former instance, the early part of the twentieth in the latter. The Montreal evidence supports this general case. Although the city's population grew rapidly during the later nineteenth century, the urban economy remained imprisoned by the limited markets available for its goods and services. Here, too, the proportion of women in the labor force declined over time. The birth weight mean reflected prevailing economic conditions, particularly as they affected women, in all three communities.

Yet, structural change in these urban economies did not invariably produce such results. In Boston and Vienna, the two cities at either ends of the development spectrum, the evolving character of economic organization left little impact on newborn size. Rapid growth and expanding job opportunities for

Table 7.5   Women's labor force participation (Percentage)

	Census decade						
	1860s	1870s	1880s	1890s	1900s	1910s	1920s
Boston							
Labor force female	—	24.2	26.1	28.4	28.0	—	—
Women 15+ employed	—	—	27.9	33.5	33.4	—	—
Dublin							
Labor force female	—	37.5	37.5	36.1	33.7	30.2	32.1
Women 15 + employed	—	49.8	48.3	45.5	42.1	36.3	37.6
Edinburgh							
Labor force female	39.0	38.9	35.3	35.8	36.3	37.1	34.4
Women 15+ employed	46.5	47.3	41.7	43.1	42.1	41.2	40.3
Montreal							
Labor force female	—	32.8	37.7	—	—	21.6	—
Women 15+ employed	—	34.5	38.2	—	—	—	—
Vienna							
Labor force female	—	—	35.9	36.1	35.4	36.3	36.4
Women 14 + employed[a]	—	—	48.4	48.9	45.5	46.3	43.4

Sources: United States, *Census,* 1870–1900; Wright, *Working Girls of Boston,* 6–15; Great Britain, *Census of Ireland,* 1871–1911; Ireland, *Census of Ireland,* 1926; Great Britain, *Census of Scotland,* 1861–1921; Canada, *Census of Canada,* 1871, 1881, 1911; Austria, *Die Bevölkerung der im Reichsrathe vertretenen Königreiche und Länder nach Beruf und Erwerb,* 1880; Rigler, *Frauenleitbild und Frauenarbeit in Österreich,* 57, 147.

Note: The proportion of women aged fourteen or fifteen and over in the labor force was obtained by dividing the total number of females employed by the total number of females in the given age group. In each city a significant number of younger girls was employed, the number being greater during the nineteenth century than later. It proved impossible to segregate them from the adult female labor force, thus introducing a possible upward bias in the estimate. This effect, however, was offset by the inclusion of elderly women in the potential adult labor pool, very few of whom likely worked for wages.

[a]Women fifteen and over from 1900 onward.

women neither raised nor lowered average weight at birth to any significant extent, and this fact points us to an obvious conclusion. By itself industrial growth seems to have had little effect on birth weight, and thus on the welfare of poor women.

The crucial variable was the level of economic development characteristic of each city. In varying degrees the two New-World cities were prosperous urban centers, Boston especially so. Victorian and Edwardian Dublin and Edinburgh stood on the periphery of British growth, insulated from the worst horrors of industrial life yet deprived of some of its benefits as well. Vienna lay at the heart of a late and unevenly industrializing empire, and the benefits of its great wealth were unequally distributed within urban society, too. Here, of course, we must be cautious. The nutritional standards of working-class women were affected by much more than economic forces. Local dietary tastes and customs, access to garden plots, relatives living in the neighboring countryside, and power relations within the family might all mediate between purchasing power and what people ate. But by reflecting the nutritional well-being of pregnant working-class women, mean size at birth ultimately assesses the level of economic development of these five diverse cities.

APPENDIX 1:
SOURCES AND SAMPLES

The data bases created for this study were drawn from the patient records of seven lying-in hospitals or maternity clinics in these five cities. This appendix describes each set of records, the criteria used to create each data set, and the definition of the population on which each multiple regression analysis was performed. It also assesses the reliability of the information on fetal weight and length found in these clinical records.

Boston

The clinical records of the Boston Lying-in inpatient and outpatient services, and those of the New England Hospital maternity unit, are housed in the Rare Book Room, Francis A. Countway Library of Medicine, Harvard University, Boston, Massachusetts. While the information found in these records varied somewhat from one hospital to the next, each set of records was consistent throughout the period under review. Four data bases were established, one consisting exclusively of white patients for each of the three clinics and one composed of all black patients from both services of the Boston Lying-in.

The four sample populations were constituted in the following ways. The clinical records of the New England Hospital's maternity clinic exist in continuous series from 1872 to 1900. All births were recorded because there were fewer than 200 deliveries annually. The patient registers of the Boston Lying-in inpatient service span the years 1886 to 1900, with a gap in 1893 and 1894. A random sample of 200 cases was chosen for each year. The same procedure was followed at the outpatient clinic, whose case files extend from 1884 to

1900, excepting those years in which all were recorded because fewer births occurred, and a short period when all cases were noted even though they totalled more than 200. Because the number of black patients was small, and because the birth weight experience of blacks was distinctive in some important respects, a fourth file was created consisting of all blacks in the Lying-in inpatient and outpatient records. The preliminary data bases consisted of 3480, 2503, 3654, and 373 cases, respectively. The birth weight means in the Lying-in inpatient sample are accurate to 79 grams, and those of the outpatient clinic sample to 65 grams, at the 95 percent confidence level.

Dublin

The Dublin patients are a random sample of those found in the clinical records of the hospital. Case files were compiled from two sources, the Register of Patients, which included the administrative record of each patient, and the Master's Ward Book, which noted the medical circumstances of each case. These records exist in continuous series during the years with which this study is concerned, and only minor changes occurred in the categories of information collected. Most of these documents were held by the Rotunda Hospital when they were consulted for this project, but all of them have now been transferred to the Public Record Office of Ireland in Dublin. As birth weights were first recorded in July 1869, 100 cases were selected for that year. In all subsequent years 200 cases were chosen. The preliminary data base consisted of 12,454 cases. The weight and length means in the sample are accurate to 84 grams and 0.4 centimeter at a confidence level of 95 percent.

Edinburgh

The data analyzed in this study were taken from two sources, the Register of Births and the Indoor Casebooks of the Edinburgh Royal Maternity Hospital. The bulk of the records are kept in the Medical Archives Centre, University of Edinburgh, in Edinburgh, although the Library of the Royal College of Physicians in Edinburgh holds the Indoor Casebook for 1844–71. In 1877 the hospital adopted a new form for taking case records, introducing a discontinuity into the time series created for this study. The most significant change was a loss of some information about the social and economic backgrounds of hospital patients.[1] In years when fewer than 200 patients were admitted to hospital all cases were recorded. In other years a random sample of 200 patients was selected for analysis. Patient records were missing for 1852–53 and 1858–63. In all, 13,488 cases were chosen for preliminary analysis. The newborn weights and lengths in the sample are accurate to 91 grams and 0.6 centimeter at the 95 percent confidence level.

Montreal

The Montreal cases were transcribed from the Register of Patients of the University Lying-in Hospital, a large leather-bound ledger now kept in the McGill University Archives, Montreal, Quebec. Because the number of patients was small, all case records were coded. The series runs from 1843 to 1900. Unfortunately, the information for the period 1843 to 1850 is too limited to support systematic analysis. In 1901 the hospital adopted a new form of taking case records although the data gathered remained consistent with previous practice. Unfortunately, this information was not collected as thoroughly as had been the practice before the turn of the century. The series ends abruptly and inexplicably in 1905. The initial data base included 8216 cases.

Vienna

The *Geburtsprotokolle* of the Allgemeines Krankenhaus are preserved in the Wiener Stadt- und Landesarchiv in Vienna. The primary data base for 1872 to 1930 consists of an annual sample of 200 cases chosen randomly from the records of Clinic I. (The single exception was 1882, when weights were missing for a three-month period and, in order to preserve the same seasonal distribution found elsewhere in the data base, only 150 cases were selected.) The patient records of Clinic I exist in continuous series with no significant changes in content throughout this period. The birth weight and length means in the sample are accurate to 76 grams and 0.4 centimeter at the 95 percent confidence level. In order to extend the span of time investigated, the records of Clinic I were supplemented by those of Clinic III, the first obstetric unit in the hospital in which birth dimensions were recorded routinely. It functioned only for the academic year (October to June) and it also accommodated far fewer patients annually than did Clinic I. The smaller number of patients attending Clinic III and the gaps in its records necessitated a different sampling procedure. For clinic years 1865–66 to 1868–69 the first two of every three cases in which a live birth occurred and for which a weight was listed were recorded. In 1869–70 cases were selected on the same basis as for Clinic I. For these reasons the Clinic III records have significant deficiencies not found in those of Clinic I and may be somewhat less reliable.

Sample definition and regression analysis

The data bases created for this study were defined in identical ways in order to facilitate the comparison of birth size in the five cities. The principal difficulty to be overcome was the absence of systematic, reliable information on the date of last menses for patients in most clinics. The University Lying-in recorded this fact in Montreal and the record appears to be reasonably accurate. But the remaining hospitals either failed to note this information or did so only sporadically. Consequently, it was not possible to calculate a gestational age for most of the newborns in these samples. As noted in chapter 1, several measures of newborn maturity coexisted in nineteenth-century medical practice, and physicians were much more likely to base their assessment of an infant's developmental stage on its physiological features than on its mother's recollection of her menstrual history.

Ideally it would have been best to limit the sample populations to infants within a defined range of gestational ages in order to permit closer comparison on the basis of fetal maturity. This not being possible, two alternatives remained. One was to regard all live births as the study population, the other to limit the samples in accordance with some other criteria common to them all. The incidence of multiple births (which usually yielded abnormally light infants), and also of very low birth weight, varied from city to city and from one year to the next. This problem introduced an unacceptable distributional variation into time series analysis. For this reason, and in order to provide a standardized body of data common to all samples, multiple births and very low birth weight newborns were excluded. Only live, singleton infants who were born in hospital and who weighed 1500 grams or more were incorporated in the final samples used for multiple and linear regression analysis. All live deliveries, however, were considered in the analysis of low birth weight and all births, live or dead, in the calculation of stillbirth rates.

The exact procedures used to weigh and measure newborns in these various hospitals are unknown. The clinical protocols routinely employed have not survived in any instance. But it can safely be assumed that the practices which we know to have been followed elsewhere during these years were employed in these settings as well. Not only were they noted in the scientific literature of the period, but the elaborate dialogue about the basis and meaning of newborn size (which predated the period of this study and continues up to the present) was based on the need for careful comparison among different populations and therefore, in turn, commonly accepted procedures for measuring infant weight and length. The high degree of consistency in these measurements within and between these clinical settings over time also offers indirect evidence of their reliability. Standard practice was to weigh newborns soon after birth, bathed and unclothed, on one of a number of commercially available scientific scales.[2] The accuracy of birth length measurements, however, is open to some question. The physical task of taking the length of a newborn child is more difficult than that of determining its weight, if for no other reason than that the legs of neonates often cannot be fully extended. Thus clinicians were more likely to underestimate than overestimate newborn lengths, and as a result the measurements found in these hospital records may be biased downward slightly.

In this inquiry, therefore, newborn weight is superior to length as a measure of infant well-being, just as it has been considered in investigations of neonatal size from the early nineteenth century to the present. The correlations between weight and length in the three data sets which include both measures are as follows:

	r[a]	N
Dublin (1900–1930)	.738	4771
Edinburgh (1886–1920)	.591	4566
Vienna (1869–1930)	.846	10103

[a]1-Tail significance = .001.

APPENDIX 2: ANNUAL BIRTH WEIGHT MEANS

Year	Weight (g)	S.D.[a] (g)	N	Year	Weight (g)	S.D.[a] (g)	N
	Edinburgh				Edinburgh (*cont.*)		
1847	3203	499	164	1878	3333	556	148
1848	3267	545	125	1879	3243	506	144
1849	3312	488	130	1880	3419	540	140
1850	3392	521	144	1881	3273	519	166
1851	3262	505	129	1882	3317	518	162
				1883	3208	636	171
1854	3180	505	121	1884	3319	532	104
1855	3198	428	146	1885	3075	572	152
1856	3293	480	111	1886	3309	500	146
1857	3353	383	63	1887	3246	546	151
				1888	3218	596	224
1864	3451	604	104	1889	3359	569	134
1865	3530	453	115	1890	3282	616	140
1866	3452	577	84	1891	3304	554	212
1867	3390	529	70	1892	3167	509	141
1868	3390	490	145	1893	3167	491	155
1869	3220	529	96	1894	3061	527	154
1870	3206	541	119	1895	3158	526	160
1871	3540	634	43	1896	2997	494	145
1872	3394	516	93	1897	3194	612	157
1873	3708	564	72	1898	3102	603	140
1874	3283	570	115	1899	3183	463	131
1875	3305	551	140	1900	3161	526	161
1876	3221	503	146	1901	3145	554	155
1877	3301	532	156	1902	3116	543	153

Year	Weight (g)	S.D.[a] (g)	N	Year	Weight (g)	S.D.[a] (g)	N
	Edinburgh (*cont.*)				Vienna (*cont.*)		
1903	3081	530	154	1888	3079	462	174
1904	3047	550	142	1889	3085	453	169
1905	3125	531	153	1890	3152	445	176
1906	3087	555	168	1891	3132	509	177
1907	3191	582	143	1892	3125	442	178
1908	3221	523	140	1893	3051	459	165
1909	3211	510	141	1894	3142	385	176
1910	3144	497	150	1895	3116	440	172
1911	3203	600	123	1896	3151	436	166
1912	3324	431	108	1897	3184	481	175
1913	3142	565	136	1898	3144	457	177
1914	3222	542	126	1899	3096	472	171
1915	3192	566	114	1900	3105	490	170
1916	3188	508	144	1901	3173	507	177
1917	3162	551	135	1902	3146	488	170
1918	3133	575	130	1903	3177	483	165
1919	3158	525	137	1904	3165	521	157
1920	3191	497	70	1905	3084	483	169
				1906	3149	463	158
Mean/Total	3231	546	8891	1907	3137	463	162
				1908	3101	466	151
				1909	3153	468	126
	Vienna			1910	3143	584	134
1865	3221	461	159	1911	3060	503	131
1866	3200	428	45	1912	3112	540	135
1867	3242	514	133	1913	3101	546	143
1868	3207	447	193	1914	3149	490	144
1869	3187	488	114	1915	3139	484	146
1870	3044	520	83	1916	3124	503	148
				1917	3088	480	162
1872	3158	452	181	1918	3056	442	127
1873	3182	493	173	1919	3055	501	126
1874	3138	455	182	1920	3012	498	125
1875	3167	499	184	1921	2991	517	123
1876	3166	441	181	1922	3015	475	138
1877	3180	445	181	1923	3201	524	141
1878	3096	491	178	1924	3292	464	119
1879	3140	451	183	1925	3211	494	132
1880	3123	457	174	1926	3234	531	129
1881	3136	452	184	1927	3304	555	136
1882	3130	443	128	1928	3227	514	138
1883	3093	439	179	1929	3215	516	142
1884	3114	426	183	1930	3275	581	146
1885	3077	493	184				
1886	3066	482	176	Mean/Total	3137	483	10111
1887	3064	474	187				

Year	Weight (g)	S.D.[a] (g)	N	Year	Weight (g)	S.D.[a] (g)	N
Dublin				Dublin (*cont.*)			
1869	3252	549	85	1915	3316	500	157
1870	3299	516	168	1916	3388	528	158
1871	3290	485	166	1917	3303	461	168
1872	3299	486	164	1918	3284	600	157
1873	3239	546	172	1919	3344	506	158
1874	3244	538	173	1920	3305	483	143
1875	3190	516	169	1921	3356	533	154
1876	3212	531	161	1922	3332	559	160
1877	3197	578	151	1923	3343	500	154
1878	3186	517	140	1924	3368	563	160
1879	3283	491	156	1925	3276	465	167
1880	3207	521	163	1926	3341	552	158
1881	3215	529	161	1927	3337	522	148
1882	3240	476	139	1928	3448	559	168
1883	3227	533	146	1929	3308	559	148
1884	3318	475	150	1930	3411	511	156
1885	3187	475	151				
1886	3196	531	158	Mean/Total	3299	528	9535
1887	3215	485	114				
1888	3231	549	138	Boston			
1889	3190	526	154				
1890	3260	501	139	New England Hospital			
1891	3270	527	142	1872	3742	575	29
1892	3250	486	144	1873	3501	534	83
1893	3304	471	146	1874	3538	557	107
1894	3164	563	149	1875	3604	493	86
1895	3261	563	153	1876	3647	542	87
1896	3284	532	148	1877	3506	612	108
1897	3371	523	148	1878	3497	661	89
1898	3280	538	149	1879	3444	603	88
1899	3275	560	145	1880	3637	566	84
1900	3402	543	156	1881	3616	777	105
1901	3222	519	151	1882	3506	507	69
1902	3420	496	148	1883	3557	654	100
1903	3370	531	158	1884	3545	621	87
1904	3330	581	158	1885	3423	567	104
1905	3294	494	164	1886	3443	550	59
1906	3366	532	149	1887	3437	477	99
1907	3376	539	166	1888	3558	582	96
1908	3354	563	164	1889	3606	533	93
1909	3425	488	163	1890	3533	615	108
1910	3340	540	168	1891	3496	649	144
1911	3518	523	151	1892	3498	489	161
1912	3300	496	171	1893	3514	580	143
1913	3272	553	156	1894	3508	616	123
1914	3396	546	156	1895	3389	537	148

Year	Weight (g)	S.D.[a] (g)	N	Year	Weight (g)	S.D.[a] (g)	N
Boston (*cont.*)				Boston (*cont.*)			
1896	3255	491	181	Boston black patients			
1897	3419	570	171	1886	3062	481	2
1898	3305	603	67	1887	3208	318	7
1899	3446	593	77	1888	2951	709	11
1900	3333	518	213	1889	3048	547	19
Mean/Total	3480	581	3109	1890	3086	423	27
				1891	3033	529	42
Boston Lying-in inpatients				1892	3031	659	10
1886	3293	524	185	1895	3134	516	26
1887	3318	503	183	1896	3133	502	54
1888	3228	494	177	1897	3160	589	48
1889	3337	485	179	1898	3178	443	45
1890	3315	543	176	1899	3197	435	28
1891	3345	510	161	1900	3243	436	20
1892	3354	545	180	Mean/Total	3126	506	339
1895	3351	554	168				
1896	3287	529	163	Montreal			
1897	3352	530	179				
1898	3349	542	166	1851	3656	542	48
1899	3411	538	168	1852	3634	486	107
1900	3353	512	176	1853	3563	471	112
				1854	3606	600	88
Mean/Total	3330	524	2261	1855	3567	568	104
				1856	3608	586	76
Boston Lying-in outpatients				1857	3501	444	78
1884	3730	545	19	1858	3511	491	59
1885	3517	655	35	1859	3418	390	67
1886	3507	576	90	1860	3386	395	90
1887	3439	550	176	1861	3368	478	63
1888	3519	608	256	1862	3415	556	98
1889	3410	566	305	1863	3461	537	120
1890	3456	563	287	1864	3617	458	100
1891	3463	538	342	1865	3589	570	113
1892	3511	575	318	1866	3461	516	99
1893	3505	533	182	1867	3484	417	114
1894	3391	562	188	1868	3623	489	98
1895	3487	556	189	1869	3645	511	137
1896	3485	528	185	1870	3636	540	134
1897	3522	530	190	1871	3526	581	102
1898	3467	547	182	1872	3500	565	104
1899	3575	577	174	1873	3576	530	114
1900	3475	514	175	1874	3608	511	109
Mean/Total	3479	558	3294	1875	3587	581	101
				1876	3550	533	111

Year	Weight (g)	S.D.[a] (g)	N	Year	Weight (g)	S.D.[a] (g)	N
	Montreal (*cont.*)				Montreal (*cont.*)		
1877	3523	524	93	1893	3257	468	97
1878	3500	621	93	1894	3180	551	122
1879	3518	576	79	1895	3314	514	77
1880	3313	650	75	1896	3173	568	111
1881	3437	552	69	1897	3317	655	118
1882	3411	504	66	1898	3216	588	135
1883	3402	521	59	1899	3130	539	91
1884	3331	552	78	1900	3166	486	43
1885	3345	503	54	1901	3124	549	61
1886	3387	596	69	1902	3202	509	102
1887	3377	635	44	1903	2980	539	27
1888	3301	521	99	1904	3124	541	135
1889	3222	506	75	Mean/Total	3423	557	4877
1890	3298	545	61				
1891	3281	515	90				
1892	3256	519	105				

[a]S.D. = standard deviation

APPENDIX 3: ONE-WAY ANALYSIS OF VARIANCE

Source of variation	F ratio	F probability	Degrees of freedom	Variable	N	Mean (g or cm)[a]
			Edinburgh birth weight			
Categorical variable						
Sex	105.22	.000	1, 8061	male	4163	3281
				female	3900	3158
State of health	46.46	.000	1, 8081	well	7990	3226
				ill	93	2841
Pregnancy history	2.32	.128	1, 6128	previous miscarriage(s)	880	3185
				no miscarriage	5250	3215
Occupation	7.16	.000	13, 7972	mother unskilled	550	3070
				mother skilled	179	3041
				mother domestic	2296	3237
				mother clerical	287	3166
				mother food handling	376	3211
				mother unemployed	254	3186
				mother miscellaneous	93	3105
				father unskilled	1130	3236
				father skilled	1313	3239
				father domestic	190	3323
				father clerical	848	3277
				father professional	63	3176
				father food handling	348	3241
				father miscellaneous	59	3272

Source of variation	*F* ratio	*F* probability	Degrees of freedom	Variable	*N*	Mean (g or cm)[a]
			Edinburgh birth weight (*cont.*)			
Season	9.08	.003	1, 8076	autumn	1921	3254
				other	6157	3212
Address	5.73	.000	5, 6750	working-class Edinburgh	3549	3188
				charitable institution	502	3231
				upper-class Edinburgh	1623	3235
				Leith	617	3237
				other Scotland	348	3332
				other	117	3219
Years	30.85	.000	4, 8078	1847–57	887	3270
				1863–73	800	3386
				1874–99	3582	3224
				1900–1913	1970	3150
				1914–20	844	3174
Birth place	5.35	.000	10, 7367	Highlands	600	3306
				northeast	275	3214
				north/north islands	142	3314
				Borders	344	3249
				east Lowlands	1284	3250
				west Lowlands	476	3236
				Edinburgh	2491	3178
				Leith	421	3193
				other cities	475	3161
				England	528	3168
				Ireland	342	3267
Marital status	0.26	.609	1, 8081	single	5489	3224
				married	2594	3217
Continuous variable						
Number of births	6.50	.000	1, 6993			
Age	1.87	.002	1, 7981			
			Edinburgh birth length			
Categorical variable						
Sex	59.84	.000	1, 4561	male	2323	50.8
				female	2240	50.0
State of health	10.56	.001	1, 4564	well	4484	50.5
				ill	82	49.2
Pregnancy history	0.44	.508	1, 3418	previous miscarriage(s)	435	50.4
				no miscarriage	2985	50.3
Occupation	1.89	.027	13, 4546	mother unskilled	418	49.9
				mother skilled	135	49.8

Source of variation	F ratio	F probability	Degrees of freedom	Variable	N	Mean (g or cm)[a]
			Edinburgh birth length (*cont.*)			
				mother domestic	1520	50.5
				mother clerical	223	50.3
				mother food handling	328	50.5
				mother unemployed	113	50.7
				mother miscellaneous	91	51.0
				father unskilled	569	50.4
				father skilled	503	50.6
				father domestic	62	51.1
				father clerical	400	50.7
				father professional	30	50.1
				father food handling	142	50.5
				father miscellaneous	26	50.8
Season	6.65	.010	1, 4564	autumn	1071	50.7
				other	3495	50.4
Address	2.86	.014	5, 3893	working-class Edinburgh	2236	50.3
				charitable institution	349	51.0
				upper-class Edinburgh	816	50.6
				Leith	377	50.2
				other Scotland	71	50.8
				other	50	50.6
Years	59.94	.000	2, 4563	1886–99	1815	49.8
				1900–1913	1944	51.0
				1914–20	807	50.6
Birth place	1.65	.086	10, 4269	Highlands	312	50.9
				northeast	163	50.4
				north/north islands	88	50.7
				Borders	176	50.4
				east lowlands	794	50.6
				west lowlands	294	50.7
				Edinburgh	1427	50.4
				Leith	246	50.2
				other cities	283	49.9
				England	367	50.5
				Ireland	130	50.3
Marital status	3.57	.059	1, 4564	single	2834	50.4
				married	1732	50.6
Continuous variable						
Number of births	1.67	.054	1, 3911			
Age	1.22	.175	1, 4493			

Source of variation	F ratio	F probability	Degrees of freedom	Variable	N	Mean (g or cm)[a]
			Vienna birth weight			
Categorical variable						
Sex	197.72	.000	1, 10186	male	5284	3202
				female	4904	3069
Occupation	3.19	.002	7, 9928	unskilled	3016	3120
				skilled	434	3173
				domestic	5204	3140
				clerical	357	3157
				professional	77	3257
				food handling	352	3197
				unemployed	419	3089
				miscellaneous	77	3194
Season	13.42	.000	1, 10175	autumn	2436	3169
				other	7741	3128
Address	1.22	.299	3, 9578	working-class Vienna	3438	3129
				upper-class Vienna	4365	3148
				Lower Austria	1625	3127
				other	154	3141
Years	21.33	.000	5, 10105	1865–73	1081	3186
				1874–99	4560	3121
				1900–1915	2438	3132
				1916–19	563	3083
				1920–22	386	3006
				1923–30	1083	3245
Ethnic group	0.06	.979	3, 9784	Austrian	5614	3136
				Hungarian	527	3130
				Czech	3125	3140
				other	522	3138
Marital status	33.92	.000	1, 9885	single	8226	3123
				married	1661	3198
Religion	0.36	.695	2, 10057	Roman Catholic	9656	3138
				Evangelical	178	3131
				Jewish	226	3110
Continuous variable						
Birth	23.24	.000	1, 10123			
Age	8.03	.000	1, 10102			
Days in hospital	1.78	.000	1, 9957			
			Vienna birth length			
Categorical variable						
Sex	195.30	.000	1, 10097	male	5237	50.3
				female	4862	49.6
Occupation	4.14	.000	7, 9845	unskilled	2999	49.8

Source of variation	F ratio	F probability	Degrees of freedom	Variable	N	Mean (g or cm)[a]
			Vienna birth length *(cont.)*			
				skilled	431	49.9
				domestic	5148	50.0
				clerical	354	49.9
				professional	77	50.1
				food handling	349	50.0
				unemployed	419	49.4
				miscellaneous	76	49.8
Season	4.71	.030	1, 10088	other	7672	49.9
				autumn	2418	50.0
Address	0.48	.698	3, 9520	working-class Vienna	3418	49.9
				upper-class Vienna	4333	50.0
				Lower Austria	1619	49.9
				other	154	50.1
Years	13.58	.000	5, 10022	1865–73	1013	49.8
				1874–99	4548	50.0
				1900–1915	2438	50.2
				1916–19	562	49.6
				1920–22	384	49.4
				1923–30	1083	49.7
Ethnic group	0.96	.409	3, 9707	Austrian	5582	49.9
				Hungarian	523	50.0
				Czech	3087	50.0
				other	519	50.0
Marital status	0.26	.610	1, 9801	single	8147	49.9
				married	1656	50.0
Religion	0.15	.858	2, 9973	Roman Catholic	9573	49.9
				Evangelical	178	49.9
				Jewish	225	49.9
Continuous variable						
Birth	13.55	.000	1, 10035			
Age	5.46	.000	1, 10016			
Days in hospital	1.68	.000	1, 9876			
			Dublin birth weight			
Categorical variable						
Sex	119.06	.000	1, 9533	male	4867	3357
				female	4668	3239
State of health	32.72	.000	1, 9533	well	9486	3302
				ill	49	2870
Occupation	1.84	.087	6, 9521	unskilled	4686	3289
				skilled	1919	3318
				domestic	351	3335
				clerical	1364	3311

Source of variation	F ratio	F probability	Degrees of freedom	Variable	N	Mean (g or cm)[a]
			Dublin birth weight (*cont.*)			
				professional	61	3248
				food handling	428	3325
				miscellaneous	719	3265
Season	3.22	.022	3, 9531	winter	2295	3273
				spring	2627	3303
				summer	2413	3299
				autumn	2200	3322
Address	7.53	.000	4, 8326	North Dublin	3875	3296
				South Dublin	1633	3285
				Dublin suburbs	1508	3357
				Dublin poor core	1154	3254
				other Ireland	161	3357
Years	24.23	.000	4, 9530	1869–73	755	3278
				1874–99	3887	3240
				1900–1913	2223	3356
				1914–20	1097	3334
				1921–30	1573	3353
Marital status	8.16	.004	1, 9444	single	462	3231
				married	8984	3303
Religion	0.00	.967	1, 9511	Roman Catholic	8536	3300
				Protestant	977	3299
Continuous variable						
Birth	17.31	.000	1, 9491			
Age	6.37	.000	1, 9499			
Days in hospital	0.62	.935	1, 9505			
			Dublin birth length			
Categorical variable						
Sex	63.96	.000	1, 4769	male	2452	49.9
				female	2319	49.3
State of health	14.62	.000	1, 4769	well	4766	49.6
				ill	5	45.2
Occupation	1.11	.351	6, 4763	unskilled	2424	49.6
				skilled	763	49.7
				domestic	109	49.9
				clerical	777	49.6
				professional	37	49.1
				food handling	240	49.6
				miscellaneous	420	49.4
Season	1.15	.326	3, 4767	winter	1092	49.5
				spring	1286	49.6
				summer	1229	49.6
				autumn	1164	49.7
Address	4.30	.002	4, 4237	North Dublin	2095	49.5
				South Dublin	620	49.5

Source of variation	F ratio	F probability	Degrees of freedom	Variable	N	Mean (g or cm)[a]
Dublin birth length (*cont.*)						
				Dublin suburbs	1056	49.8
				Dublin poor core	383	49.4
				other Ireland	88	50.1
Year	7.05	.001	2, 4768	1900–1913	2122	49.7
				1914–20	1083	49.3
				1921–30	1566	49.7
Marital status	1.21	.272	1, 4729	single	258	49.4
				married	4473	49.6
Religion	1.12	.290	1, 4760	Roman Catholic	4343	49.6
				Protestant	419	49.7
Continuous variable						
Birth	3.89	.000	1, 4731			
Age	2.12	.000	1, 4736			
Days in hospital	1.59	.037	1, 4747			
Boston birth weight New England Hospital						
Categorical variable						
Sex	23.82	.000	1, 3100	male	1580	3530
				female	1522	3429
State of health	4.51	.034	1, 3107	well	3022	3484
				ill	87	3350
Pregnancy history	4.25	.039	1, 3107	previous miscarriage(s)	691	3520
				no miscarriage	2418	3469
Occupation	2.25	.036	6, 2911	unskilled	296	3415
				skilled	55	3639
				domestic	1219	3483
				clerical	115	3397
				professional	122	3402
				housewife	993	3498
				food handling	118	3496
Season	0.74	.528	3, 3105	winter	700	3503
				spring	768	3458
				summer	869	3480
				autumn	772	3482
Address	0.49	.740	4, 2941	Boston suburbs	335	3466
				other Boston	1876	3482
				North End & East Boston	192	3513
				South Boston	135	3512
				New England	408	3455
Years	9.70	.000	5, 3103	1872–73	112	3563
				1874–79	565	3538

Source of variation	F ratio	F probability	Degrees of freedom	Variable	N	Mean (g or cm)[a]
			Vienna birth length (*cont.*)			
				1880–82	258	3594
				1883–85	291	3505
				1886–92	760	3511
				1893–1900	1123	3389
Marital status	13.57	.000	1, 3028	single	949	3422
				married	2081	3505
Continuous variable						
Birth	7.33	.000	1, 2908			
Age	2.18	.000	1, 3032			
			Boston Lying-in Hospital Inpatient Clinic			
Categorical variable						
Sex	18.94	.000	1, 2259	male	1110	3378
				female	1151	3283
Season	0.29	.833	3, 2257	winter	570	3338
				spring	677	3318
				summer	630	3326
				autumn	384	3345
Address	1.97	.096	4, 2208	Boston suburbs	167	3399
				other Boston	1113	3344
				North End & East Boston	666	3309
				South Boston	118	3290
				New England	149	3264
Year	3.00	.084	1, 2259	1886–92	1241	3312
				1893–1900	1020	3351
Marital status	16.03	.000	1, 2175	single	970	3276
				married	1207	3366
Birth place	5.55	.000	5, 2248	New England	776	3268
				other USA	116	3250
				Canada	511	3334
				Ireland	482	3413
				Russia	32	3346
				other	337	3369
Fee payment	0.12	.732	1, 2218	fee paid	620	3338
				no fee paid	1600	3329
Continuous variable						
Birth	7.43	.000	1, 2244			
Age	2.61	.000	1, 2228			

Source of variation	F ratio	F probability	Degrees of freedom	Variable	N	Mean (g or cm)[a]
			Dublin birth weight (*cont.*)			
			Boston Lying-in Hospital Outpatient Clinic			
Categorical variable						
Sex	49.85	.000	1, 3287	male	1665	3547
				female	1624	3410
State of health	13.48	.000	1, 3292	well	3152	3487
				ill	142	3311
Season	0.88	.449	3, 3290	winter	834	3491
				spring	777	3464
				summer	817	3499
				autumn	866	3463
Address	4.74	.001	4, 3218	Boston suburbs	4	3745
				other Boston	873	3481
				North End & East Boston	2000	3460
				South Boston	343	3597
				New England	3	3667
Year	1.36	.256	2, 3291	1884–85	55	3580
				1886–92	1774	3469
				1893–1900	1465	3488
Marital status	4.77	.029	1, 3246	single	74	3339
				married	3174	3483
Birth place	6.78	.000	5, 3253	New England	386	3457
				other USA	94	3416
				Canada	225	3488
				Ireland	589	3595
				Russia	1233	3439
				other	732	3478
Continuous variable						
Birth	7.00	.000	1, 3262			
Age	3.08	.000	1, 3148			
			Boston black maternity patients			
Categorical variable						
Sex	1.42	.238	1, 337	male	160	3161
				female	179	3095
Season	0.73	.537	3, 335	winter	80	3058
				spring	97	3131
				summer	91	3170
				autumn	71	3140
Address	1.05	.370	3, 320	Boston suburbs	22	3036
				other Boston	154	3102

Source of variation	F ratio	F probability	Degrees of freedom	Variable	N	Mean (g or cm)[a]
				North End & East Boston	129	3170
				New England	19	3256
Years	4.06	.045	1, 337	1886–92	118	3051
				1893–1900	221	3166
Fee payment	0.63	.429	1, 331	fee paid	102	3154
				no fee paid	231	3107
Continuous variable						
Age	1.58	.041	1, 313			

Montreal birth weight

Source of variation	F ratio	F probability	Degrees of freedom	Variable	N	Mean (g or cm)[a]
Categorical variable						
Sex	38.89	.000	1, 4875	male	2517	3470
				female	2360	3371
State of health	11.56	.001	1, 4875	well	4832	3425
				ill	45	3142
Season	2.81	.038	3, 4873	winter	1130	3413
				spring	1312	3460
				summer	1264	3401
				autumn	1171	3413
Years	45.39	.000	9, 4867	1851–56	535	3600
				1857–59	204	3477
				1860–62	251	3393
				1863–64	220	3532
				1865–73	1015	3565
				1874–79	586	3551
				1880–82	210	3385
				1883–85	191	3357
				1886–92	543	3295
				1893–1904	1122	3198
National group	10.88	.000	8, 4687	Irish (religion unknown)	180	3487
				English	615	3383
				Scots	231	3439
				Canadian	2097	3383
				American	279	3419
				European	133	3367
				Irish Catholic	804	3530
				Irish Protestant	324	3607
				other	33	3280
Marital status	4.16	.041	1, 3211	single	2169	3456
				married	1044	3498
Religion	0.33	.723	2, 3114	Roman Catholic	1547	3489
				Protestant	1561	3475
				other	9	3411

Source of variation	F ratio	F probability	Degrees of freedom	Variable	N	Mean (g or cm)[a]
Continuous variable						
Birth	8.14	.000	1, 4817			
Age	2.28	.000	1, 4725			
Days in hospital	1.15	.109	1, 4733			

[a]Mean birth weight in grams, mean birth weight in centimeters.

ABBREVIATIONS

Acta Obstet. Gynecol. Scand.	Acta Obstetricia Gynecologica Scandinavica
Acta Paediatr. Scand.	Acta Paediatrica Scandinavica
Am. Hist. Rev.	American Historical Review
Am. J. Clin. Nutr.	American Journal of Clinical Nutrition
Am. J. Dis. Child.	American Journal of Diseases of Children
Am. J. Epidemiol.	American Journal of Epidemiology
Am. J. Med. Sci.	American Journal of the Medical Sciences
Am. J. Obstet. Gynecol.	American Journal of Obstetrics and Gynecology
Am. J. Public Health	American Journal of Public Health
Anat. Rec.	Anatomical Record
Ann. demog. hist.	Annales de démographie historique
Ann. gynecol.	Annales de gynécologie
Ann. hyg.	Annales d'hygiène publique et de médecine légale
Ann. Hum. Biol.	Annals of Human Biology
Arch. Gynak.	Archiv für Gynäkologie
Arch. Sozial.	Archiv für Sozialgeschichte
Arch. Dis. Child.	Archives of Disease in Childhood
Bost. Med. Surg. J.	Boston Medical and Surgical Journal
Br. Am. J.	British American Journal
Br. For. Med. Rev.	British and Foreign Medico-Chirurgical Review
Br. J. Ind. Med.	British Journal of Industrial Medicine
Br. J. Ob. Gyn.	British Journal of Obstetrics and Gynaecology
Br. Med. Bull.	British Medical Bulletin

Br. Med. J.	*British Medical Journal*
Bull. Acad. Med.	*Bulletin de l'Académie de Médicine*
Bull. Hist. Med.	*Bulletin of the History of Medicine*
Bull. WHO.	*Bulletin of the World Health Organization*
Can. Med. Assoc. J.	*Canadian Medical Association Journal*
Can. Natur.	*Canadian Naturalist*
Clin. Genet.	*Clinical Genetics*
Clin. Nutrit.	*Clinical Nutrition*
Deut. Med. Woch.	*Deutsche Medizinische Wochenschrift*
Dev. Med. Child Neurol.	*Developmental Medicine and Child Neurology*
Dev. Pharmacol. Ther.	*Developmental Pharmacology and Thera-putics*
Dub. Qu. J. Med. Sci.	*Dublin Quarterly Journal of Medical Science*
Early Hum. Dev.	*Early Human Development*
Ec. Hist. Rev.	*Economic History Review*
Edinb. Med. Surg. J.	*Edinburgh Medical and Surgical Journal*
Edinb. Med. J.	*Edinburgh Medical Journal*
Explor. Ec. Hist.	*Explorations in Economic History*
H. s./S. H.	*Histoire sociale/Social History*
Hist. Meth.	*Historical Methods*
Int. J. Epidemiol.	*International Journal of Epidemiology*
Ir. Ec. Soc. Hist.	*Irish Economic and Social History*
Ir. Hist. S.	*Irish Historical Studies*
Ir. J. Med. Sci.	*Irish Journal of Medical Science*
J. Appl. Physiol.	*Journal of Applied Physiology*
J. Am. Hist.	*Journal of American History*
J. Biosoc. Sci.	*Journal of Biosocial Science*
J. Ec. Hist.	*Journal of Economic History*
J. Epidemiol. Commun. Health	*Journal of Epidemiology and Community Health*
J. Eur. Ec. Hist.	*Journal of European Economic History*
J. Hist. Med.	*Journal of the History of Medicine and Allied Sciences*
J. Interdisc. Hist.	*Journal of Interdisciplinary History*
J. Ob. Gyn. Br. Emp./Comm.	*Journal of Obstetrics and Gynaecology of the British Empire/Commonwealth*
J. Pediatr.	*Journal of Pediatrics*
J. R. Coll. Surg. Edinb.	*Journal of the Royal College of Surgeons of Edinburgh*
J. Reprod. Med.	*Journal of Reproductive Medicine*
J. Soc. Hist.	*Journal of Social History*
J. A. M. A.	*Journal of the American Medical Association*
J. Trop. Med. Hyg.	*Journal of Tropical Medicine and Hygiene*
J. Trop. Pediatr.	*Journal of Tropical Pediatrics*
Maand. Kind.	*Maandschrift voor Kindergeneeskunde*
Med. Care	*Medical Care*

Monat. Geburt. Gynak.	*Monatsschrift für Geburtshülfe und Gynäkologie*
Monat. Geburt. Frauen.	*Monatsschrift für Geburtskunde und Frauenkrankheiten*
Monat. Kinder.	*Monatsschrift für Kinderheilkunde*
N. Eng. J. Med.	*New England Journal of Medicine*
N. Eng. J. Med. Surg.	*New England Journal of Medicine and Surgery*
Nutr. Rev.	*Nutrition Reviews*
Obstet. J. Gt. Br.	*Obstetrical Journal of Great Britain and Ireland*
Phil. Trans. R. Soc. Lond.	*Philosophical Transactions of the Royal Society of London*
Pop. Stud.	*Population Studies*
Public Health Rep.	*Public Health Reports*
R. H. A. F.	*Revue d'histoire de l'Amérique française*
Scot. Ec. Soc. Hist.	*Scottish Economic and Social History*
Sem. Perinatol.	*Seminars in Perinatology*
Soc. Sci. Med.	*Social Science and Medicine*
Ther. Monat.	*Therapeutische Monatshefte*
Trans. Edinb. Obstet. Soc.	*Transactions of the Edinburgh Obstetrical Society*
Trans. R. Soc. Trop. Med. Hyg.	*Transactions of the Royal Society for Tropical Medicine and Hygiene*
Ulst. Med. J.	*Ulster Medical Journal*
Viertel. Gerich. Med.	*Vierteljahrsschrift für Gerichlichten Medizin*
Wien. Klin. Woch.	*Wiener Klinische Wochenschrift*
Wien. Med. Woch.	*Wiener Medizinische Wochenschrift*
World Health Stat. Q.	*World Health Statistics Quarterly*
Zeit. Geburt. Gynak.	*Zeitschrift für Geburtshilfe und Gynäkologie*
Zeit. Ges. Med.	*Zeitschrift für die gesamte Medizin*
Zent. Gynak.	*Zentralblatt für Gynäkologie*

NOTES

Introduction

1. Tanner, *A History of the Study of Human Growth;* Eveleth and Tanner, *Worldwide Variation in Human Growth.*

2. The longstanding British standard of living debate provides the best-known example. For a brief introduction see Taylor, *The Standard of Living in Britain in the Industrial Revolution.*

3. Oddy and Miller, *The Making of the Modern British Diet,* 11–100; Hémardinquer, *Pour une histoire de l'alimentation,* 43–78; Teuteberg, "The General Relationship between Diet and Industrialization."

4. Teuteberg, "The General Relationship between Diet and Industrialization," 98–101; Hémardinquer, *Pour une histoire de l'alimentation;* Oddy and Miller, *Making of the Modern British Diet,* 103–85; Johnston, *Diet in Workhouses and Prisons, 1835–1895;* Oddy, "Working-Class Diets in Late Nineteenth-Century Britain"; Oddy, "A Nutritional Analysis of Historical Evidence"; Oddy, "Food, Drink and Nutrition"; Teuteberg, "Die Nahrung der sozialen Unterschichten"; Burnett, *Plenty and Want;* Teuteberg, "Der Verzehr von Nahrungsmitteln in Deutschland"; Flandrin, Hyman, and Hyman, *Le Cuisinier françois.*

5. McKeown, *The Modern Rise of Population.*

6. McKeown, *The Modern Rise of Population,* 153–54.

7. For example see Floud, Wachter, and Gregory, *Height, Health and History.*

8. Livi-Bacci, *Population and Nutrition,* especially chapter 6.

9. Floud, Wachter, and Gregory, *Height, Health and History;* Fogel, "Nutrition and the Decline in Mortality since 1700"; Fogel, "Physical Growth as a Measure of the Economic Well-being of Populations"; Fogel et al., "Secular Changes in American and British Stature and Nutrition"; Komlos, *Nutrition and Economic Development in the Eighteenth-Century Habsburg Monarchy.* For an important exception see Steckel, "A Peculiar Population"; Steckel, "Growth, Depression and Recovery."

10. World Health Organization, "The Incidence of Low Birth Weight."

11. For an introduction to the European literature see Kaelble, *Industrialisation and Social Inequality in Nineteenth-Century Europe*. Much of the literature cited elsewhere in this introduction addresses these broad issues. For other recent works related to this study see Lebergott, *The American Economy;* Williamson and Lindert, *American Inequality;* Williamson, *Did British Capitalism Breed Inequality?* For a critique of Williamson see Feinstein, "The Rise and Fall of the Williamson Curve."

12. For an introduction to the literature in those countries with which this study is concerned see Appelt, *Von Ladenmädchen, Schreibfräulein und Gouvernanten;* Daly, "Women in the Irish Workforce"; Ehmer, "Frauenarbeit und Arbeiterfamilie in Wien"; Goldin, *Understanding the Gender Gap;* Prentice, *Canadian Women;* Rigler, *Frauenleitbild und Frauenarbeit in Österreich.*

Chapter One

1. Hytten and Leitch, *The Physiology of Human Pregnancy*, 289.

2. Brenner, Edelman, and Hendricks, "A Standard of Fetal Growth for the United States of America," 558. The curve represents the median weekly weight gain observed in an urban American clinical setting and has been accepted as a standard for American births since the mid-1970s. It should be noted, however, that the information is based upon cases of abortion and premature birth and therefore it may not reflect normal circumstances precisely.

3. Stein and Susser, "Intrauterine Growth Retardation."

4. In recent years the perinatal mortality rate has declined dramatically in developed countries, thus lowering the level of risk at any weight well below 2500 grams. New thresholds have been defined to identify these risk levels, very low birth weight infants weighing 1500 grams or less and extremely low birth weight newborns 1000 grams or less. The latter is increasingly recognized as the upper boundary of poor neonatal outcome. Gould, "The Low-Birth-Weight Infant." But although the probability of survival has greatly increased for low birth weight children in industrial societies, a large number of newborns weighing less than 2500 grams require intensive medical care in order to survive, and therefore the low birth weight designation continues to be extremely important clinically. In underdeveloped societies it remains the primary index of risk assessment and therapeutic practice.

5. World Health Organization, "The Incidence of Low Birth Weight," 197.

6. World Health Organization, "The Incidence of Low Birth Weight." Most of the data come from the late 1960s and 1970s.

7. World Health Organization Working Group, "Use and Interpretation of Anthropometric Indicators of Nutritional Status"; Mahner, "Birth-weight as a New Development Indicator."

8. Magnus, "Causes of Variation in Birth Weight"; Magnus, "Further Evidence for a Significant Effect of Fetal Genes on Variation in Birth Weight"; Magnus et al., "Parental Determinants of Birth Weight."

9. Roberts, "The Genetics of Human Fetal Growth," 137, 139.

10. Robson, "The Genetics of Birth Weight," 293; Kline, Stein, and Susser, *Conception to Birth*, 232.

11. Hytten and Leitch, *Physiology of Human Pregnancy*, 300; Ounsted and

Ounsted, *On Fetal Growth Rate,* 18; Musaiger, "Factors Associated with Birth Weight in Bahrain"; Osuhor, "Birthweights in Southern Zaria."

12. Ounsted and Ounsted, *On Fetal Growth Rate,* 19–22.

13. Hytten and Leitch, *Physiology of Human Pregnancy,* 307–8. Fathers contribute to the birth weight of their children through their role in fetal sex selection. Some recent experimental evidence, derived from comparing the birth weights of both mothers and fathers with those of their offspring, suggests that maternal and paternal genotypes also have a minor but similar influence upon weight at birth. Magnus et al., "Parental Determinants of Birth Weight." It should also be noted that maternal height is influenced by nutritional as well as genetic factors, and the relative effects of these influences upon newborn size cannot easily be distinguished from one another.

14. Alexander et al., "Racial Differences in the Relation of Birth Weight and Gestational Age to Neonatal Mortality"; Chetcuti, Sinha, and Levene, "Birth Size in Indian Ethnic Subgroups"; Dawson, Golder, and Jonas, "Birth Weight by Gestational Age"; Shiono et al., "Birth Weight among Women of Different Ethnic Groups."

15. Kline, Stein, and Susser, *Conception to Birth,* 223–25.

16. Hytten and Leitch, *Physiology of Human Pregnancy,* 301–3; Ounsted and Ounsted, *On Fetal Growth Rate,* 14–15.

17. Ounsted and Ounsted, *On Fetal Growth Rate,* 17.

18. Miller, "Determinants of Intrauterine Growth Retardation"; Fortney and Higgins, "The Effect of Birth Interval on Perinatal Survival and Birth Weight."

19. Meyer, "Effects of Maternal Smoking and Altitude on Birth Weight"; Moore et al., "Infant Birth Weight Is Related to Maternal Arterial Oxygenation."

20. Hytten and Leitch, *Physiology of Human Pregnancy,* 320–21; Roberts, "Environment and the Fetus."

21. Ounsted and Ounsted, *On Fetal Growth Rate,* 9–12; Niswander, "Obstetric Factors Related to Prematurity"; Goldstein, "Factors Related to Birth Weight and Perinatal Mortality"; Peters et al., *"Plus ça change:* Predictors of Birthweight in Two National Studies."

22. Cnattingius et al., "Factors Influencing Birthweight for Gestational Age." A woman who has had a previous preterm infant has an increased probability of bearing another, though a history of growth retardation is not associated with an increased likelihood of preterm birth.

23. Ounsted and Ounsted, *On Fetal Growth Rate,* 22.

24. Hytten and Leitch, *Physiology of Human Pregnancy,* 319–20; Ounsted and Ounsted, *On Fetal Growth Rate,* 13–14; Kline, Stein, and Susser, *Conception to Birth,* 214–15.

25. Anderson et al., "Determinants of Size at Birth in a Canadian Population."

26. Rubin et al., "Effect of Passive Smoking on Birth-Weight."

27. Rush and Cassano, "Relationship of Cigarette Smoking and Social Class to Birth Weight."

28. Kline, Stein, and Susser, *Conception to Birth,* 214–15.

29. Kline, Stein, and Susser, *Conception to Birth,* 215; Olsen, Rachootin, and Schiødt, "Alcohol Use, Conception Time and Birthweight"; Wright et al., "Alcohol Consumption, Pregnancy and Low Birthweight"; Mills et al., "Maternal Alcohol Consumption and Birth Weight."

30. Martorell and González-Cossío, "Maternal Nutrition and Birth Weight."

31. Hytten and Leitch, *Physiology of Human Pregnancy,* 311–13; Dowding, "Distribution of Birth Weight in Seven Dublin Maternity Units"; Ericson et al., "Socio-economic Variables and Pregnancy Outcome"; Garn, Shaw, and McCabe, "Effects of Socioeconomic Status and Race on Weight-Defined and Gestational Prematurity"; Stein et al., "Social Adversity, Low Birth Weight, and Preterm Delivery."

32. Thomson, Billewicz, and Hytten, "The Assessment of Fetal Growth."

33. Anderson et al., "Determinants of Size at Birth in a Canadian Population."

34. Ericson et al., "Socio-economic Variables and Pregnancy Outcome."

35. Donaldson and Billy, "The Impact of Prenatal Care on Birth Weight"; Showstack, Budetti, and Minkler, "Factors Associated with Birthweight."

36. Pinard, "Note pour servir à l'histoire de la puériculture intra-utérine"; Pinard, *Clinique obstétricale;* Letourneur, *De l'influence de la profession de la mère sur le poids de l'enfant;* Bachimont, *Documents pour servir à l'histoire de la puériculture intra-utérine;* Sarraute-Lourié, *De l'influence du repos sur la durée de la gestation.*

37. Saurel-Cubizolles and Kaminski, "Work in Pregnancy."

38. Poerksen and Petitti, "Employment and Low Birth Weight in Black Women"; Saurel-Cubizolles and Kaminski, "Work in Pregnancy," 438, 439.

39. McDonald et al., "Prematurity and Work in Pregnancy"; Saurel-Cubizolles and Kaminski, "Work in Pregnancy," 438.

40. Tafari, Naeye, and Gobezie, "Effects of Maternal Undernutrition and Heavy Physical Work during Pregnancy on Birth Weight"; Roberts et al., "Seasonal Changes in Activity, Birth Weight and Lactational Performance"; Bantje and Niemeyer, "Rainfall and Birthweight Distribution in Rural Tanzania"; Launer et al., "The Effect of Maternal Work on Fetal Growth."

41. Ericson et al., "Socio-economic Variables and Pregnancy Outcome."

42. Kline, Stein, and Susser, *Conception to Birth,* 228.

43. Metcoff, "Association of Fetal Growth with Maternal Nutrition."

44. Metcoff, "Association of Fetal Growth with Maternal Nutrition," 333.

45. Manocha, *Malnutrition and Retarded Human Development,* 169.

46. Worthington-Roberts, "Nutrition during Pregnancy and Lactation."

47. Martorell, "Interrelationships between Diet, Infectious Disease, and Nutritional Status," 84.

48. Villar and González-Cossío, "Nutritional Factors Associated with Low Birth Weight and Short Gestational Age."

49. Antonov, "Children Born during the Siege of Leningrad in 1942."

50. Susser, "Prenatal Nutrition, Birthweight, and Psychological Development," 794.

51. Dean, "The Size of the Baby at Birth and the Yield of Breast Milk." At least forty studies of fetal development were done in Europe during and immediately after World War I, the great majority of them in Germany and Austria. The primary object of most was to determine if the nutritional conditions of wartime, which often included rationing and reductions in the availability of food, affected birth weight. Over all, the results of these inquiries were inconclusive. The majority found that wartime nutrition had no adverse effect on fetal development while a minority found that it did. While some of the findings were later questioned on methodological grounds, as a group

these investigations yielded no substantial conclusions about the role of nutrition in fetal growth. Peller and Bass, "Die Rolle exogener Faktoren in der intrauterinen Entwicklung des Menschen"; Bruce Murray, *Effect of Maternal Social Conditions and Nutrition upon Birth-Weight.*

52. Bergner and Susser, "Low Birth Weight and Prenatal Nutrition."

53. Phillips and Johnson, "The Impact of Quality of Diet and Other Factors on Birth Weight"; Martorell and González-Cossío, "Maternal Nutrition and Birth Weight," 207.

54. Susser, "Prenatal Nutrition, Birthweight, and Psychological Development"; Martorell and González-Cossío, "Maternal Nutrition and Birth Weight," 208–9.

55. Martorell and González-Cossío, "Maternal Nutrition and Birth Weight," 209–13.

56. Lechtig et al., "Effect of Food Supplementation during Pregnancy on Birth Weight"; Lechtig, Delgado, and Lasky, "Maternal Nutrition and Fetal Growth"; Villar and Rivera, "Nutritional Supplementation during Two Consecutive Pregnancies."

57. Villar and Repke, "Calcium Supplementation during Pregnancy."

58. Tchernia et al., "Maternal Folate Status, Birthweight and Gestational Age"; Worthington-Roberts, "Nutrition during Pregnancy," 247–52. For an instructive historical study of the relationship between iron-folate dietary improvements among pregnant women and declining infant mortality in eighteenth-century France see Dresch, "Maternal Nutrition and Infant Mortality Rates."

59. Lechtig et al., "Influence of Maternal Nutrition on Birth Weight."

60. Villar and González-Cossío, "Nutritional Factors Associated with Low Birth Weight," 78; Rooth, "Low Birth Weight Revised."

61. World Health Organization, "The Incidence of Low Birth Weight," 202–18.

62. Stein and Susser, "Intrauterine Growth Retardation," 6–7.

63. Stein and Susser, "Intrauterine Growth Retardation," 7.

64. Gould, "The Low-Birth-Weight Infant," 392. First trimester malnutrition may also be a factor in preterm delivery and in this sense may also influence fetal growth. Kline, Stein, and Susser, *Conception to Birth,* 247, 251.

65. Villar et al., "A Health Priority for Developing Countries"; Gould, "The Low-Birth-Weight Infant," 404–10; Martorell and González-Cossío, "Maternal Nutrition and Birth Weight," 203; Kline, Stein, and Susser, *Conception to Birth,* 251–52.

66. Villar et al., "The Differential Neonatal Morbidity of the Intrauterine Growth Retardation Syndrome."

67. Cone, *"De Pondere Infantum Recens Natorum."* Roederer found that on average the eighteen males weighed 6 pounds 9 ounces (Göttingen measure) and the nine females weighed 6 pounds 2.5 ounces (or 6 pounds 12 ounces and 6 pounds 5 ounces avoirdupois, respectively).

68. Clarke, "Observations on Some Causes of the Excess of the Mortality of Males."

69. Hamilton, Midwifery Casebook; Hamilton, *Select Cases in Midwifery.*

70. Tanner, *A History of the Study of Human Growth,* 255–56.

71. Denman, *An Introduction to the Practice of Midwifery,* 192–93.

72. For example see Flamm, "Gewicht und Grösse Neugeborener betreffend," who reported the stillbirth of a 14.5 pound male in Warsaw.

73. Simpson, "Memoir on the Sex of the Child."

74. Storer, "An Abstract of 500 Cases of Midwifery"; Storer, "Statistics of the Boston Lying-in Hospital."

75. "Foetus."

76. Quetelet, "Recherches sur le poids de l'homme aux différens ages"; Quetelet, *Sur l' homme et le développement des facultés;* Tanner, *A History of the Study of Human Growth,* 122–38.

77. Frankenhäuser, "Über einige Verhältnisse, die Einfluss auf die stärkere oder schwächere Entwickelung der Frucht während der Schwangerschaft haben"; Siebold, "Über die Gewichts- und Längenverhältnisse der neugeborenen Kinder"; Veit, 1855, "Beiträge zur geburtshülflichen Statistik"; Veit, 1856, "Beiträge zur geburtshülflichen Statistik"; Van Heddeghem, *De oude Bijlokematerniteit,* 153–80.

78. Siebold, "Über die Gewichts- und Längenverhältnisse der neugeborenen Kinder," 340.

79. Hecker and Buhl, *Klinik der Geburtskunde,* 44–51; Ogston, "Table of Cases"; Tardieu, *Étude médico-légale sur l'infanticide;* Ahlfeld, "Bestimmungen der Grösse und des Alters der Frucht vor der Geburt"; Pfannkuch, "Über die Körperform der Neugeborenen."

80. Elaesser, "Nouveau-nés," 206–10.

81. Hecker, "Zur geburtshülflichen Statistik;" Hecker, "Über das Gewicht des Fötus."

82. Cone, *"De Pondere Infantum Recens Natorum,"* 497.

83. Siebold, "Über die Gewichts- und Längenverhältnisse der neugeborenen Kinder"; Winckel, "Untersuchungen über die Gewichtsverhältnisse bei hundert Neugeborenen"; Haake, "Über die Gewichtsveränderung der Neugeborenen"; Odier, *Recherches sur la loi d'accroissement des nouveau-nés;* Theis, *Über die Gewichtsveränderung der Neugeborenen;* Sobbe, *Über Gewichts- und Längenverhältnisse der Neugeborenen;* de Franco, *Études historiques et recherches sur le poids et la loi de l'accroissement du nouveau-né;* Fleischmann, "Über Ernährung und Körperwägungen der Neugeborenen."

84. Veit, 1855, "Beiträge zur geburtshülflichen Statistik"; Veit, 1856, "Beiträge zur geburtshülflichen Statistik." For an account of Veit's career see Engel, *Leben und Werk des Bonner Frauenarztes Gustav von Veit.*

85. Frankenhäuser, "Über einige Verhältnisse, die Einfluss auf die stärkere oder schwächere Entwickelung der Frucht während der Schwangerschaft haben," 170–79.

86. Duncan, "On the Weight and Length of the Newly-Born Child"; Hecker, "Über Gewicht und Länge der neugeborenen Kinder."

87. Segond, "Du poids des nouveau-nés"; Pinard, "Foetus. I. Anatomie et physiologie"; "Nouveau-né."

88. Ingerslev, "On the Weight of New Born Children"; Ogston, "On the Average Length and Weight of Mature Newborn Scotch Children"; Körber, "Die Durchschnittsmasse ausgetragener Neugeborener und ihre Lebensfähigkeit"; Schaetzel, *Über den Einfluss des Alters der Mutter und der Zahl der voraufgegangenen Schwangerschaften auf Länge und Gewicht der Neugeborenen;* Pies, "Zur Physiologie des Neugeborenen"; Benestad, "Die Gewichtsverhältnisse reifer norwegischer Neugeborener."

89. Issmer, "Zwei Hauptmerkmale der Reife Neugeborener und deren physiologische Schwankungen."

90. Piering, "Uber die Grenzen des Körpergewichtes Neugeborener."

91. Frank, "Über den Werth der einzelnen Reifezeichen der Neugeborenen"; Holzbach, "Über den Wert der Merkmale zur Bestimmung der Reife des Neugeborenen"; Kline, Stein, and Susser, *Conception to Birth*, 165–68.

92. Pinard, "Note pour servir à l'histoire de la puériculture intra-utérine"; Pinard, *Clinique obstétricale*.

93. Letourneur, *De l'influence de la profession de la mère sur le poids de l'enfant;* Bachimont, *Documents pour servir à l'histoire de la puériculture intra-utérine;* Sarraute-Lourié, *De l'influence du repos sur la durée de la gestation;* Péchin, *Contribution à l'étude de la puériculure avant la naissance;* Grenier, *Quelques documents concernant la durée de la gestation et le poids de l'enfant à terme.*

94. Stewart, *Women, Work and the French State*, 178–90.

95. Au point de vue de l'humanité, au point de vue de l'augmentation de la population, au point de vue de l'évolution de la race française, il est nécessaire, il est urgent que les pouvoirs publics interviennent pour protéger la femme enceinte pendant les trois derniers mois de sa grossesse et le foetus pendant les trois derniers mois de sa vie intra-utérine. Bachimont, *L'histoire de la puériculture intra-utérine*, 56; Pinard, *Clinique obstétricale*, 60.

96. Fuchs, *Die Abhängigkeit des Geburtsgewichtes des Neugeborenen vom Stand und der Beschäftigung der Mutter.*

97. Schaeffer, "Über die Schwankungsbreite der Gewichtsverhältnisse von Säuglingen"; Mackenzie, *The Health of the School Child*, 38; Franqué, "Fürsorge für Schwangere und Wöchnerinnen"; Ashby, *Infant Mortality*, 30–33.

98. Oakley, *The Captured Womb*, 11.

99. Green, "The Care of Women in Pregnancy."

100. Oakley, *The Captured Womb*, 46–50; Ballantyne, *Manual of Antenatal Pathology and Hygiene*, 465–76.

101. Franqué, "Fürsorge für Schwangere und Wöchnerinnen," 542.

102. Meckel, *Save the Babies*, 159–77.

103. Oakley, *The Captured Womb*, 50–59.

104. Napheys, *The Physical Life of Woman*, 173–74.

105. For example see *Cyclopaedia of Obstetrics and Gynecology*, 307; Winckel, *A Text-book of Obstetrics*, 123; Norris, *An American Text-Book of Obstetrics*, 180; Evans, *Obstetrics: A Manual for Students and Practitioners*, 60; Bandler, *The Expectant Mother*, 46.

106. Hytten and Leitch, *Physiology of Human Pregnancy*, 461–68.

107. Prochownick, "Über Ernährungscuren in der Schwangerschaft."

108. Mussey, "Nutrition and Human Reproduction," 1041–42.

109. Guggenheim and Wolinsky, *Nutrition and Nutritional Diseases*, 150–54.

110. Ballantyne, *Expectant Motherhood*, 183.

111. Scharlieb, *The Welfare of the Expectant Mother*, 18–20.

112. Momm, "Hat die eiweiss- und fettarme Nahrung einen Einfluss auf die Entwicklung der Frucht?"

113. Oakley, *The Captured Womb*, 28–30; Donnison, *Midwives and Medical Men*, 18, 25–27.

114. Kerr, Johnstone, and Phillips, *Historical Review of British Obstetrics and Gynaecology,* 340; Cianfrani, *A Short History of Obstetrics and Gynecology,* 411.

115. Kerr, Johnstone, and Phillips, *Historical Review of British Obstetrics and Gynaecology,* especially 87–132, 390–405; Cianfrani, *A Short History of Obstetrics and Gynecology,* 399–419.

116. Issmer, "Zwei Hauptmerkmale der Reife Neugeborener," 280.

117. Siebold, "Über die Gewichts- und Längenverhältnisse der neugeborenen Kinder," 340.

118. Odier and Blache, *Quelques considérations sur les causes de la mortalité des nouveau-nés,* 20–21; Odier, *Recherches sur la loi d'accroissement des nouveau-nés,* 53–54.

119. The Wellcome Museum of the History of Medicine in London, England, holds a small collection of these scales dating from 1848. All of them were manufactured in England. See accession numbers A73065, A200718, A602015, A602029, A602073, A604038, and A655834. See also Galante et Fils, *Catalogue,* 110–11; Allen & Hanburys, *Catalogue,* 871; Maw, Son & Sons, *Catalogue,* 362.

Chapter Two

1. Flinn, *Scottish Population History,* 312.

2. Flinn, *Scottish Population History,* 309–11.

3. Butt, "The Changing Character of Urban Employment," 216; Campbell, *The Rise and Fall of Scottish Industry,* 81.

4. Hunt, *Regional Wage Variations in Britain,* 53; Campbell, *Rise and Fall of Scottish Industry,* 87–91; Smout, *A Century of the Scottish People,* 112–14.

5. Rodger, "Employment, Wages and Poverty in the Scottish Cities," 37; Gray, *The Labour Aristocracy in Victorian Edinburgh,* 44.

6. Rodger, "Employment, Wages and Poverty in the Scottish Cities," 43.

7. Rodger, "The Invisible Hand," 200.

8. Gray, *The Labour Aristocracy in Victorian Edinburgh,* 51.

9. Matthews, Feinstein, and Odling-Smee, *British Economic Growth,* 5–6, 21, 26–27, 606.

10. Gray, *The Labour Aristocracy in Victorian Edinburgh,* 51, 55.

11. Rodger, "Employment, Wages and Poverty in the Scottish Cities," 39.

12. Lee, "Modern Economic Growth and Structural Change in Scotland," 21–22.

13. Bradby and Black, "Women Compositors and the Factory Acts."

14. The Edinburgh Lying-in Institution provided medical care in childbirth to married women in their homes between 1824 and 1933. *Edinburgh Lying-in Institution for Delivering Poor Married Women at Their Own Homes.* The Royal Maternity Hospital was the successor institution to the Edinburgh General Lying-in Hospital, founded in 1793 by Alexander Hamilton, the professor of midwifery at the University of Edinburgh. A proprietary hospital, it remained in the possession of the Hamilton family until 1842. Sturrock, "Early Maternity Hospitals in Edinburgh," 122–25.

15. Edinburgh Royal Maternity Hospital, House Committee Minutes, 18 February 1895.

16. Edinburgh Royal Maternity Hospital, Director's Minutes, 25 January 1896; Ferguson, *Scottish Social Welfare,* 512.

17. Edinburgh Royal Maternity Hospital, Director's Minutes, 8 December 1876.

18. Edinburgh Royal Maternity Hospital, Director's Minutes, 3 March 1881 and 7 October 1884.

19. The proportion of married patients rose from 27 percent between 1891 and 1895 to 59 percent between 1916 and 1920.

20. *Rules & Bye-Laws of the Edinburgh Maternity Hospital.*

21. Edinburgh Royal Maternity Hospital, Director's Minutes, 8 April 1874.

22. Edinburgh Royal Maternity Hospital, Director's Minutes, 8 January, 25 January, and 13 April 1896.

23. Miller, "A Short Record of the Edinburgh Royal Maternity and Simpson Memorial Hospital," 9; Edinburgh Royal Maternity Hospital, *Annual Report,* 1907, 6.

24. Mackenzie, *Scottish Mothers and Children,* 69–89; Edinburgh Royal Maternity Hospital, Director's Minutes, 25 July 1913. The first agreements signed were with the Heart of Midlothian Lodge of the National Independent Order of Odd Fellows, the Scottish Order of Oddfellows Friendly Society, the East of Scotland Brassfounders Society, and the Burgh of Edinburgh and Burgh of Leith insurance committees.

25. *Scotsman,* 6 May 1914; Edinburgh Royal Maternity Hospital, Medical Board Minutes, 24 September and 12 November 1913.

26. Ferguson, "Some Twentieth-Century Problems in Relation to Marriage and Childbirth."

27. Edinburgh Royal Maternity Hospital, Director's Minutes, 9 April 1915; Edinburgh Royal Maternity Hospital, Medical Board Minutes, 22 February 1916; Sturrock, "The Edinburgh Royal Maternity and Simpson Memorial Hospital," 180; Oakley, *The Captured Womb,* 50–53.

28. The definition of class-based patterns of residence in Edinburgh was based upon the categories employed by Gordon in "The Status Areas of Edinburgh in 1914," 168–96. For the purposes of this study, Gordon's lowest residential category was considered the working-class area of the city.

29. The birth weight means published during the nineteenth century varied between 3100 and 3400 grams. In 1844 James Young Simpson reported a mean weight of 3295 grams for fifty male and fifty female newborns delivered at the Edinburgh Lying-in Hospital. He later recorded an average of 3103 grams for 337 singleton births in hospital between 1844 and 1846. In 1864 another Edinburgh obstetrician J. Matthews Duncan, noted a birth weight mean of 3277 grams for 2053 infants. During the late 1870s Charles Roberts, a physician and early student of human growth, indicated a birth weight mean of 3352 grams for 100 male and 100 female children of the artisan class born at full term at the Royal Maternity. Another physician, Francis Ogston, reported a series of statistics on size at birth in 1881. The mean weight of the 145 liveborn infants noted in his study was 3402 grams. It should be noted that these samples were constituted in different fashions and therefore are not precisely comparable. Simpson, "Memoir on the Sex of the Child as a Cause of Difficulty and Danger in Human Parturition," 405; Simpson, *The Obstetric Memoirs,* 847–48; Duncan, "On the Weight and Length of the Newly-Born Child," 498; Roberts, *A Manual of Anthropometry,* 79; Ogston, "On the Average Length and Weight of Mature Newborn Scotch Children."

30. Table 2.2 includes only those variables associated with statistically significant

variation in newborn weight. Similarly, all subsequent tables incorporating the results of multiple regression analysis of birth weight and length in each of the five cities include only significant variables. The preliminary results of the analysis of variance in birth weight and length performed on the entire range of variables in each urban data base are summarized in appendix 3.

31. Kitchin and Passmore, *The Scotsman's Food*, 37–52; Campbell, "Diet in Scotland," 47–60; Steven, *The Good Scots Diet*, 91–106; Mitchison, "Malnutrition in Scotland since 1700."

32. The definition of time intervals as regression variables for Edinburgh and the other cities in this study is somewhat problematic. The limitations of a single statistic in representing the experiences and conditions of diverse economic and social groups is a general problem and requires no discussion here. More specific to this study, the indices which define business cycles for these five communities exist only at the national level. Economic cycles are affected, however, by local and regional as well as national and international factors; consequently, the capacity of national indices to reflect the circumstances of individual cities is approximate at best. For the most part, therefore, I have attempted to define these time intervals broadly, guided by the economic historians of each country. Those for Edinburgh were derived from Matthews, Feinstein, and Odling-Smee, *British Economic Growth*, 5–6, 21, 26–27, 606.

33. Winter, *The Great War and the British People*, 215–29, 244–45; Dwork, *War is Good for Babies*, 208–15.

34. Martorell and González-Cossío, "Maternal Nutrition and Birth Weight."

35. No attempt has been made in this study to examine the relationship between birth weight trends on one hand and those in infant mortality or the health of young children on the other. The principal difficulty lies in the fact that, apart from data on mortality, there are no reliable indices of infant and child morbidity in any of these five communities during the period under consideration. Thus, mortality rates provide the only available measure of the health conditions of the very young. But infant morbidity and mortality are influenced by postnatal as well as prenatal factors, and the relative weight of each set of influences varies with the developmental stage of the newborn. The relationship between birth weight and infant health is strongest during the first weeks of life; thereafter a host of additional factors come gradually to exert the dominant force over a child's well-being. Unfortunately, most of the available historic information on infant mortality rates treats the first year of life as an undifferentiated whole; it does not permit us to distinguish between the immediate postnatal period and the later months of a child's first year, a distinction crucial to an understanding of the relationship between trends in infant mortality and those in newborn weight.

36. While it appears from table 2.3 that there was a higher proportion of low birth weight infants among food workers, the difference was not statistically significant.

37. Bowley, *Wages and Income in the United Kingdom since 1860*, 30, 122–23; Feinstein, *National Income, Expenditure and Output of the United Kingdom*, T140–T141.

38. The following equation expresses the relation (t-statistics are in parentheses):

$$B = 14454.0 + 6.960 \, \Delta E - 5.964 \, Y$$
$$(9.694) \qquad (3.199) \qquad (7.519)$$

Adjusted r^2 = .485; degrees of freedom = 56; Durbin-Watson = 1.771; B = birth weight; ΔE = change in earnings; and Y = year.

39. Floud, Wachter, and Gregory, *Height, Health and History,* 282, 307–9.

40. This observation rests on three facts. First, the annual means of the lengths recorded up to 1885 fluctuated more widely than they did after that time. Second, mean length rose in 1886 from 48 centimeters to 51 centimeters and thereafter remained well above the levels experienced in previous years. The size and abruptness of this increase strongly suggests the introduction of new procedures for measuring infant lengths. Third, Rohrer's index for the annual means lay above the ninetieth percentile for most years before 1886. This index (100 × weight / length^3) measures the relationship between newborn weight and length and is an indicator of newborn nutritional status. See Lubchenco, Hansman, and Boyd, "Intrauterine Growth in Length and Head Circumference"; Brandt, "Postnatal Growth of Preterm and Full-term Infants"; Mueller and Pollitt, "The Bacon Chow Study."

41. At least one inquiry has noted the independence of change in birth weight and that of length in some circumstances, an observation based on the findings of a nutritional supplementation study conducted in Taiwan during the early 1970s. Mueller and Pollitt, "The Bacon Chow Study."

42. Levitt and Smout, *The State of the Scottish Working Class in 1843,* 22.

43. Littlejohn, *Report on the Sanitary Condition of the City of Edinburgh,* 59–60.

44. Great Britain, *Report of the Royal Commission on Physical Training (Scotland),* 24.

45. Great Britain, *Report of the Inter-Departmental Committee on Physical Deterioration,* 149, 274.

46. Paton, Dunlop, and Inglis, *A Study of the Diet of the Labouring Classes in Edinburgh,* 70–82.

47. Kitchin and Passmore, *The Scotsman's Food,* 37–38; Steven, *The Good Scots Diet;* Smout, *A Century of the Scottish People,* 124–31; Campbell, "Diet in Scotland"; Oddy, "Working-Class Diets in Late Nineteenth-Century Britain."

48. Dewey, "Nutrition and Living Standards in Wartime Britain," 199–200.

49. Dewey, "Nutrition and Living Standards in Wartime Britain," 203–12.

50. A tuberculosis mortality rate for young adult women (or in its absence a more general measure) has been used as a proxy index for the infectious disease environment of Edinburgh and each of the other four cities. Like all proxies this one has been used in the absence of a superior measure, an index of the morbidity condition within the target population. Nonetheless, tuberculosis is a particularly suitable measure for this purpose. It was the leading cause of death among women of childbearing age in western Europe and North America during the late nineteenth and early twentieth centuries, and this fact alone justifies the attempt to examine the relationship between the course of the disease and the trend in newborn weight in each of these communities.

Tuberculosis mortality rates were in decline, however, throughout much of Europe and North America from at least the mid-nineteenth century onward (although Ireland was a notable exception). The reasons for this decline have long been in dispute, but nutritional and environmental conditions are among them. These factors are related to fetal development as well. But given the complex and diverse influences which affect each phenomenon, close parallelism between a community's tuberculosis mortality rates and its birth weight means should not be expected.

The literature on the history of tuberculosis is voluminous. For a brief introduction which captures the flavor of recent debate see Dubos and Dubos, *The White Plague;* McKeown and Record, "Reasons for the Decline of Mortality in England and Wales"; Cronjé, "Tuberculosis and Mortality Decline in England and Wales"; Tomes, "The White Plague Revisited"; Wilson, "Historical Decline of Tuberculosis in Europe and America."

Chapter Three

1. Helczmanovszki, "Die Entwicklung der Bevolkerung Österreichs in den letzten hundert Jahren," 120, 122–23.

2. Berend and Ranki, *The European Periphery and Industrialization,* 144.

3. Rudolph, "The Pattern of Austrian Industrial Growth from the Eighteenth to the Early Twentieth Centuries"; Rudolph, *Banking and Industrialization in Austria-Hungary,* 6–38; Komlos, *The Habsburg Monarchy as a Customs Union,* 90–111; Good, *The Economic Rise of the Habsburg Empire,* 11–95; Rudolph, "Social Structure and the Beginning of Austrian Economic Development."

4. Good, *The Economic Rise of the Habsburg Empire,* 237–56; Rudolph, *Banking and Industrialization in Austria-Hungary,* 13; Gross, "The Industrial Revolution in the Habsburg Monarchy," 273.

5. Milward and Saul, *The Development of the Economies of Continental Europe,* 321.

6. Rudolph, *Banking and Industrialization in Austria-Hungary,* 13.

7. This description is based on Rudolph, "Austria, 1800–1914."

8. Sandgruber, *Österreichische Agrarstatistik 1750–1918,* 186, table 135; Walré de Bordes, *The Austrian Crown.*

9. Rothschild, *Austria's Economic Development between the Two Wars,* 16–18. On the wartime and postwar economy see also Gulick, *Austria from Habsburg to Hitler,* 144–77; Kernbauer, März, and Weber, "Die wirtschaftliche Entwicklung," 343–79; März, *Österreichische Bankpolitik in der Zeit der grossen Wende;* Berger, "The Austrian Economy, 1918–1938," 270–84.

10. Feldbauer, *Stadtwachtstum und Wohnungsnot,* 30–35.

11. Ehmer, "Frauenarbeit und Arbeiterfamilie in Wien," 449–54, 465–68.

12. Lesky, *The Vienna Medical School of the Nineteenth Century,* 52–59. For a history of obstetrics in Vienna from a physician's perspective see Fischer, *Geschichte der Geburtshilfe in Wien.* On the history of the women's clinics see Chrobak and Schauta, *Geschichte und Beschreibung des Baues der Neuen Frauenkliniken in Wien.*

13. Hofmeister, "Austria," 302–6, 318–19, 356.

14. O'Connell, "Obstetrics in Vienna."

15. Kaup, "Säuglingssterblichkeit und Bevölkerungspolitik."

16. Peller, "Längengewichtsverhältnis der Neugeborenen und Einfluss der Schwangerenernährung auf die Entwicklung des Fötus"; Peller, "Die Masse der Neugeborenen und die Kriegsernährung der Schwangeren"; Peller, "Rückgang der Geburtsmasse als Folge der Kriegsernährung."

17. Wegs, "Working Class Respectability," 629.

18. Vienna expanded rapidly until the eve of World War I. The city extended its boundaries in 1890 to embrace its swollen suburbs, increasing the number of districts

(*Bezirke*s) from ten to nineteen and later to twenty-one. In order to standardize the address data for purposes of analysis, the city was considered a single metropolitan unit throughout this period, and the areas which constituted the eleven wards added after 1889 were recorded by their eventual designation from 1865 onward. The twenty-one districts of the city can be divided into two broad groups: working-class wards comprise *Bezirke*s 5, 11 to 17, 20, and 21 and the upper-class wards consist of *Bezirke*s 1 to 4, 6 to 10, 18, and 19.

19. In identifying the origins of the patients the hospital took political citizenship as its definition of origin. In many (probably most) instances this would have been the patient's birthplace, but in some cases it was that of her father or mother, or even a more remote ancestor. Unfortunately, the proportion of patients in these several categories is unknown. Despite this disadvantage, the practice held a hidden benefit for this study. By specifying origins in this fashion, the records provide more reliable information on the ethnicity of the patients than would otherwise have been the case.

20. Hytten and Leitch, *The Physiology of Human Pregnancy,* 300–303.

21. Ehmer, "Frauenarbeit und Arbeiterfamilie in Wien," 450.

22. The mean weight of servants' children born in winter and spring was 3135 grams, those born in summer and fall 3146 grams. The mean weights of nondomestics' newborns were 3113 grams and 3163 grams, respectively.

23. The time intervals entered into the Viennese regressions were broadly similar to those employed in Edinburgh and Dublin with the following exceptions. The economic slump of 1913 was not as severe in Austria as it was in the British Isles and North America and therefore 1915, the eve of the deepening wartime economic crisis, was chosen as the end point for the interval. In addition, the postwar economic collapse had no parallels in Great Britain and Ireland, and therefore an additional time interval (1920–22) was introduced into these regressions.

24. As figure 3.2 reveals, the proportion of low birth weight infants rose sharply after 1909, at a time when the proportion of Viennese births occurring in hospital began to rise. The possibility exists that this change introduced an increasing proportion of patients with obstetric and other health problems into the sample, thus inflating the number of low-weight newborns and stillbirths. While this possibility cannot be entirely discounted, the rising trend of low-weight births existed previously. As a result, any change in the character of the hospital population which introduced a greater number of problem births merely reinforced an existing tendency. We should also note that the rising trend of hospital stillbirths in the sample paralleled the same pattern in civic births generally, and this also indicates that the trends identified in the sample reflected changes in the population at large rather than in the sample's composition.

25. The rising number of stillbirths in the hospital was not a disguised form of abortion. Medical opinion in early twentieth-century Vienna strongly opposed abortion, which outside the hospital environment was thought to be high. The patient records list very few instances of dilation and curettage. Wegs, "Working Class Respectability," 629; Schauta, "Der Kampf gegen den gewollten Abortus."

26. The exception is an association between ethic origin and low birth weight. Czech women from laboring occupations delivered significantly fewer low birth weight infants than expected. The association noted here is slight and may be the product of a minor distributional anomaly. It is important to note that no similar effect was

detected among Czech domestics, who constituted almost two-thirds of all Czech women in the sample.

27. The influence of distributional changes among sample variables on the birth weight trend was limited. A small rise in the mean age of patients during the postwar years placed slight upward pressure on the birth weight trend in the 1920s because older women bore the heaviest children. But because of the small numbers of older mothers and the relatively small contribution made to birth weight by advancing age, the effect was small as well. The changing occupational structure of the patient population may also have introduced an upward bias to the trend. After the turn of the century a growing number of middle-class women delivered in hospital. While their numbers were limited throughout this period, they too may have helped to raise the trend slightly.

28. In this instance two cost of living indices covering different spans of time were combined to produce a single index for the whole period under review. That for 1865 to 1913 was taken from a general index developed by the Austrian economic historians Mühlpeck, Sandgruber, and Woitek and reported by Good; that for 1914 to 1930 is reported by Mitchell. Because 1914 = 100 in the Mühlpeck index whereas 1914 = 90 in the Mitchell index, I multiplied the Mitchell index by 10/9 to align it with the former. Good, *The Economic Rise of the Habsburg Empire,* 171; Mitchell, *European Historical Statistics,* 779, 781.

29. The following equation expresses the relation (t-statistics are in parentheses):

$$B = 1531.8 - 0.030\Delta C - 79.498D_1 + 0.854Y$$
$$(1.109) \quad (-1.804) \quad (2.449) \quad (1.172)$$

Adjusted r^2 = .462; degrees of freedom = 61; Durbin-Watson = 1.933; B = birth weight; ΔC = change in cost of living; D_1 = dummy variable, 1916 to 1923; and Y = year.

30. An annual Rohrer's index, which expressed the relationship between newborn weight and length, was calculated for each year under consideration. It normally ranged between the twenty-fifth and seventy-fifth centile of the ratios for modern full-term infants, and the ponderal index for the entire series fell approximately at the thirty-fifth centile. Lubchenco, Hansman, and Boyd, "Intrauterine Growth in Length and Head Circumference."

31. Sandgruber, *Die Anfänge der Konsumgesellschaft,* 150, 162.

32. Sandgruber, *Die Anfänge der Konsumgesellschaft,* 263.

33. Sandgruber, *Österreichische Agrarstatistik,* 186.

34. Rothschild, *Austria's Economic Development,* 16–18. See also Walré de Bordes, *The Austrian Crown.*

35. Sieder, "Behind the Lines."

36. The decline was from 49.0 to 28.3 deaths per ten thousand females aged fifteen to forty-four between 1891 and 1914.

37. Parentheses enclose t-statistics:

$$B = 3077.7 + .6456D$$
$$(51.551) \quad (.406)$$

$r^2 = .007$; degrees of freedom $= 22$; B $=$ birth weight; and D $=$ tuberculosis death rate.

38. Hytten and Leitch, *Physiology of Human Pregnancy,* 317.

Chapter Four

1. Sources on the size of the urban population in 1926 disagree. O'Brien indicates a population of 317,000, Vaughan and Fitzpatrick one of 394,000. The discrepancy seems due to differing definitions of the city boundary. O'Brien, *Dear, Dirty Dublin,* 284; Vaughan and Fitzpatrick, *Irish Historical Statistics,* 28–29, 42.

2. Daly, *Dublin: The Deposed Capital,* 16.

3. Daly, *Dublin: The Deposed Capital,* 4.

4. For a brief overview of the period see Kennedy, Giblin, and McHugh, *The Economic Development of Ireland in the Twentieth Century,* 34–40.

5. Daly, *Dublin: The Deposed Capital,* 4, 15–16, 18–49; Daly, "Social Structure of the Dublin Working Class," 121–23.

6. Daly, *Dublin: The Deposed Capital,* 53, 68; Daly, "Social Structure of the Dublin Working Class," 130.

7. Daly, *Dublin: The Deposed Capital,* 56–64.

8. Daly, "Women in the Irish Workforce," 75–77; Daly, "Women, Work and Trade Unionism," 71.

9. Hearn, "Domestic Servants in Dublin, 1880–1920," 86.

10. Daly, "Women in the Irish Workforce," 78.

11. Browne, "The Rotunda Hospital and its Founder"; Browne, *The Story of the Rotunda Hospital;* Browne, *The Rotunda Hospital, 1745–1945;* Ross, "The Early Years of the Dublin Lying-in Hospital."

12. The others were the Coombe Hospital, Sir Patrick Dun's Hospital, and the National Maternity Hospital. Established in 1829, the Coombe functioned throughout this period, offering intern and extern services. Sir Patrick Dun's provided extern maternity services between 1868 and 1902 only, while the National Maternity opened its doors in 1885. Feeney, *The Coombe Lying-in Hospital; Story of the National Maternity Hospital.*

13. *Clinical Report of the Rotunda,* 1869, 6; Rotunda Hospital, *Report of the Rotunda Hospital,* 1893, 13; Rotunda Hospital, Board of Governors, Minutes, 14 October 1904.

14. Phelan, "Observations on the Comparative Advantages of Affording Obstetric Attendance," 82–84.

15. *Clinical Report of the Rotunda,* 1870, 4.

16. Rotunda Hospital, *Report of the Rotunda Hospital,* 1880, 7–8.

17. Sinclair and Johnston, *Practical Midwifery,* 9–10. How long these admission procedures were followed is not clear.

18. Bigger, *Report on the Physical Welfare of Mothers and Children,* 63–65.

19. Rotunda Hospital, Board of Governors, Minutes, 8 October 1920, Master's Report on Expenditure and Income.

20. Browne, *The Story of the Rotunda Hospital,* 12; *Clinical Reports of the Rotunda,* 1920, 1.

21. Connell, "Illegitimacy Before the Famine," 51; Connolly, "Illegitimacy and Pre-Nuptial Pregnancy in Ireland before 1864."

22. Daly, *Dublin: The Deposed Capital,* 126–27.

23. The boundaries of this slum are identified on the front endpaper of O'Brien, *Dear, Dirty Dublin.*

24. Because very few women spent more than a short time in hospital before delivery, the multiple regression analysis included all patients, regardless of the duration of their prenatal hospital care.

25. Burnett, *Plenty and Want,* 182–85; Oddy, "Food, Drink and Nutrition," 271–73.

26. Because of the high degree of integration of the Irish and British economies, the time variables entered into the Dublin multiple regression analysis were broadly similar to those used in the Edinburgh analysis, the exception being that the Dublin data begin and end somewhat later than the Edinburgh. For this reason some of the Edinburgh time intervals were dropped entirely or in part in the Dublin analysis, while a new interval was introduced at the end of the period (1921–30).

27. Daly, *Dublin: The Deposed Capital,* 56–64.

28. In the following discussion, the principal concern is with the general trend of the birth weight curve. On a year-to-year basis it reveals considerable fluctuation, in large part because the sample size is relatively small and significant year-to-year variation can therefore be expected.

29. O'Flanagan, "Dublin City in an Age of War and Revolution," 9–64.

30. Bowley, *Wages and Income in the United Kingdom since 1860,* 30. Bowley's estimates extend from 1880 to the later 1930s, excluding the years 1915 to 1923.

31. Floud, Wachter, and Gregory, *Height, Health and History,* 282, 307–9.

32. The equation is as follows (t-statistics in parentheses):

$$B = 2957.9 + 3.599W$$
$$(36.593)   (4.333)$$

Adjusted r^2 = .3024; degrees of freedom = 40; Durbin-Watson = 1.910; B = birth weight; and W = real wages.

33. *Tuberculosis in Ireland,* 31–32.

34. Stafford, "Note on the Social Condition of Certain Working Class Families in Dublin," 148–58.

35. Cameron, *How the Poor Live.*

36. Thompson, *War and the Food of the Dublin Labourer,* 1–14.

37. Dockeray and Fearon, "Antenatal Nutrition in Dublin."

38. Clarkson and Crawford, "Diet and Health in Ireland," 69–75; Crawford, "Death Rates from Diabetes Mellitus in Ireland."

39. Drolet, "Epidemiology of Tuberculosis," A-5; *Tuberculosis in Ireland,* following p. 32.

40. Daly, *Dublin: The Deposed Capital,* 244.

41. Clarke, *Causes and Prevention of Tuberculosis,* 133–57.

Chapter Five

1. Thernstrom, *The Other Bostonians*, 24.

2. Davis et al., *American Economic Growth*, 34.

3. David and Solar, "History of the Cost of Living in America," 28–39.

4. Davis et al., *American Economic Growth*, 52.

5. Adams, "The Canal and Railroad Enterprise of Boston."

6. Handlin, *Boston's Immigrants*, 74–81.

7. Ward, "Nineteenth Century Boston," 90, 208–13.

8. Atkinson, "Boston as a Centre of Manufacturing Capital," 98–101; Handlin, *Boston's Immigrants*, 74–81; Ward, "Nineteenth Century Boston," 345.

9. Ward, "Nineteenth Century Boston," 87, 342.

10. Ward, "Nineteenth Century Boston," 352.

11. Keyssar, *Out of Work*, 47.

12. Wright, *Working Girls of Boston*, 98–102.

13. Wright, *Working Girls of Boston*, 128–29.

14. Wright, *Working Girls of Boston*, 128.

15. Drachman, *Hospital with a Heart*.

16. The trend to hospital birth in the United States did not accelerate until after the turn of the century, particularly during the interwar years. Leavitt, *Brought to Bed*, 171–95.

17. The New England Hospital also provided home attendance for women in childbirth, at least during the 1870s, but the numbers of patients served is not known. A third maternity hospital, St. Mary's Infant Asylum and Lying-in Hospital, was established in suburban Dorchester by the Roman Catholic archbishop of Boston during the 1870s. Little is now known about it but the number of patients it served seems to have been small. Cheney, *History and Description of the New England Hospital;* Vogel, *The Invention of the Modern Hospital*, 13; Ryan, *Beyond the Ballot Box*, 26.

18. Ward, "Nineteenth Century Boston," 230–32.

19. Quoted in Morantz and Zschoche, "Professionalism, Feminism and Gender Roles," 576.

20. New England Hospital, *Reference Book of Standing Rules; Medical Police and Rules and Regulations of the Boston Medical Association*, 23–24.

21. Drachman, *Hospital with a Heart*, 61–62.

22. New England Hospital, *Annual Report*, 1874, 11; New England Hospital, *Annual Report*, 1891, 11; *Memoir of Susan Dimock*, 37; *History of the New England Hospital for Women and Children*, 26, 33, 39.

23. Ward, "Nineteenth Century Boston," 187–90.

24. Boston Lying-in Hospital, *Annual Report*, 1884, inside cover.

25. Boston Lying-in Hospital, *Annual Report*, 1900, 26; Boston Lying-in Hospital, Minutes of the Executive Committee, 30 December 1897.

26. Boston Lying-in Hospital, Matron's Journal, 23 December 1881.

27. Boston Lying-in Hospital, Matron's Journal, 14 October and 27 December 1876, 24 November 1885; Boston Lying-in Hospital, *Annual Report*, 1890, 14.

28. Boston Lying-in Hospital, *Annual Report*, 1875, 6–7.

29. Ward, "Nineteenth Century Boston," 223–28.

30. Boston Lying-in Hospital, *Annual Report*, 1882, 7, and *Annual Report*, 1888, 11.

31. Underhill, "Public Health," 79.

32. In 1843 the Boston obstetrician D. H. Storer reported means of 3856 grams for thirty newborns recently delivered in his private practice. In 1850 he noted a mean of 3314 grams for 406 infants born in the Boston Lying-in during the previous four years. He attributed the difference to the fact that virtually all of the former were borne by Americans while most of the latter were the children of foreigners. In 1847 the Massachusetts physician J. G. Metcalf published a birth weight mean of 3771 grams for 836 infants lately born in his private practice and those of several colleagues. S. W. Abbott, another Massachusetts doctor, reported a mean of 3762 grams for 205 infants in 1879. Storer, "An Abstract of 500 Cases of Midwifery," 16; Storer, "Statistics of the Boston Lying-in Hospital," 350; Metcalf, "Statistics in Midwifery," 314; Abbott, "The Evidence of Still-birth," 261.

33. The short time span for which much of the Boston clinical data was available restricts the analysis of business cycle influences on birth weight variation. For comparative reasons, and because of the close integration of the Canadian and American economies during these years, the time variables entered into the Boston multiple regressions were based on the cycles identified by Keyssar and on those employed in the Montreal analysis. They accord generally with the broader intervals employed in Edinburgh, Vienna, and Dublin, but they also reflect somewhat shorter-term variation. Keyssar, *Out of Work*, 47.

34. In this instance, only those variables common to all four sample populations were included in the regression equation. This restriction was necessary because the program used for analysis excludes all cases for which there is a missing variable and, therefore, a standardized data base is required.

35. Pleck, *Black Migration and Poverty*, 122–60.

36. Kline, Stein, and Susser, *Conception to Birth*, 183–84, 223.

37. Boston Lying-in Hospital, *Annual Report*, 1877, 9; Boston Lying-in Hospital, Matron's Journal, 17 April 1886.

38. Boston Lying-in Hospital, *Annual Report*, 1900, 24–26.

39. David and Solar, "History of the Cost of Living in America," 16, 59.

40. The following equations express the relationships (t-statistics are in parentheses).

a) Boston Lying-in inpatients:

$$B = 3796.6 \quad - \quad 4.3867C$$
$$(19.373) \quad\quad (-2.383)$$

Adjusted $r^2 = .281$; degrees of freedom $= 11$; Durbin-Watson $= 2.353$; $B =$ birth weight; and $C =$ consumer prices.

b) Boston Lying-in black patients:

$$B = 4099.8 \quad - \quad 9.2861C$$
$$(11.379) \quad\quad (-2.7438)$$

Adjusted r^2 = .352; degrees of freedom = 11; Durbin-Watson = 1.990; B = birth weight; and C = consumer prices.

41. During the later nineteenth century, the height of children and adults also was greater in Boston than it was in northwestern Europe, a fact which further underscores the nutritional advantages generally enjoyed by Americans. Tanner, *A History of the Study of Human Growth,* 185–96.

42. Atwater, *Investigations on the Chemistry and Economy of Food.*

43. Atwater, *Investigations on the Chemistry and Economy of Food,* 212.

44. Atwater, *Investigations on the Chemistry and Economy of Food,* 214–22.

45. Levenstein, *Revolution at the Table,* 23–24.

46. Levenstein, *Revolution at the Table,* 7.

47. Levenstein, *Revolution at the Table,* 26.

Chapter Six

1. Four annexations during the 1880s and 1890s added an estimated 28,000 to the urban population. Blanchard, *L'Ouest du Canada français,* 292–96; Canada, *Census of Canada,* 1881 and 1891.

2. Canada, *Census of Canada,* 1851, vol. 1, appendix 3; *Census of Canada,* 1901, vol. 1, table 11.

3. Robert, "Urbanisation et population."

4. Chambers and Bertram, "Urbanization and Manufacturing in Central Canada," 239.

5. Chambers and Bertram, "Urbanization and Manufacturing in Central Canada," 242–53.

6. Firestone, *Canada's Economic Development,* 172–73; Marr and Paterson, *Canada: An Economic History,* 375–90.

7. Bradbury, "The Family Economy and Work in an Industrializing City," 76.

8. Ames, *The City Below the Hill,* 20.

9. The institution was renamed the Montreal Maternity Hospital in 1887.

10. Sainte-Mechtilde, "La fille-mère," 172–73.

11. Ward, "Unwed Motherhood in Nineteenth Century English Canada;" Ward, "Introduction."

12. Sainte-Mechtilde, "La fille-mère," 185–86.

13. The Dutch mean fell to 3000 grams while the Russian average declined even further to 2800 grams. Antonov, "Children Born during the Siege of Leningrad in 1942"; Susser, "Prenatal Nutrition, Birthweight, and Psychological Development."

14. In this instance the time intervals entered into the regression were based upon Marr and Paterson's description of Canadian business cycles. Marr and Paterson, *Canada: An Economic History,* 375–90.

15. Taylor and Michell, *Statistical Contributions to Canadian Economic History,* vol. 2, 55–56.

16. Lapointe-Roy, *Charité bien ordonnée,* 273–89.

17. Denstedt, "A Chronicle of the Montreal Diet Dispensary"; *Short History of the Diet Dispensary, 1879–1906.*

18. Montreal, *Report of the Sanitary State,* 1881, 15; *Report of the Sanitary State,* 1885, 17–19; *Report of the Sanitary State,* 1887, 19–20; *Report of the Sanitary State,* 1892, 14.

19. La nourriture est tellement chère et les moyens de l'ouvrier sont si restreints que la famille pauvre achète des aliments de qualité inférieure et avariés. Quoted in Tétreault, "Les maladies de la misère," 521–22.

Chapter Seven

1. Eveleth and Tanner, *Worldwide Variation in Human Growth,* 191–207.

2. Ó Gráda, *The Great Irish Famine,* 26–27.

3. Daly, *Dublin: The Deposed Capital,* 80–81.

4. Bowley, *Wages and Income in the United Kingdom since 1860;* Floud, Wachter, and Gregory, *Height, Health and History,* 282, 307–9; Komlos, *Nutrition and Economic Development,* 47–49; Fogel, "Nutrition and the Decline in Mortality," 497.

5. Because the variances of these populations were unequal, statistical significance was tested by the Kruskal-Wallis one-way analysis of variance. The test was for differences between the three categories of duration of hospitalization. The following results were obtained:

	N	Chi-Square[a]	Significance
Edinburgh	1936	27.924	.000
Montreal	4877	47.193	.000
Vienna (weight)	7763	71.869	.000
Vienna (length)	7693	67.792	.000

[a]Corrected for ties.

6. T-Test for the equality of two means, pooled variance estimate: *t* value = 1.75, 2-Tail probability = .080.

7. In each instance, statistical significance was tested by a T-Test for the equality of two means (marital status, residence, and season) or by the Kruskal-Wallis one-way analysis of variance (age, parity, and occupation). The findings are as follows:

	Separate variance estimate *t* value			Age[d]		Parity[e]		Occupation[f]	
	Marital status[a]	Residence[b]	Season[c]	N	Chi-square[g]	N	Chi-square[g]	N	Chi-square[g]
Edinburgh	4.05	4.24		1932	6.667	1622	23.010		
	(.000)	(.000)			[.036]		[.000]		
Montreal	11.14		3.35	4759	34.734	4833	97.655		
	(.000)		(.001)		[.000]		[.000]		
Vienna	13.11	19.86	3.95	10,001	13.160	10,008	124.649	9813	245.814
	(.000)	(.000)	(.000)		[.001]		[.000]		[.000]

[a]Married compared with unmarried.

[b]Urban residents compared with others.

[c]Winter compared with other seasons.

[d]Age groups: under 20, 20 to 34, 35 and older.

eParity: 1, 2 through 4, 5 or more.
fOccupations: domestics and unemployed compared with others.
gCorrected for ties.
2-Tail probability scores in parentheses.
Significance values in square brackets.

8. See chapter 1, pages 16, 25–26.

9. Sieder, "Behind the Lines."

10. Foisy, *De quelques applications de la balance à l'étude physiologique et clinique des nouveau-nés;* Sobbe, *Über Gewichts- und Längenverhältnisse der Neugeborenen.*

11. Goldin and Margo, "The Poor at Birth."

12. Rosenberg, "Birth Weights in Three Norwegian Cities." In this study the sample population was constructed to answer questions about the patients' breast-feeding histories. It therefore included a disproportionately large number of multiparous mothers, a factor which would raise birth weight means slightly above the levels of a normal population of newborns.

13. Brudevoll, Liestøl, and Walløe, "Menarcheal Age in Oslo during the Last 140 Years"; Liestøl, "Social Conditions and Menarcheal Age"; Komlos, "The Age at Menarche in Vienna."

14. This pattern is broadly similar to that observed by Floud and others in the average heights of Irish and Scottish military recruits to the British army and the Royal Marines. The mean height of Scottish enlistees exceeded that of the Irish for all birth cohorts before that of the 1860s. Thereafter these positions were reversed, and average Irish heights exceeded those of the Scots. According to Floud and colleagues, the trends reflected changes in the nutritional status of the two communities rather than genetic differences. The greater birth weight disadvantage of Dublin mothers had been overcome by 1884, just at that time when the height cohorts born in the 1860s were reaching their maturity, and Irish superiority was firmly established within the next decade. Floud, Wachter, and Gregory, *Height, Health and History,* 200, 206–7. Both height and birth weight indices point to a fundamental shift in the relative nutritional status of the Irish and the Scots during the 1870s and 1880s.

15. The proportion of patients in the sample who delivered infants dropped from 90 percent to approximately 75 percent annually during the first decade of the new century, and it remained close to this level until 1930. This change reflects an increase in the proportion of patients suffering from obstetric and gynecological complaints and indicates that the medical functions of the Geburtskliniken broadened somewhat during these years.

16. We should also note the likely connection between the incidence of low birth weight and infant mortality at a time when infant mortality rates in western Europe and North America had begun to decline. Because low birth weight is both a predisposing and a causal factor in early infant death, it was almost certainly a leading factor in sustaining high infant mortality rates, at least in communities where low birth rates were high or rising.

17. Van Wieringen, "Secular Growth Changes"; Eveleth and Tanner, *Worldwide Variation in Human Growth,* 205–7; Floud, Wachter, and Gregory, *Height, Health and History,* 20.

18. Floud, Wachter, and Gregory, *Height, Health and History;* Fogel, "Nutrition and the Decline in Mortality," 439–527; Komlos, *Nutrition and Economic Development.*

19. Komlos, *Nutrition and Economic Development,* table B.1, 242.

20. Fogel, "Nutrition and the Decline in Mortality," 465, 511.

21. Floud, Wachter, and Gregory, *Height, Health and History,* 205–7, 216.

22. Sieder, " 'Vata, derf i aufstehen?' "; Sieder, "Behind the Lines." Similar family food consumption patterns were characteristic of working-class life in the United Kingdom. Floud, Wachter, and Gregory, *Height, Health and History,* 280; Burnett, *Plenty and Want,* 182–85; Oddy, "Food, Drink and Nutrition," 271–73.

23. Other evidence supports this conclusion. Hartmut Kaelble argues that growing inequality characterized the general living conditions of European men and women between the mid-nineteenth century and the early twentieth century. He suggests that, although both sexes enjoyed improvements in food, housing, medicine, and hygiene, women benefited less than men because of deterioration in other working and living conditions. Kaelble, *Industrialisation and Social Inequality in Nineteenth-Century Europe,* 134.

24. Fogel, "Nutrition and the Decline in Mortality," 496.

25. The mean birth weight of 768 singleton infants was 2973 grams. Their mothers were selected for the study because they were identified as being at high risk of bearing a low birth weight child. Susser, "Prenatal Nutrition, Birthweight, and Psychological Development."

26. World Health Organization, "The Incidence of Low Birth Weight," 199.

27. World Health Organization, "The Incidence of Low Birth Weight," 202–3.

28. Villar and Belizán, "The Relative Contribution of Prematurity and Fetal Growth Retardation to Low Birth Weight."

Appendix 1

1. Simpson, "Method of Case-Taking in Midwifery."

2. Issmer, "Zwei Hauptmerkmale der Reife Neugeborener," 280.

REFERENCES AND
ADDITIONAL SOURCES

The following list includes those works referred to in the endnotes as well as other major sources which informed the study.

Abbott, S. W. 1879. "The Evidence of Still-birth." *Bost. Med. Surg. J.* 10, no. 8: 259–64.

Adams, Charles Francis. 1881. "The Canal and Railroad Enterprise of Boston." *The Memorial History of Boston.* Vol. 4, ed. Justin Windsor. Boston: James R. Osgood.

Ahlfeld, F. 1871. "Bestimmungen der Grösse und des Alters der Frucht vor der Geburt." *Arch. Gynak.* 2:353–72.

Alexander, G. R., M. E. Tompkins, J. M. Altekruse, and C. A. Hornung. 1985. "Racial Differences in the Relation of Birth Weight and Gestational Age to Neonatal Mortality." *Public Health Rep.* 100, no. 5:539–47.

Allen & Hanburys, London. c. 1910. *Catalogue.*

Ames, Herbert. [1897] 1972. *The City Below the Hill.* Reprint. Toronto: University of Toronto Press.

Anderson, G. D., I. N. Blidner, S. McClemont, and J. C. Sinclair. 1984. "Determinants of Size at Birth in a Canadian Population." *Am. J. Obstet. Gynecol.* 150, no. 3:236–44.

Annual Report of the Directors of the Edinburgh General Lying-in Hospital. 1832.

Antonov, A. N. 1947. "Children Born during the Siege of Leningrad in 1942." *J. Pediatr.* 30:250–59.

Appelt, Erna. 1985. *Von Ladenmädchen, Schreibfräulein und Gouvernanten: Die weiblichen Angestellten Wiens zwischen 1900 und 1934.* Vienna: Verlag für Gesellschaftskritik.

Arbuckle, T. E., and G. S. Sherman. 1989. "An Analysis of Birth Weight by Gestational Age in Canada." *Can. Med. Assoc. J.* 140, no. 2:157–60.

Ashby, H. T. 1915. *Infant Mortality.* Cambridge: Cambridge University Press.

Atkinson, Edward. 1881. "Boston as a Centre of Manufacturing Capital." *The Memorial History of Boston.* Vol. 4, ed. Justin Windsor. Boston: James R. Osgood.

Atwater, W. O. 1895. *Methods and Results of Investigations on the Chemistry and Economy of Food.* U.S. Department of Agriculture, Office of Experiment Stations, Bulletin No. 21. Washington, D.C.: Government Printing Office.

Austria. *Berufsstatistik nach den Ergebnissen der Volkszählung von 31. December 1890. Österreichische Statistik* vol. 33, no. 2.

Austria. *Berufsstatistik nach den Ergebnissen der Volkszählung von 31. December 1900. Österreichische Statistik.* Vol. 66, no. 2.

Austria. *Berufsstatistik nach den Ergebnissen der Volkszählung von 31. December 1910. Österreichische Statistik.* N.s., vol. 3, no. 2.

Austria. *Die Bevölkerung der im Reichsrathe vertretenen Königreiche und Länder nach Beruf und Erwerb,* 1880. Österreichische Statistik. Vol. 1, no. 3.

Bachimont, F. -C. 1898. *Documents pour servir à l'histoire de la puériculture intra-utérine.* M.D. thesis, Faculté de médecine de Paris.

Baird, D. 1980. "Environment and Reproduction." *Br. J. Obstet. Gynaecol.* 87, no. 12:1057–67.

Baird, D. 1974. "The Epidemiology of Low Birth Weight: Changes in Incidence in Aberdeen, 1948–72." *J. Biosoc. Sci.* 6:323–41.

Ballantyne, J. W. 1914. *Expectant Motherhood: Its Supervision and Hygiene.* London: Cassell.

Ballantyne, J. W. 1902. *Manual of Antenatal Pathology and Hygiene: The Foetus.* Edinburgh: William Green and Sons.

Bandler, S. W. 1916. *The Expectant Mother.* Philadelphia and London: W. B. Saunders.

Bantje, H., and R. Niemeyer. 1984. "Rainfall and Birthweight Distribution in Rural Tanzania." *J. Biosoc. Sci.* 16:375–84.

Barker, D. J. P., A. R. Bull, C. Osmond, and S. J. Simmonds. 1990. "Fetal and Placental Size and Risk of Hypertension in Adult Life." *Br. Med. J.* 301, no. 6746: 259–62.

Barr, A. 1956. "A Short Account of Tuberculosis in Ireland, 1850–1900." *Ir. J. Med. Sci.* 6th series, no. 362:58–67.

Barrington, Ruth. 1987. *Health, Medicine and Politics in Ireland, 1900–1970.* Dublin: Institute of Public Administration.

Barron, S. L. 1983. "Birthweight and Ethnicity." *Br. J. Obstet. Gynaecol.* 90:289–90.

Benestad, G. 1914. "Die Gewichtsverhältnisse reifer norwegischer Neugeborener in den ersten 12 Tagen nach der Geburt." *Arch. Gynak.* 101:292–350.

Berend, I. T., and G. Ranki. 1974. *Economic Development in East Central Europe in the 19th and 20th Centuries.* New York: Columbia University Press.

Berend, I. T., and G. Ranki. 1982. *The European Periphery and Industrialization, 1780–1914.* Cambridge: Cambridge University Press.

Berger, Peter. 1990. "The Austrian Economy, 1918–1938." *Economic Development in the Habsburg Monarchy and in the Successor States,* ed. John Komlos. Boulder, Colo.: East European Monographs.

Bergner, L., and M. W. Susser. 1970. "Low Birth Weight and Prenatal Nutrition: An Interpretive Review." *Pediatrics* 46, no. 6:946–66.

Bernier, Jacques. 1973. "La condition des travailleurs, 1851–1896." In *Les travailleurs québécois*, ed. Jean Hamelin, 31–60. Montréal: Les Presses de l'Université du Québec.

Bigger, E. Coey. 1917. *Report on the Physical Welfare of Mothers and Children*. Dublin: Carnegie United Kingdom Trust.

Blanchard, Raoul. 1953. *L'Ouest du Canada français*. Vol. 1, *Montréal et sa région*. Montreal: Beauchemin.

Blidner, I., S. McClemont, G. D. Anderson, and J. C. Sinclair. 1984. "Size-at-birth Standards for an Urban Canadian Population." *Can. Med. Assoc. J.* 130:133–40.

Board of Superintendence of Dublin Hospitals. *Report*. 1868–69 to 1900.

Boldman, R., and D. M. Reed. 1977. "Worldwide Variations in Low Birth Weight." In *The Epidemiology of Prematurity*, ed. D. M. Reed and F. J. Stanley, 39–51. Baltimore and Munich: Urban and Schwarzenberg.

Bolognese-Leuchtenmüller, Birgit, ed. 1978. *Bevölkerungsentwicklung und Berufsstruktur, Gesundheits- und Fürsorgewesen in Österreich, 1750–1918*. Vol. 1, *Wirtschafts- und Sozialstatistik Österreich-Ungarns*. Vienna: Verlag für Geschichte und Politik Wien.

Bolognese-Leuchtenmüller, Birgit. 1979. "Unterversorgung und mangelnde Betreuung der Kleinkinder in den Unterschichtenfamilien als soziales Problem des 19. Jahrhunderts." *Wirtschaft- und sozialhistorische Beiträge. Festschrift für Alfred Hoffman zum 75. Geburtstag*, ed. Herbert Knittler, 410–30. Vienna: Verlag für Geschichte und Politik Wien.

Boston. *Annual Report of the Board of Health*. 1876–1900.

Boston Lying-in Hospital. *Annual Report*. 1875–1900.

Boston Lying-in Hospital. 1873. *Bylaws of the Boston Lying-in Hospital*. Boston: Rockwell & Churchill.

Boston Lying-in Hospital. Matron's Journal. Rare Book Room, Countway Library, Harvard University.

Boston Lying-in Hospital. Minutes of the Executive Committee. Rare Book Room, Countway Library, Harvard University.

Bowditch, H. P. 1877. *The Growth of Children*. Boston: Wright.

Bowley, A. L. 1937. *Wages and Income in the United Kingdom since 1860*. Cambridge: Cambridge University Press.

Bradbury, Bettina. 1979. "The Family Economy and Work in an Industrializing City: Montreal in the 1870s." Canadian Historical Association, *Historical Papers*, 71–96.

Bradbury, Bettina. 1982. "The Fragmented Family: Family Strategies in the Face of Death, Illness, and Poverty—Montreal, 1860–1885." In *Childhood and Family in Canadian History*, ed. Joy Parr, 109–28. Toronto: McClelland and Stewart.

Bradby, L. Barbara, and Anne Black. 1899. "Women Compositors and the Factory Acts." *The Economic Journal* 9:261–66.

Brandt, I. 1980. "Postnatal Growth of Preterm and Full-term Infants." In *Human Physical Growth and Maturation: Methodologies and Factors*, ed. F. E. Johnston, A. F. Roche, and C. Susanne, 139–60. New York and London: Plenum Press.

Brenner, W. E., D. A. Edelman, and C. H. Hendricks. 1976. "A Standard of Fetal Growth for the United States of America." *Am. J. Obstet. Gynecol.* 126, no. 5: 555–64.

Browne, Alan D. H. 1977. "The Rotunda Hospital and Its Founder." In *Essays in Honour of J. D. H. Widness,* ed. Eoin O'Brian, 143–56. Dublin: Cityview Press.

Browne, Alan D. H. 1979. *The Story of the Rotunda Hospital.* Dublin: Rotunda Hospital.

Browne, O'Donel T. D. 1947. *The Rotunda Hospital, 1745–1945.* Edinburgh: Livingston.

Bruce Murray, M. 1924. *The Effect of Maternal Social Conditions and Nutrition upon Birth-Weight and Birth-Length.* London: His Majesty's Stationery Office.

Brudevoll, J. E., K. Liestøl, and L. Walløe. 1979. "Menarcheal Age in Oslo during the Last 140 Years." *Ann. Hum. Biol.* 6, no. 5:407–16.

Bryder, Linda. 1988. *Below the Magic Mountain: A Social History of Tuberculosis in Twentieth-Century Britain.* Oxford: Clarendon Press.

Burnett, John. 1979. *Plenty and Want: A Social History of Diet in England from 1815 to the Present Day.* London: Scolar Press.

Butt, John. 1985. "The Changing Character of Urban Employment 1901–1981." In *Perspectives of the Scottish City,* ed. G. Gordon, 212–35. Aberdeen: Aberdeen University Press.

Cameron, Charles. 1908. *How the Poor Live.* Dublin: Falconer.

Campbell, R. H. 1966. "Diet in Scotland: An Example of Regional Variation." In *Our Changing Fare: Two Hundred Years of British Food Habits,* ed. T. C. Barker, J. C. McKenzie, and John Yudkin, 47–60. London: MacGibbon & Kee.

Campbell, R. H. 1980. *The Rise and Fall of Scottish Industry.* Edinburgh: John Donald.

Canada. *Census of Canada,* 1851–1911.

Canada. Statistics Canada, Canadian Centre for Health Information. 1990. *Health Reports,* supplement 14, vol. 2, no. 1 (1990), *Births, 1978–88,* 29–36. Ottawa: Minister of Supply and Services.

Carpenter, Philip P. 1859. "On the Relative Value of Human Life in Different Parts of Canada." *Can. Natur.* 4:173–86.

Carpenter, Philip P. 1869. "On Some of the Causes of Excessive Mortality of Young Children in the City of Montreal." *Can. Natur.* 4:188–206.

Carpenter, Philip P. 1866. "On the Vital Statistics of Montreal." *Can. Natur.* New series, 3:134–56.

Chambers, E. J., and G. W. Bertram. 1966. "Urbanization and Manufacturing in Central Canada, 1870–1890." In *Canadian Political Science Association, Conference on Statistics, 1964: Papers on Regional Statistical Studies,* ed. Sylvia Ostry and T. K. Rymes, 225–58. Toronto: University of Toronto Press.

Cheney, Ednah Dow. 1876. *History and Description of the New England Hospital for Women and Children.* Boston.

Chetcuti, P., S. H. Sinha, and M. I. Levene. 1985. "Birth Size in Indian Ethnic Subgroups Born in Britain." *Arch. Dis. Child.* 60:868–70.

Chrobak, Rudolf, and Friedrich Schauta. 1911. *Geschichte und Beschreibung des Baues der Neuen Frauenkliniken in Wien.* Berlin and Vienna: Urban and Schwarzenberg.

Cianfrani, Theodore. 1960. *A Short History of Obstetrics and Gynecology.* Springfield, Ill.: Charles C. Thomas.

Clarke, Brice R. 1952. *Causes and Prevention of Tuberculosis,* 133–57. Baltimore: Williams and Wilkins.

Clarke, J. 1786. "Observations on Some Causes of the Excess of the Mortality of Males above That of Females." *Phil. Trans. R. Soc. Lond.*:349–64.

Clarkson, L. A., and E. M. Crawford. 1989. "Diet and Health in Ireland: 1600–1900." *Professional Horticulture* 3:69–75.

Clinical Report of the Rotunda Lying-in Hospital. 1869–1930.

Cnattingius, S., O. Axelsson, G. Eklund, G. Lindmark, and O. Meirik. 1984. "Factors Influencing Birthweight for Gestational Age with Respect to Risk Factors for Intrauterine Growth Retardation." *Early Hum. Dev.* 10:45–55.

Cone, T. E. 1961. *"De Pondere Infantum Recens Natorum:* The History of Weighing the Newborn Infant." *Pediatrics* 28:490–98.

Connell, K. H. 1968. "Illegitimacy Before the Famine." In *Irish Peasant Society: Four Historical Essays,* 51–86. Oxford: Oxford University Press.

Connolly, S. J. 1979. "Illegitimacy and Pre-Nuptial Pregnancy in Ireland before 1864: The Evidence of Some Catholic Parish Registers." *Ir. Ec. Soc. Hist.* 6:5–23.

Cooper, J. I. 1956. "The Social Structure of Montreal in the 1850's." Canadian Historical Association, *Report,* 63–73.

Copp, Terry. 1974. *The Anatomy of Poverty: The Condition of the Working Class in Montreal, 1897–1929.* Toronto: McClelland and Stewart.

Crawford, E. M. 1987. "Death Rates from Diabetes Mellitus in Ireland 1833–1983: A Historical Commentary." *Ulst. Med. J.* 56, no. 2:109–15.

Cronjé, Gillian. 1984. "Tuberculosis and Mortality Decline in England and Wales, 1851–1910." *Urban Disease and Mortality in Nineteenth-Century England,* ed. Robert Woods and John Woodward, 79–101. London: Batsford.

Cross, D. Suzanne. 1973. "The Neglected Majority: The Changing Role of Women in Nineteenth-Century Montreal." *H. s./S. H.* 6:202–23.

Cyclopaedia of Obstetrics and Gynecology. Vol. 1. 1887. New York: William Wood. [Vol. 1 of A. Charpentier. 1887. *A Practical Treatise on Obstetrics.*]

Daly, Mary E. 1984. *Dublin: The Deposed Capital: A Social and Economic History, 1860–1914.* Cork: Cork University Press.

Daly, Mary E. 1982. "Social Structure of the Dublin Working Class, 1871–1911." *Ir. Hist. S.* 23, no. 90:121–33.

Daly, Mary E. 1981. "Women in the Irish Workforce from Pre-Industrial to Modern Times." *Saothar* 7:74–82.

Daly, Mary E. 1978. "Women, Work and Trade Unionism." *Women in Irish Society: The Historical Dimension,* ed. Margaret MacCurtain and Donncha O'Corrain, 71–81. Dublin: Arlen Houx.

D'Arcy, Fergus A. 1988. "Wages of Labourers in the Dublin Building Industry, 1667–1918." *Saothar* 14:17–32.

David, Paul A., and Peter Solar. 1977. "A Bicentenary Contribution to the History of the Cost of Living in America." In *Research in Economic History: An Annual Compilation of Research,* vol. 2, 1–80. Greenwich, Conn.: JAI Press.

Davis, Lance E., Richard E. Easterlin, William N. Parker, Dorothy S. Brady, Albert Fishlow, Robert E. Gallman, Stanley Lebergott, Robert E. Lipsey, Douglass C. North, Nathan Rosenberg, Eugene Smolensky, and Peter Temin. 1972. *American*

Economic Growth: An Economist's History of the United States. New York: Harper and Row.

Dawson, I., R. Y. Golder, and E. G. Jonas. 1982. "Birthweight by Gestational Age and Its Effect on Perinatal Mortality in White and in Punjabi Births: Experience at a District General Hospital in West London 1967–1975." *Br. J. Ob. Gyn.* 89: 896–99.

Dean, R. F. A. 1951. "The Size of the Baby at Birth and the Yield of Breast Milk." In *Studies of Undernutrition, Wuppertal 1946–9.* Medical Research Council, Special Report Series, no. 275, 346–78. London: His Majesty's Stationery Office.

Denman, T. 1816. *An Introduction to the Practice of Midwifery.* 5th ed. London: Bensley and Son.

Denstedt, Orville F. "A Chronicle of the Montreal Diet Dispensary." [Typescript in possession of the Montreal Diet Dispensary].

Dewey, P. E. 1988. "Nutrition and Living Standards in Wartime Britain." In *The Upheaval of War: Family, Work and Welfare in Europe, 1914–1918,* ed. Richard Wall and Jay Winter, 197–220. Cambridge: Cambridge University Press.

Dockeray, G. C., and W. R. Fearon. 1939. "Antenatal Nutrition in Dublin: A Preliminary Survey." *Ir. J. Med. Sci.* 6th series, no. 158:80–84.

Donaldson, P. J., and J. O. G. Billy. 1984. "The Impact of Prenatal Care on Birth Weight: Evidence from an International Data Set." *Med. Care* 22, no. 2:177–88.

Donnison, Jean. 1977. *Midwives and Medical Men: A History of Inter-Professional Rivalries and Women's Rights.* New York: Schocken.

Dougherty, C. R. S., and A. D. Jones. 1982. "The Determinants of Birthweight." *Am. J. Obstet. Gynecol.* 144, no. 2:190–200.

Dowding, V. M. 1982. "Distributions of Birth Weight in Seven Dublin Maternity Units." *Br. Med. J.* 284:1901–4.

Drachman, Virginia G. 1984. *Hospital with a Heart: Women Doctors and the Paradox of Separatism at the New England Hospital 1862–1969.* Ithaca, N.Y.: Cornell University Press.

Dresch, Catherine. 1990. "Maternal Nutrition and Infant Mortality Rates: An Evaluation of the Bourgeoisie of 18th-Century Montbélard." *Food and Foodways* 4, no. 1:1–38.

Drolet, Godias J. 1946. "Epidemiology of Tuberculosis." In *Clinical Tuberculosis,* ed. B. Goldberg, A-3–A-9. Philadelphia: F. A. Davis.

Dublin. *Reports and Printed Documents of the Corporation of Dublin.* 1869–1900.

Dubos, René, and Jean Dubos. [1952] 1987. *The White Plague: Tuberculosis, Man and Society.* 2d ed. New Brunswick, N.J.: Rutgers University Press.

Dumont, Micheline, Michèle Jean, Marie Lavigne, and Jennifer Stoddart. 1987. *Quebec Women: A History.* Toronto: Women's Press.

Duncan, J. M. 1864. "On the Weight and Length of the Newly-Born Child in Relation to the Mother's Age." *Edinb. Med. J.* 10:497–502.

Duncan, J. M. 1871. "Practice in the Prediction of the Day of Confinement." *Trans. Edinb. Obstet. Soc.* 2:259–69.

Dunn, H. G. 1984. "Social Aspects of Low Birth Weight." *Can. Med. Assoc. J.* 130:1131–40.

Dwork, Deborah. 1987. *War is Good for Babies and Other Young Children: A History of the Infant and Child Welfare Movement in England, 1898–1918*. London: Tavistock.

Edinburgh Lying-In Institution for Delivering Poor Married Women at Their Own Homes. 1824. Edinburgh: Murray and Mitchell.

Edinburgh Royal Maternity Hospital. *Annual Report*. 1870–1921.

Edinburgh Royal Maternity Hospital. Constitutions, Bylaws, etc. Medical Archives Centre University of Edinburgh.

Edinburgh Royal Maternity Hospital. Director's Minutes. Medical Archives Centre University of Edinburgh.

Edinburgh Royal Maternity Hospital. House Committee Minutes. Medical Archives Centre University of Edinburgh.

Edinburgh Royal Maternity Hospital. Medical Board Minutes. Medical Archives Centre University of Edinburgh.

Ehmer, Josef. 1981. "Frauenarbeit und Arbeiterfamilie in Wien: Vom Vormärz bis 1934." *Geschichte und Gesellschaft* 7:438–73.

Ehmer, Josef. 1991. "The Making of the 'Modern Family' in Vienna 1780–1930." *History & Society in Central Europe* 1, no. 1:7–27.

Elaesser, M., 1843. "Nouveau-nés." *Archiv Générale de Médicine*. 4th series, 3: 206–10.

Engel, Carola. 1983. *Leben und Werk des Bonner Frauenarztes Gustav von Veit*. M.D. diss., Friedrich-Wilhelms-Universität zu Bonn.

Ericson, A., M. Eriksson, B. Källén, and R. Zetterström. 1989. "Socio-economic Variables and Pregnancy Outcome: Birthweight in Singletons." *Acta Paediatr. Scand.* Supplement 360:37–42.

Evans, D. J. 1909. *Obstetrics. A Manual for Students and Practitioners*. Philadelphia and New York: Lea and Febiger.

Eveleth, P. B., and J. M. Tanner. 1990. *Worldwide Variation in Human Growth*. 2d ed. Cambridge: Cambridge University Press.

Feeney, J. K. 1983. *The Coombe Lying-in Hospital*. Dublin.

Feinstein, C. H. 1972. *National Income, Expenditure and Output of the United Kingdom, 1855–1965*. Cambridge: Cambridge University Press.

Feinstein, C. H. 1988. "The Rise and Fall of the Williamson Curve." *J. Ec. Hist.* 48, no. 3:699–729.

Feldbauer, Peter. 1977. *Stadtwachstum und Wohnungsnot: Determinaten unzureichender Wohnungsversorgung in Wien 1848 bis 1914*. Vienna: Verlag für Geschichte und Politik Wien.

Fenwick, George E. 1861. "The Medical Statistics of the City of Montreal." *Br. Am. J.* 2:390–94, 439–42, 489–93, 527–31.

Fenwick, George E. 1862. "The Medical Statistics of the City of Montreal." *Br. Am. J.* 3:33–37.

Ferguson, J. H. 1913. "Some Twentieth-Century Problems in Relation to Marriage and Childbirth." *Trans. Edinb. Obstet. Soc.* 38:3–39.

Ferguson, Thomas. 1958. *Scottish Social Welfare, 1864–1914*. Edinburgh: Livingston.

Firestone, O. J. 1958. *Canada's Economic Development, 1867–1953*. London: Bowes and Bowes.

Fischer, J. 1909. *Geschichte der Geburtshilfe in Wien.* Leipzig and Vienna: Franz Deuticke.

Fitzpatrick, David. 1987. "The Modernisation of the Irish Female." *Rural Ireland 1600–1900: Modernisation and Change,* ed. Patrick O'Flanagan, Paul Ferguson, and Kevin Whelan, 162–80. Cork: Cork University Press.

Flamm. 1844. "Gewicht und Grösse Neugeborener betreffend." *Zeit. Ges. Med.* 27:362–70.

Flandrin, Jean-Louis, Philip Hyman, and Mary Hyman, eds. 1983. *Le Cuisinier françois.* Paris: Montalba.

Fleetwood, John F. 1983. *The History of Medicine in Ireland.* 2d ed. Dublin: Skellig Press.

Fleischmann, L. 1877. "Über Ernährung und Körperwägungen der Neugeborenen und Säuglinge." *Wiener Klinik* 3:145–94.

Flinn, D. Edgar. 1906. *Official Report on the Sanitary Circumstances and Administration of the City of Dublin with Special Reference to the Causes of the High Death Rate.* Dublin: His Majesty's Stationery Office.

Flinn, Michael, ed. 1977. *Scottish Population History from the 17th Century to the 1930's.* Cambridge: Cambridge University Press.

Floud, Roderick, Kenneth Wachter, and Annabel Gregory. 1990. *Height, Health and History: Nutritional Status in the United Kingdom, 1750–1980.* Cambridge: Cambridge University Press.

"Foetus." In *Dictionnaire des sciences médicales* 16:49–80. Paris, 1816.

Fogel, Robert William. 1986. "Nutrition and the Decline in Mortality since 1700: Some Preliminary Findings." In *Long-Term Factors in American Economic Growth,* ed. Stanley L. Engerman and Robert E. Gallman, 439–555. Chicago: University of Chicago Press.

Fogel, Robert William. 1986. "Physical Growth as a Measure of the Economic Well-being of Populations: The Eighteenth and Nineteenth Centuries." In *Human Growth: A Comprehensive Treatise.* 2d ed. Vol. 3, *Methodology: Ecological, Genetic and Nutritional Effects on Growth,* ed. Frank Falkner and J. M. Tanner, 263–81. New York and London: Plenum Press.

Fogel, Robert W., Stanley L. Engerman, Roderick Floud, Gerald Friedman, Robert A. Margo, Kenneth Sokoloff, Richard H. Steckel, T. James Trussell, Georgia Villaflor, and Kenneth W. Wachter. 1983. "Secular Changes in American and British Stature and Nutrition." *J. Interdisc. Hist.* 14, no. 2:445–81.

Foisy, L. -H. -G. 1873. *De quelques applications de la balance à l'étude physiologique et clinique des nouveau-nés.* M.D. thesis, Faculté de médecine de Paris.

Fortney, J. A., and J. E. Higgins. 1984. "The Effect of Birth Interval on Perinatal Survival and Birth Weight." *Public Health* 98:73–83.

Franco, L. de. 1874. *Études historiques et recherches sur le poids et la loi de l'accroissement du nouveau-né.* M.D. thesis, Faculté de médecine de Paris.

Frank, M. 1895. "Über den Werth der einzelnen Reifezeichen der Neugeborenen." *Arch. Gynak.* 48:163–200.

Frankenhäuser. 1859. "Über einige Verhältnisse, die Einfluss auf die stärkere oder schwächere Entwickelung der Frucht während der Schwangerschaft haben." *Monat. Geburt. Frauen.* 13:170–79.

Franqué, O. von. 1911. "Fürsorge für Schwangere und Wöchnerinnen." *Zeit. Geburt. Gynak.* 69:530–43.

Friedlander, M. 1815. *De l'éducation physique de l'homme.* Paris.

Fuchs, K. 1899. *Die Abhängigkeit des Geburtsgewichtes des Neugeborenen vom Stand und der Beschäftigung der Mutter.* M.D. diss., Friedrichs-Universität, Hall-Wittenburg.

Galante, H., et Fils, Paris. 1885. *Catalogue.*

Garn, S. M., H. A. Shaw, and K. D. McCabe. 1977. "Effects of Socioeconomic Status and Race on Weight-Defined and Gestational Prematurity in the United States." In *The Epidemiology of Prematurity,* ed. D. M. Reed and F. J. Stanley, 127–43. Baltimore and Munich: Urban and Schwarzenberg.

Goldin, Claudia. 1990. *Understanding the Gender Gap: An Economic History of American Women.* New York: Oxford University Press.

Goldin, Claudia, and Robert A. Margo. 1989. "The Poor at Birth: Birth Weights and Infant Mortality at Philadelphia's Almshouse Hospital, 1848–1873." *Explor. Ec. Hist.* 26:360–79.

Goldstein, H. 1981. "Factors Related to Birth Weight and Perinatal Mortality." *Br. Med. Bull.* 37 no. 3:259–64.

Good, David F. 1976. "The Cost of Living in Austria, 1874–1913." *J. Eur. Ec. Hist.* 5:391–400.

Good, David F. 1984. *The Economic Rise of the Habsburg Empire, 1750–1914.* Berkeley: University of California Press.

Gordon, George. 1983. "The Status Areas of Edinburgh in 1914." In *Scottish Urban History,* ed. G. Gordon and B. Dicks, 168–96. Aberdeen: Aberdeen University Press.

Gossage, Peter. 1987. "Les enfants abandonnés à Montréal au 19ᵉ siècle: La crèche d'Youville des Soeurs Gris, 1820–1871." *R. H. A. F.* 40, no. 4:537–59.

Gould, Jeffrey B. 1986. "The Low-Birth-Weight Infant." *Human Growth: A Comprehensive Treatise.* 2d ed., vol. 1, *Developmental Biology, Prenatal Growth,* ed. Frank Falkner and J. M. Tanner, 391–413. New York and London: Plenum Press.

Gray, R. Q. 1976. *The Labour Aristocracy in Victorian Edinburgh.* Oxford: Oxford University Press.

Great Britain. *Census of Ireland, 1871–1911.*

Great Britain. *Census of Scotland, 1841–1921.*

Great Britain. Parliament. *Report of the Committee of Inquiry; Together with Minutes of Evidence and Appendices.* C. 5042. 1887 [Committee appointed in 1885 to inquire into the management of Dublin Hospitals.]

Great Britain. Parliament. *Report of the Inter-Departmental Committee on Physical Deterioration.* Vol. 32. 1904.

Great Britain. Parliament. *Report of the Royal Commission on Physical Training (Scotland).* Vol. 30. 1903.

Great Britain. Registrar-General of Scotland. *Detailed Annual Report of the Registrar General of Births, Deaths and Marriages in Scotland.* 1820–1919.

Green, C. M. 1892. "The Care of Women in Pregnancy." *Bost. Med. Surg. J.* 126, no. 8:186–90, 194–96.

Grenier, E. 1913. *Quelques documents concernant la durée de la gestation et le poids de l'enfant à terme.* Bordeaux: A. Destout.

Grois, Bernhard. 1965. *Das Allgemeine Krankenhaus in Wien und seine Geschichte.* Vienna: W. Maudrich.

Gross, Nachum T. 1983. "Austria-Hungary in the World Economy." In *Economic Development in the Habsburg Monarchy in the Nineteenth Century: Essays,* ed. John Komlos, 1–46. Bouldèr, Colo.: East European Monographs.

Gross, Nachum T. 1976. "The Industrial Revolution in the Hapsburg Monarchy, 1750–1914." In *The Emergence of Industrial Societies—Part One,* ed. Carlo M. Cipolla. Vol. 4, *The Fontana Economic History of Europe.* Hassocks, England and New York: Harvester Press, Barnes & Noble.

Guggenheim, Karl Y., and Ira Wolinsky. 1981. *Nutrition and Nutritional Diseases: The Evolution of Concepts.* Lexington, Mass.: D. C. Heath.

Gulick, Charles A. 1948. *Austria From Habsburg to Hitler.* Vol. 1, *Labor's Workshop of Democracy.* Berkeley: University of California Press.

Gutman, R. 1959. *Birth and Death Registration in Massachusetts, 1639–1900.* New York: Millbank Memorial Fund.

Haake, H. 1862. "Über die Gewichtsveränderung der Neugeborenen." *Monat. Geburt. Frauen.* 19:339–54.

Hamelin, Jean, and Yves Roby. 1971. *Histoire économique du Québec, 1851–1896.* Montreal: Fides.

Hamilton, David. 1981. *The Healers: A History of Medicine in Scotland.* Edinburgh: Canongate.

Hamilton, James. Midwifery Casebook, 1793–94. Royal College of Physicians Library and Archives, Edinburgh.

Hamilton, James. 1795. *Select Cases in Midwifery: Extracted from the Records of the Edinburgh General Lying-in Hospital.* Edinburgh: P. Hill.

Handlin, Oscar. 1959. *Boston's Immigrants: A Study in Acculturation.* Revised edition. Cambridge, Mass.: Harvard University Press, Belknap Press.

Hardy, J. B., and E. D. Mellits. 1977. "Relationship of Low Birth Weight to Maternal Characteristics of Age, Parity, Education and Body Size." In *The Epidemiology of Prematurity,* ed. D. M. Reed and F. J. Stanley, 105–17. Baltimore and Munich: Urban and Schwarzenberg.

Hareven, Tamara K., and Maris A. Vinovskis. 1975. "Marital Fertility, Ethnicity, and Occupation in Urban Families: An Analysis of South Boston and the South End in 1880." *J. Soc. Hist.* 8:69–93.

Hautmann, Hans. 1978. "Hunger ist ein schlechter Koch: Die Ernährungslage der österreichischen Arbeiter im Ersten Weltkrieg." In *Bewegung und Klass: Studien zur österreichischen Arbeitsgeschichte,* ed. G. Botz. Vienna: Euroverlag.

Hearn, Mona. 1984. "Domestic Servants in Dublin, 1880–1920." Ph.D. thesis, Trinity College, University of Dublin.

Hearn, Mona. 1989. "Life for Domestic Servants in Dublin, 1880–1920." In *Women Surviving,* ed. Maria Luddy and Cliona Murphy, 148–79. Swords, Co. Dublin: Poolbeg.

Hecker, C. von. 1864. "Zur geburtshülflichen Statistik." *Monat. Geburt. Frauen.* 24:401–12.

Hecker, C. von. 1866. "Über das Gewicht des Fötus und seiner Anhänge in den verschiedenen Monaten der Schwangerschaft." *Monat. Geburt. Frauen.* 27:286–99.

Hecker, C. von. 1865. "Über Gewicht und Länge der neugeborenen Kinder im Verhältniss zum Alter der Mutter." *Monat. Geburt. Frauen.* 26:348–63.

Hecker, C. von., and L. Buhl. 1861. *Klinik der Geburtskunde.* Vol. 1. Leipzig: Wilhelm Engelmann.

Helczmanovszki, Heimold. 1979. "Austria-Hungary." In *European Demography and Economic Growth,* ed. W. R. Lee, 27–78. London: Croom Helm.

Helczmanovszki, Heimold. 1973. "Die Entwicklung der Bevolkerung Österreichs in den letzten hundert Jahren nach den wichtigsten demographischen Komponenten." *Beiträge zur Bevölkerungs- und Sozialgeschichte Österreichs. Nebst einem Überblick über die Entwicklung der Bevölkerungs- und Sozialstatistik,* ed. Heimold Helczmanovszki, 113–66. Vienna: Verlag für Geschichte und Politik Wien.

Hémardinquer, J. -J., ed. 1970. *Pour une histoire de l'alimentation.* Paris: A. Colin.

Henripin, Jacques, and Yves Péron. 1972. "The Demographic Transition of the Province of Quebec." *Population and Social Change,* ed. D. V. Glass and R. Revelle, 213–31. London: Edward Arnold.

Hershberg, T., and R. Dockhorn. 1976. "Occupational Classification." *Hist. Meth.* 9, nos. 2 and 3:58–98.

History of the New England Hospital for Women and Children, 1859–1899. 1899. Boston.

Hofmeister, Herbert. 1982. "Austria." In *The Evolution of Social Insurance 1881–1981: Studies of Germany, France, Great Britain, Austria and Switzerland,* ed. Peter A. Köhler and Hans F. Zacher in collaboration with Martin Partington, 265–383. London: Francis Pinter.

Holzbach, E. 1906. "Über den Wert der Merkmale zur Bestimmung der Reife des Neugeborenen." *Monat. Geburt. Gynak.* 24:430–45.

Huggins, Nathan Irvin. 1971. *Protestants Against Poverty: Boston's Charities, 1870–1900.* Westport, Conn.: Greenwood.

Hunt, E. H. 1973. *Regional Wage Variations in Britain, 1850–1914.* Oxford: Clarendon Press.

Hytten, F. E., and I. Leitch. 1971. *The Physiology of Human Pregnancy.* 2d. ed. Oxford: Blackwells.

Ingerslev, E. 1876. "On the Weight of New Born Children." *Obstet. J. Gt. Br.* 3, no. 35:705–15; no. 36:777–99.

Ireland. *Census of Ireland.* 1926.

Issmer, E., 1887. "Zwei Hauptmerkmale der Reife Neugeborener und deren physiologische Schwankungen." *Arch. Gynak.* 30:277–315.

Jellett, Henry. 1913. *A Short Practice of Midwifery, Embodying the Treatment Adopted at the Rotunda Hospital, Dublin.* London: Churchill.

Johnston, Valerie J. 1985. *Diet in Workhouses and Prisons, 1835–1895.* New York and London: Garland.

Kaelble, Hartmut. 1986. *Industrialisation and Social Inequality in 19th-Century Europe.* Leamington Spa: Berg.

Kaup, Ignaz. 1919. "Säuglingssterblichkeit und Bevölkerungspolitik." Österreich,

Bundesministerium für Soziale Verwaltung, Österreiches Volfarhtswesen. *Mitteilungen des Volksgesundheitsamtes* 3:76–89.

Keen, D. V., and R. G. Pearse. 1985. "Birthweight between 14 and 42 Weeks Gestation." *Arch. Dis. Child.* 60:440–46.

Kenneally, R. R. 1983. "The Montreal Maternity, 1843–1926: Evolution of a Hospital." Master's thesis, McGill University.

Kennedy, Kieran A., Thomas Giblin, and Deirdre McHugh. 1988. *The Economic Development of Ireland in the Twentieth Century.* London: Routledge.

Kernbauer, Hans, Eduard März, and Fritz Weber. 1983. "Die wirtschaftliche Entwicklung." In *Österreich 1918–1938: Geschichte der Ersten Republik.* Vol. 1, ed. Erika Weinzierl and Kurt Skalnik, 343–80. Vienna: Styria.

Kerr, J. M. Munro, R. W. Johnstone, and Miles H. Phillips. 1954. *Historical Review of British Obstetrics and Gynaecology, 1800–1950.* Edinburgh: E. & S. Livingstone.

Kessel, S. S., J. Villar, H. W. Berendes, and R. P. Nugent. 1984. "The Changing Pattern of Low Birth Weight in the United States, 1970–1980." *J. A. M. A.* 251, no. 15:1978–82.

Keyssar, Alexander. 1986. *Out of Work: The First Century of Unemployment in Massachusetts.* Cambridge: Cambridge University Press.

Kitchin, A. H., and R. Passmore. 1949. *The Scotsman's Food: An Historical Introduction to Modern Food Administration.* Edinburgh: Livingstone.

Kleinman, J. C., and J. H. Madans. 1985. "The Effects of Maternal Smoking, Physical Stature, and Educational Attainment on the Incidence of Low Birth Weight." *Am. J. Epidemiol.* 121, no. 6:843–55.

Kline, J., Z. Stein, and M. Susser. 1989. *Conception to Birth: Epidemiology of Prenatal Development.* New York: Oxford University Press.

Komlos, John. 1989. "The Age at Menarche in Vienna: The Relationship between Nutrition and Fertility." *Historical Methods* 22, no. 4:158–63.

Komlos, John. 1983. *The Habsburg Monarchy as a Customs Union: Economic Development in Austria-Hungary in the Nineteenth Century.* Princeton, N.J.: Princeton University Press.

Komlos, John. 1989. *Nutrition and Economic Development in the Eighteenth-Century Habsburg Monarchy: An Anthropometric History.* Princeton, N.J.: Princeton University Press.

Körber. 1884. "Die Durchschnittsmasse ausgetragener Neugeborener und ihre Lebensfähigkeit, berechnet aus den Jahresberichten der Findelhäuser in St. Petersburg und Moskau." *Viertel. Gerich. Med.* 40:225–42.

Kramer, M. S., F. H. McLean, M. Olivier, D. M. Willis, and R. H. Usher. 1989. "Body Proportionality and Head and Length 'Sparing' in Growth-Retarded Neonates: A Critical Reappraisal." *Pediatrics* 84, no. 4:717–23.

Landicho, B., A. Lechtig, and R. E. Klein. 1985. "Anthropometric Indicators of Low Birth Weight." *J. Trop. Pediatr.* 31:301–5.

Lapointe-Roy, Huguette. 1987. *Charité bien ordonnée: Le premier réseau de la lutte contre la pauvreté à Montréal au 19e siècle.* Montreal: Boréal.

Launer, L. J., J. Villar, E. Kestler, and M. De Onis. 1990. "The Effect of Maternal

Work on Fetal Growth and Duration of Pregnancy: A Prospective Study." *Br. J. Ob. Gyn.* 97, no. 1:62–70.

Lavigne, Marie, and Jennifer Stoddart. 1983. "Ouvrières et travailleuses montréalaises, 1900–1940." *Travailleuses et féministes: Les femmes dans la société québécoise,* ed. Marie Lavigne and Yolande Pinard, 99–113. Montreal: Boréal.

Leavitt, Judith Walzer. 1986. *Brought to Bed: Child-Bearing in America, 1750–1950.* New York: Oxford University Press.

Lebergott, Stanley. 1976. *The American Economy: Income, Wealth, and Want.* Princeton, N.J.: Princeton University Press.

Lebergott, Stanley. 1966. "Labor Force and Employment, 1800–1960." *Output, Employment, and Productivity in the United States after 1800,* 117–210. New York: National Bureau of Economic Research.

Lechtig, A. 1976. "The Influence of Maternal Food Supplements on Birthweight in Guatemala." *Nutr. Rev.* 34, no. 6:169–72.

Lechtig, A., H. Delgado, R. E. Lasky, R. E. Klein, P. L. Engle, C. Yarborough, and J. -P. Habicht. 1975. "Maternal Nutrition and Fetal Growth in Developing Societies." *Am. J. Dis. Child.* 129:434–37.

Lechtig, A., J. -P. Habicht, H. Delgado, R. E. Klein, C. Yarborough, and R. Martorell. 1975. "Effect of Food Supplementation during Pregnancy on Birth Weight." *Pediatrics* 56, no. 2:508–20.

Lechtig, A., C. Yarborough, H. Delgado, J. -P. Habicht, R. Martorell, and R. E. Klein. 1975. "Influence of Maternal Nutrition on Birth Weight." *Am. J. Clin. Nutr.* 28:1223–33.

Lee, C. H. 1979. *British Regional Employment Statistics, 1841–1971.* Cambridge: Cambridge University Press.

Lee, C. H. 1983. "Modern Economic Growth and Structural Change in Scotland: The Service Sector Reconsidered." *Scot. Ec. Soc. Hist.* 3:5–35.

Lesky, Erna. 1976. *The Vienna Medical School of the 19th Century.* Baltimore: Johns Hopkins University Press.

Letourneur, L. 1897. *De l'influence de la profession de la mère sur le poids de l'enfant (étude statistique).* M.D. thesis, Faculté de medecine de Paris.

Levenstein, Harvey. 1988. *Revolution at the Table: The Transformation of the American Diet, 1880–1930.* New York: Oxford University Press.

Levitt, I. 1979. "The Scottish Poor Law and Unemployment, 1890–1929." *The Search for Wealth and Stability: Essays on Economic and Social History, Presented to M. W. Flinn,* ed. T. C. Smout, 263–82. London: Macmillan.

Levitt, I., and C. Smout. 1979. *The State of the Scottish Working Class in 1843: A Statistical and Spatial Enquiry Based on the Data from the Poor Law Commission Report of 1844.* Edinburgh: Scottish Academic Press.

Liestøl, K. 1982. "Social Conditions and Menarcheal Age: The Importance of Early Years of Life." *Ann. Hum. Biol.* 9:521–37.

Lindblad, B. S., and R. Zetterström. 1971. "Causes of Impaired Fetal Growth." In *Proceedings of the 2nd. European Congress of Perinatal Medicine,* 181–90. Basel: Karger.

Littlejohn, H. D. 1865. *Report on the Sanitary Condition of the City of Edinburgh.* Edinburgh: Colston and Son.

Livi-Bacci, Massimo. 1991. *Population and Nutrition: An Essay on European Demographic History.* Cambridge: Cambridge University Press.

Lubchenco, L. O., C. Hansman, and E. Boyd. 1966. "Intrauterine Growth in Length and Head Circumference as Estimated from Live Births at Gestational Ages from 26 to 42 Weeks." *Pediatrics* 37, no. 3:403–8.

McCollum, Elmer Verner. 1957. *A History of Nutrition: The Sequence of Ideas in Nutrition Investigations.* Boston: Houghton Mifflin.

McCormick, M. C. 1985. "The Contribution of Low Birth Weight to Infant Mortality and Childhood Morbidity." *N. Eng. J. Med.* 312:82–90.

McDonald, A. D., J. C. McDonald, B. Armstrong, N. M. Cherry, A. D. Nolin, and D. Robert. 1988. "Prematurity and Work in Pregnancy." *Br. J. Ind. Med.* 45:56–62.

McKeown, Thomas. 1976. *The Modern Rise of Population.* London: Edward Arnold.

McKeown, Thomas, and R. G. Record. 1962. "Reasons for the Decline of Mortality in England and Wales during the Nineteenth Century." *Pop. Stud.* 16:94–122.

Mackenzie, W. L. 1906. *The Health of the School Child.* London: Methuen.

Mackenzie, W. L. 1917. *Scottish Mothers and Children.* East Port, Dunfermline: Carnegie United Kingdom Trust.

Magnus, P. 1984. "Causes of Variation in Birth Weight: A Study of Offspring of Twins." *Clin. Genet.* 25:15–24.

Magnus, P. 1984. "Further Evidence for a Significant Effect of Fetal Genes on Variation in Birth Weight." *Clin. Genet.* 26:289–96.

Magnus, P., K. Berg, and T. Bjerkedal. 1985. "The Association of Parity and Birth Weight: Testing the Sensitization Hypothesis." *Early Hum. Dev.* 12:49–54.

Magnus, P., K. Berg, T. Bjerkedal, and W. E. Nance. 1984. "Parental Determinants of Birth Weight." *Clin. Genet.* 26:397–405.

Mahner, J. 1978. "Birth-weight as a New Development Indicator." In *Birth-weight Distribution: An Indicator of Social Development,* Report from a SAREC/WHO Workshop, ed. G. Sterky and L. Mellander, 33–39. Uppsala: Swedish Agency for Research Co-operation with Developing Countries.

Manocha, S. L. 1972. *Malnutrition and Retarded Human Development.* Springfield, Ill.: C. D. Thomas.

Manzer, Edna. 1979. "Women's Doctors: The Development of Obstetrics and Gynaecology in Boston, 1860–1930." Ph.D. thesis, Indiana University.

Marr, William L., and Donald G. Paterson. 1980. *Canada: An Economic History.* Toronto: Macmillan.

Martorell, R. 1980. "Interrelationships between Diet, Infectious Disease, and Nutritional Status." In *Social and Biological Predictors of Nutritional Status, Physical Growth and Neurological Development,* ed. L. S. Green and F. E. Johnston, 81–106. New York: Academic Press.

Martorell, R. 1981. "Notes on the History of Nutritional Anthropometry." *Federation Proceedings* 40, no. 11:2572–76.

Martorell, R., and T. González-Cossío. 1987. "Maternal Nutrition and Birth Weight." *Yearbook of Physical Anthropology.* 30:195–220.

März, Eduard. 1981. *Österreichische Bankpolitik in der Zeit der grossen Wende 1913–1923: Am Beispiel der Creditanstalt für Handel und Gewerbe.* Munich: R. Oldenbourg.

Massachusetts. *Annual Report of the State Board of Health*. 1870–1900.

Massachusetts. *Annual Report on the Vital Statistics of Massachusetts*. 1869–1900.

Massachusetts. *Report to the Legislature of Massachusetts Relating to the Registry and Return of Births, Marriages and Deaths in the Commonwealth*. 1870–1900.

Massachusetts. 1885. *Sixteenth Annual Report of the Bureau of Statistics of Labor*. Boston.

Massachusetts. *State Census*. 1855–1895.

Matis, H. 1972. *Österreichische Wirtschaft 1848–1913: Konjunkturelle Dynamik und gesellschaftlicher Wandel im Zeitalter Franz Joseph I*. Berlin: Duncker und Humbolt.

Matthews, R. C. O., C. H. Feinstein, and J. C. Odling-Smee. 1982. *British Economic Growth 1856–1973*. Oxford: Clarendon Press.

Maw, S., Son & Sons. 1913. *Catalogue*.

Meckel, Richard A. 1990. *Save the Babies: American Public Health Reform and the Prevention of Infant Mortality, 1850–1929*. Baltimore: Johns Hopkins University Press.

The Medical Police and Rules and Regulations of the Boston Medical Association, with a Catalogue of the Officers and Members, 1885. Boston: Franklin Press.

Memoir of Susan Dimock, Resident Physician of the New England Hospital for Women and Children. 1875. Boston.

Metcalf, J. G. 1847. "Statistics in Midwifery." *Am. J. Med. Sci.* 27:295–329.

Metcoff, J. 1986. "Association of Fetal Growth with Maternal Nutrition." In *Human Growth: A Comprehensive Treatise*. 2d ed., vol. 3, *Methodology: Ecological, Genetic and Nutritional Effects on Growth*, ed. Frank Falkner and J. M. Tanner, 333–88. New York and London: Plenum Press.

Metcoff, J. 1980. "Maternal Nutrition and Fetal Development." *Early Hum. Dev.* 4, no. 2:99–120.

Meyer, M. B. 1977. "Effects of Maternal Smoking and Altitude on Birth Weight and Gestation." In *The Epidemiology of Prematurity*, ed. D. M. Reed and F. J. Stanley, 81–101. Baltimore and Munich: Urban and Schwarzenberg.

Miller, D. 1938. "A Short Record of the Edinburgh Royal Maternity and Simpson Memorial Hospital." *Trans. Edinb. Obstet. Soc.* 97:1–11.

Miller, J. E. 1989. "Determinants of Intrauterine Growth Retardation: Evidence Against Maternal Depletion." *J. Biosoc. Sci.* 21, no. 2:235–43.

Mills, J. L., B. I. Graubard, E. E. Harley, G. G. Rhoads, and H. W. Berendes. 1984. "Maternal Alcohol Consumption and Birth Weight: How Much Drinking During Pregnancy Is Safe?" *J. A. M. A.* 252, no. 14:1875–79.

Milward, A., and S. B. Saul. 1977. *The Development of the Economies of Continental Europe, 1850–1914*. London: Allen & Unwin.

Milward, A., and S. B. Saul. 1979. *The Economic Development of Continental Europe, 1780–1870*. 2d ed. London: Allen & Unwin.

Mitchell, Brian R. 1981. *European Historical Statistics, 1750–1975*. 2d ed. London: Macmillan.

Mitchison, Rosalind. 1977. *British Population Change since 1860*. London: Macmillan.

Mitchison, Rosalind. 1986. "Malnutrition in Scotland since 1700, and Its Social Consequences." The Society for the Social History of Medicine, *Bulletin* 38:17–18.

Mitterauer, Michael, and Reinhard Sieder. 1982. *The European Family: Patriarchy to Partnership from the Middle Ages to the Present.* Chicago: University of Chicago Press.

Momm. 1916. "Hat die eiweiss- und fettarme Nahrung einen Einfluss auf die Entwicklung der Frucht?" *Zent. Gynak.* 40, no. 28:545–50.

Montreal. *Report of the Sanitary State of the City of Montreal,* 1877–1915.

Moore, L. G., S. S. Rounds, D. Jahnigen, R. F. Grover, and J. T. Reeves. 1982. "Infant Birth Weight is Related to Maternal Arterial Oxygenation at High Altitude." *J. Appl. Physiol.* 52:695–99.

Morantz, Regina Martell, and Sue Zschoche. 1980. "Professionalism, Feminism and Gender Roles: A Comparative Study of Nineteenth-Century Medical Therapeutics." *J. Am. Hist.* 67:568–88.

Mueller, W. H., and E. Pollitt. 1984. "The Bacon Chow Study: Effects of Maternal Nutritional Supplementation on Birth Measurements of Children, Accounting for the Size of a Previous (Unsupplemented) Child." *Early Hum. Dev.* 10:127–36.

Mühlpeck, Vera, Roman Sandgruber, and Hannelore Woitek. 1979. "Index Verbraucherpreise 1800 bis 1914." In *Geschichte und Ergebnisse der Zentralen amtlichen Statistik in Österreich 1829–1979.* Vienna: Österreichischen Statistischen Zentralamt.

Musaiger, A. O. 1985. "Factors Associated with Birthweight in Bahrain." *J. Trop. Med. Hyg.* 88:31–36.

Mussey, R. D. 1949. "Nutrition and Human Reproduction: An Historical Review." *Am. J. Obstet. Gynecol.* 57, no. 6:1037–48.

Napheys, G. H. 1875. *The Physical Life of Woman: Advice to the Maiden, Wife, and Mother.* 4th Canadian edition. Toronto: Maclear.

New England Hospital for Women and Children. *Annual Report.* 1863–1900.

New England Hospital for Women and Children. *Reference Book of Standing Rules.*

Newton, R. W., and L. P. Hunt. 1984. "Psychological Stress in Pregnancy and its Relation to Low Birth Weight." *Br. Med. J.* 288:1191–94.

Niswander, K. R. 1977. "Obstetric Factors Related to Prematurity." In *The Epidemiology of Prematurity,* ed. D. M. Reed and F. J. Stanley, 249–68. Baltimore and Munich: Urban and Schwarzenberg.

Norris, R. C., ed. 1895. *An American Text-Book of Obstetrics.* Philadelphia: Saunders.

"Nouveau-né." *Dictionnaire encyclopédique des sciences médicales.* 2d series, 1879:456–83, 711–17. Paris: Asselin et Masson.

Oakley, Ann. 1984. *The Captured Womb: A History of the Medical Care of Pregnant Women.* Oxford: Blackwell.

O'Brien, Joseph V. 1982. *Dear, Dirty Dublin: A City in Distress, 1899–1916.* Berkeley: University of California Press.

O'Connell, Patrick A. 1872. "Obstetrics in Vienna." *Bost. Med. Surg. J.* 9, no. 20:309–12.

Oddy, D. J. 1990. "Food, Drink and Nutrition." In *The Cambridge Social History of Britain.* Vol. 2, *People and Their Environment,* ed. F. M. L. Thompson, 251–78. Cambridge: Cambridge University Press.

Oddy, D. J. 1976. "A Nutritional Analysis of Historical Evidence: The Working-Class Diet, 1880–1914." In *The Making of the Modern British Diet,* ed. Derek Oddy and Derek Miller, 214–31. London: Croom Helm.

Oddy, D. J. 1970. "Working-Class Diets in Late Nineteenth-Century Britain." *Ec. Hist. Rev.* 2d series, 23:314–23.

Oddy, Derek, and Derek Miller, eds. 1976. *The Making of the Modern British Diet.* London: Croom Helm.

Odier, L. 1868. *Recherches sur la loi d'accroissement des nouveau-nés constaté par le système des pesées régulières et sur les conditions d'un bon allaitement.* M.D. thesis, Faculté de medecine de Paris.

Odier, L., and R. Blache. 1867. *Quelques considérations sur les causes de la mortalité des nouveau-nés et sur les moyens d'y remédier.* Paris: Germer-Baillière.

O'Flanagan, Neil. 1985. "Dublin City in an Age of War and Revolution, 1914–1924." Master's thesis, University College, Dublin.

Ó Gráda, Cormac. 1989. *The Great Irish Famine.* London: Macmillan.

Ogston, A. 1868. "Table of Cases, with Weights of the Bodies and Lungs of Live and Stillborn Children." *Br. For. Med. Rev.* 42:472–75.

Ogston, F. 1881. "On the Average Length and Weight of Mature Newborn Scotch Children." *Edinb. Med. J.* 26:603–15.

Olegnik, Felix, ed. 1956. *Historisch-Statistische Übersichten von Wien.* Vienna.

Olsen, Donald J. 1986. *The City as a Work of Art: London, Paris, Vienna.* New Haven, Conn.: Yale University Press.

Olsen, J., P. Rachootin, and A. V. Schiødt. 1983. "Alcohol Use, Conception Time, and Birthweight." *J. Epidemiol. Commun. Health* 37:63–65.

O'Neill, T. P. 1989. "The Food Crisis of the 1890s." In *Famine: The Irish Experience 900–1900,* ed. E. Margaret Crawford, 176–97. Edinburgh: John Donald.

Orr, John Boyd. 1937. *Food, Health and Income: Report on a Survey of Adequacy of Diet in Relation to Income.* 2d ed. London: Macmillan.

Osuhor, P. C. 1982. "Birthweights in Southern Zaria, Northern Nigeria." *J. Tropic. Pediatr.* 28:196–98.

Ounsted, M., and C. Ounsted. 1973. *On Fetal Growth Rate (Its Variations and Their Consequences).* Clinics in Developmental Medicine No. 46, Spastics International Medical Publications. London: Heinemann.

Ounsted, M., and A. Scott. 1982. "Smoking During Pregnancy: Its Association with Other Maternal Factors and Birthweight." *Acta Obstet. Gynecol. Scand.* 61: 367–71.

Paterson, Audrey. 1976. "The Poor Law in Nineteenth-Century Scotland." *The New Poor Law in the Nineteenth Century,* ed. D. Fraser, 171–93. London: Macmillan.

Paton, D. Noel, J. Craufurd Dunlop, and Elsie Maud Inglis. 1902. *A Study of the Diet of the Labouring Classes in Edinburgh.* Edinburgh: Schulze.

Péchin, G. 1908. *Contribution à l'étude de la puériculture avant la naissance: Étude statistique du poids des enfants nés à la Clinique Baudelocque de 1890 à 1907.* M.D. thesis, Faculté de medecine de Paris.

Peller, S. 1917. "Längengewichtsverhältnis der Neugeborenen und Einfluss der Schwangerenernährung auf die Entwicklung des Fötus." *Deut. Med. Woch.* 43: 847–48.

Peller, S. 1917. "Die Masse der Neugeborenen und die Kriegsernährung der Schwangeren." *Deut. Med. Woch.* 43:178–80.

Peller, S. 1919. "Rückgang der Geburtsmasse als Folge der Kriegsernährung." *Wien. Klin. Woch.* 32, no. 29:758–61.

Peller, S. 1924. "Die Saüglingssterblichkeit nach dem Kriege." *Sonderabdruck aus der Wiener Klinischen Wochenschrift,* nos. 45 and 47, 1923; nos. 4 and 5, 1924.

Peller, S., and F. Bass. 1924. "Die Rolle exogener Faktoren in der intrauterinen Entwicklung des Menschen mit besonderer Berücksichtigung der Kriegs- und Nachkriegsverhältnisse." *Arch. Gynak.* 122:208–38.

Peters, T. J., J. Golding, N. R. Butler, J. G. Fryer, C. J. Lawrence, and G. V. P. Chamberlain. 1983. *"Plus ça change:* Predictors of Birthweight in Two National Studies." *Br. J. Ob. Gyn.* 90:1040–45.

Pfannkuch, W. 1872. "Über die Körperform der Neugeborenen." *Arch. Gynak.* 4:297–310.

Phelan, Denis. 1867. "Observations on the Comparative Advantages of Affording Obstetric Attendance on Poor Women in Lying-in Hospitals and in Their Own Homes." *Dub. Qu. J. Med. Sci.* 43:70–92.

Phillips, C., and N. E. Johnson. 1977. "The Impact of Quality of Diet and Other Factors on Birth Weight of Infants." *Am. J. Clin. Nutr.* 30:215–25.

Piering, O. 1899. "Über die Grenzen des Körpergewichtes Neugeborener." *Monat. Geburt. Gynak.* 10:303–14.

Pies, W. 1910. "Zur Physiologie des Neugeborenen: Über die Dauer, die Grösse und den Verlauf der physiologischen Abnahme." *Monat. Kinder.* 10:514–43.

Pinard, A. 1899. *Clinique obstétricale.* Paris: Steinheil.

Pinard, A. 1878. "Foetus. I. Anatomie et physiologie." *Dictionnaire encyclopédique des sciences médicales.* 4th series vol. 2, 472–535. Paris: Masson.

Pinard, A. 1895. "Note pour servir à l'histoire de la puériculture intra-utérine." *Bull. Acad. Med.* 3d series. 34:593–97.

Pinard, A. 1899. "De la puériculture intra-utérine." *Clinique obstétricale,* 47–71. Paris: Steinheil.

Pleck, Elizabeth Hafkin. 1979. *Black Migration and Poverty: Boston, 1865–1900.* New York: Academic Press.

Poerksen, A., and D. B. Petitti. 1991. "Employment and Low Birth Weight in Black Women." *Soc. Sci. Med.* 33, no. 11:1281–86.

Prentice, Alison, Paula Bourne, Gail Cuthbert Brandt, Beth Light, Wendy Mitchinson, and Naomi Black. 1988. *Canadian Women: A History.* Toronto: Harcourt Brace Jovanovich.

Prochownick, L. 1901. "Über Ernährungscuren in der Schwangerschaft." *Ther. Monat.* 15:387–403, 446–63.

Prochownick, L. 1917. "Über Ernährungskuren in der Schwangerschaft." *Zent. Gynak.* 41, no. 32:785–94.

Quetelet, A. 1833. "Recherches sur le poids de l'homme aux différens ages." *Ann. hyg.* 10:5–27.

Quetelet, A. 1835. *Sur l'homme et le développment des facultés, ou essai de physique sociale.* Vol. 2. Paris: Bachelier.

Rantakallio, P., and L. von Wendt. 1985. "Prognosis for Low Birthweight Infants up to the Age of 14: A Population Study." *Dev. Med. Child Neurol.* 27:655–63.

Rees, Albert. 1961. *Real Wages in Manufacturing, 1890–1914.* Princeton, N.J.: Princeton University Press.

Rigler, Edith. 1976. *Frauenleitbild und Frauenarbeit in Österreich vom ausgehenden 19. Jahrhundert bis zum Zweiten Weltkrieg.* Vienna: Verlag für Geschichte und Politik Wien.

Robert, Jean-Claude. 1977. "Montréal, 1821–1871: Aspects de l'urbanisation," Ph.D. thesis, Université de Paris.

Robert, Jean-Claude. 1982. "Urbanisation et population: Le cas de Montréal en 1861." *R.H.A.F.* 35, no. 4:523–35.

Roberts, C. 1878. *A Manual of Anthropometry, or a Guide to the Physical Examination and Measurement of the Human Body.* London: Churchill.

Roberts, D. F. 1976. "Environment and the Fetus." *The Biology of Human Fetal Growth,* ed. D. F. Roberts and A. M. Thomson. Vol 15, Symposia of the Society for the Study of Human Growth, 267–83. London: Taylor and Francis.

Roberts, D. F. 1986. "The Genetics of Human Fetal Growth." *Human Growth: A Comprehensive Treatise.* 2d ed., vol. 3, *Methodology: Ecological, Genetic and Nutritional Effects on Growth,* ed. Frank Falkner and J. M. Tanner, 113–43. New York and London: Plenum Press.

Roberts, S. B., A. A. Paul, T. J. Cole, and R. G. Whitehead. 1982. "Seasonal Changes in Activity, Birth Weight and Lactational Performance in Rural Gambian Women." *Trans. R. Soc. Trop. Med. Hyg.* 76, no. 5:668–78.

Robson, E. B. 1978. "The Genetics of Birth Weight." *Human Growth.* Vol. 1, *Principles and Prenatal Growth,* ed. F. Falkner and J. M. Tanner, 285–97. New York and London: Plenum Press.

Rodger, R. 1985. "Employment, Wages and Poverty in the Scottish Cities 1841–1911." *Perspectives of the Scottish City,* ed. G. Gordon, 25–63. Aberdeen: Aberdeen University Press.

Rodger, R. 1983. "The Invisible Hand: Market Forces, Housing and the Urban Form in Victorian Cities." *The Pursuit of Urban History,* ed. Derek Fraser and Anthony Sutcliffe, 190–211. London: Edward Arnold.

Rooth, G. 1980. "Low Birth Weight Revised." *Lancet* no. 8169:639–41.

Rosenberg, Charles E. 1987. *The Care of Strangers: The Rise of America's Hospital System.* New York: Basic Books.

Rosenberg, M. 1988. "Birth Weights in Three Norwegian Cities, 1860–1984: Secular Trends and Influencing Factors." *Ann. Hum. Biol.* 15, no. 4:275–88.

Rosenkrantz, Barbara Gutmann. 1972. *Public Health and the State: Changing Views in Massachusetts, 1842–1936.* Cambridge, Mass.: Harvard University Press.

Ross, Ian Campbell. 1986. "The Early Years of the Dublin Lying-in Hospital." In *Public Virtue, Private Love: The Early Years of the Dublin Lying-in Hospital,* 9–52. Dublin: O'Brien.

Rothschild, K. 1946. *Austria's Economic Development Between the Two Wars.* London: Mueller.

Rotunda Hospital. Board of Governors, Minutes. 1877–1921.

Rotunda Hospital. *Report of the Rotunda Hospital.* 1869–1922.

Rubin, D. H., P. A. Krasilnikoff, J. M. Leventhal, B. Weile, and A. Berget. 1986. "Effect of Passive Smoking on Birth-Weight." *Lancet* no. 8504:415–17.

Rudolph, Richard L. 1972. "Austria, 1800–1914." In *Banking and Economic Development: Some Lessons of History,* ed. Rondo Cameron, 26–57. New York and Oxford: Oxford University Press.

Rudolph, Richard L. 1976. *Banking and Industrialization in Austria-Hungary.* Cambridge: Cambridge University Press.

Rudolph, Richard L. 1975. "The Pattern of Austrian Industrial Growth from the Eighteenth to the Early Twentieth Centuries." *Austrian History Yearbook* 9:3–25.

Rudolph, Richard L. 1990. "Social Structure and the Beginning of Austrian Economic Development." *Economic Development in the Habsburg Monarchy and in the Successor States,* ed. John Komlos, 133–47. Boulder, Colo.: East European Monographs.

Rules & Bye-Laws of the Edinburgh Maternity Hospital. c. 1844–46.

Rush, D., and P. Cassano. 1983. "Relationship of Cigarette Smoking and Social Class to Birth Weight and Perinatal Mortality among All Births in Britain, 5–11 April 1970." *J. Epidemiol. Community Health* 37:249–55.

Ryan, Denis P. 1983. *Beyond the Ballot Box: A Social History of the Boston Irish, 1845–1917.* East Brunswick, N.J.: Fairleigh Dickinson University Press.

Sainte-Mechtilde, Soeur. 1946. "La fille-mère: Ses problèmes sociaux." Diplôme en Service Social dissertation (1) Université de Montréal.

Sandgruber, Roman. 1982. *Die Anfänge der Konsumgesellschaft: Konsumgüterverbrauch, Lebensstandard und Alltagskultur in Österreich in 18. und 19. Jahrhundert.* Vienna: Verlag für Geschichte und Politik Wien.

Sandgruber, Roman. 1978. *Österreichische Agrarstatistik 1750–1918.* Vol. 2, *Wirtschafts- und Sozialstatistik Österreich-Ungarns.* Vienna: Verlag für Geschichte und Politik Wien.

Sarraute-Lourié, L. 1899. *De l'influence du repos sur la durée de la gestation (étude statistique).* M.D. thesis, Faculté de médecine de Paris.

Saurel-Cubizolles, M. J., and M. Kaminski. 1986. "Work in Pregnancy: Its Evolving Relationship with Perinatal Outcome (A Review)." *Soc. Sci. Med.* 22, no. 4:431–42.

Scammon, R. E. 1927. "The Literature on the Growth and Physical Development of the Fetus, Infant, and Child: A Quantitative Summary." *Anat. Rec.* 35, no. 3:241–67.

Schaeffer, O. 1896. "Über die Schwankungsbreite der Gewichtsverhältnisse von Säuglingen in den ersten 14 Lebenstagen und die Ursachen dieser Schwankungen." *Arch. Gynak.* 52:282–313.

Schaetzel, P. von. 1893. *Über den Einfluss des Alters der Mutter und der Zahl der voraufgegangenen Schwangerschaften auf Länge und Gewicht der Neugeborenen.* M.D. diss., Universität zu Griefswald.

Scharlieb, M. 1919. *The Welfare of the Expectant Mother.* London: Cassell.

Schauta, F. 1917. "Der Kampf gegen den gewollten Abortus." *Wien. Klin. Woch.* 24:1046–49.

Schmidtbauer, P. 1983. "The Changing Household: Austrian Household Structure from the Seventeenth to the Early Twentieth Century." In *Family Forms in Historic Europe*, ed. Richard Wall, Jean Robin, and Peter Laslett, 347–78. Cambridge: Cambridge University Press.

The Scotsman, 6 May 1914.

Segond, P. 1874. "Du poids des nouveau-nés." *Ann. gynecol.* 2:298–308, 366–75.

Seifrit, E. 1968. "Changes in Beliefs and Food Practices in Pregnancy." In *Lydia J. Roberts Award Essays*, 79–90. Chicago: American Dietetic Association.

Shiono, P. H., M. A. Klebanoff, B. I. Graubard, H. W. Berendes, and G. G. Rhoads. 1986. "Birth Weight among Women of Different Ethnic Groups." *J. A. M. A.* 255, no. 1:48–52.

A Short History of the Diet Dispensary, 1879–1906. 1906. Montreal: Gazette Printing Company.

Showstack, J. A., P. P. Budetti, and D. Minkler. 1984. "Factors Associated with Birthweight: An Exploration of the Roles of Prenatal Care and Length of Gestation." *Am. J. Public Health* 74, no. 9:1003–8.

Siebold, E. von. 1860. "Über die Gewichts- und Längenverhältnisse der neugeborenen Kinder, über die Verminderung ihres Gewichtes in den ersten Tagen und die Zunahme desselben in den ersten Wochen nach der Geburt." *Monat. Geburt. Frauen.* 15:337–54.

Sieder, Reinhard. 1988. "Behind the Lines: Working-Class Family Life in Wartime Vienna." In *The Upheaval of War: Family, Work and Welfare in Europe, 1914–1918*, ed. Richard Wall and Jay Winter, 109–38. Cambridge: Cambridge University Press.

Sieder, Reinhard. 1986. "'Vata, derf i aufstehen?': Childhood Experiences in Viennese Working-Class Families around 1900." *Continuity and Change* 1, no. 1:53–88.

Simpson, A. R. 1881. "Method of Case-Taking in Midwifery." *Edinb. Med. J.* 26:680–86.

Simpson, J. Y. 1844. "Memoir on the Sex of the Child as a Cause of the Difficulty and Danger in Human Parturition." *Edinb. Med. Surg. J.* 62:387–439.

Simpson, J. Y. 1855. *The Obstetric Memoirs and Contributions of James Y. Simpson*, ed. W. O. Priestley and H. R. Storer. Edinburgh: Black.

Sinclair, Edward B., and George Johnston. 1858. *Practical Midwifery: Comprising an Account of 13,748 Deliveries Which Occurred in the Dublin Lying-in Hospital during a Period of Seven Years, Commencing November, 1847.* London: John Churchill.

Smith, C. A. 1947. "Effects of the Hunger Winter (1944–45) in Holland upon Pregnancy and the New-Born Infant." *Maand. Kind.* 15:121–41.

Smout, T. C. 1986. *A Century of the Scottish People, 1830–1950.* London: Collins.

Sobbe, A. von. 1872. *Über Gewichts- und Längenverhältnisse der Neugeborenen mit Bezugnahme auf das Alter der Mutter.* M.D. diss., medizinischen Facultät zu Marburg.

Speert, Harold. 1980. *Obstetrics and Gynecology in America: A History.* Chicago: American College of Obstetricians and Gynecologists.

Stafford, T. J. 1910. "Note on the Social Condition of Certain Working Class Families in Dublin." Appendix 2, D. *Royal Commission on the Poor Laws and Relief of Distress.* Vol. 9, Appendix A, 1910. Great Britain. *Sessional Papers.* Vol. L:344–354.

Steckel, Richard H. 1987. "Growth, Depression and Recovery: The Remarkable Case of American Slaves." *Ann. Hum. Biol.* 14, no. 2:111–32.

Steckel, Richard H. 1986. "A Peculiar Population: The Nutrition, Health, and Mortality of American Slaves from Childhood to Maturity." *J. Ec. Hist.* 46, no. 3:721–41.

Stein, A., E. A. Campbell, A. Day, K. McPherson, and P. J. Cooper. 1987. "Social Adversity, Low Birth Weight, and Preterm Delivery." *Br. Med. J.* 295, no. 6593:291–93.

Stein, Z., and M. Susser. 1984. "Intrauterine Growth Retardation: Epidemiological Issues and Public Health Significance." *Sem. Perinatol.* 8, no. 1:5–14.

Stein, Z., M. Susser, and D. Rush. 1978. "Prenatal Nutrition and Birth Weight: Experiments and Quasi-Experiments in the Past Decade." *J. Reprod. Med.* 21, no. 5:287–97.

Stein, Z., M. Susser, G. Saenger, and F. Marolla. 1975. *Famine and Human Development: The Dutch Hunger Winter of 1944–45.* New York: Oxford University Press.

Sterky, G., and L. Mellander, eds. 1978. *Birth-Weight Distribution: An Indicator of Social Development.* Report from a SAREC/WHO Workshop. Uppsala: Swedish Agency for Research Co-operation with Developing Countries.

Steven, Maisie. 1985. *The Good Scots Diet: What Happened to It?* Aberdeen: Aberdeen University Press.

Stewart, Mary Lynn. 1989. *Women, Work and the French State: Labour Protection and Social Patriarchy, 1789–1919.* Montreal: McGill-Queen's University Press.

Storer, D. H. 1843. "An Abstract of 500 Cases of Midwifery." *N. Eng. J. Med. Surg.* 1, no. 1:15–19.

Storer, D. H. 1850. "Statistics of the Boston Lying-in Hospital." *Am. J. Med. Sci.* (October):347–68.

The Story of the National Maternity Hospital, Holles Street, Dublin. N.p., n.d.

Sturrock, J. 1958. "Early Maternity Hospitals in Edinburgh (1756–1879)." *J. Ob. Gyn. Br. Emp./Comm.* 65, no. 1:122–31.

Sturrock, J. 1980. "The Edinburgh Royal Maternity and Simpson Memorial Hospital." *J. R. Coll. Surg. Edinb.* 25:173–87.

Susser, M. 1981. "Prenatal Nutrition, Birthweight, and Psychological Development: An Overview of Experiments, Quasi-experiments, and Natural Experiments in the Past Decade." *Am. J. Clin. Nutr.* 34:784–803.

Susser, M., and Z. Stein. 1977. "Prenatal Nutrition and Subsequent Development." *The Epidemiology of Prematurity,* ed. D. M. Reed and F. J. Stanley, 177–91. Baltimore and Munich: Urban and Schwarzenberg.

Tafari, N., R. L. Naeye, and A. Gobezie. 1980. "Effects of Maternal Undernutrition and Heavy Physical Work during Pregnancy on Birth Weight." *Br. J. Ob. Gyn.* 87, no. 3:222–26.

Tanner, J. M. 1981. *A History of the Study of Human Growth.* Cambridge: Cambridge University Press.

Tardieu, A. 1868. *Étude médico-légale sur l'infanticide.* Paris: Baillère.

Tardieu, A. 1880. *Étude médico-légale sur l'infanticide.* 2d ed. Paris: Baillère.

Taylor, A. J., ed. 1975. *The Standard of Living in Britain in the Industrial Revolution.* London: Methuen.

Taylor, K. W., and H. Michell. 1931. *Statistical Contributions to Canadian Economic History.* Toronto: Macmillan.

Tchernia, G., I. Blot, A. Rey, J. P. Kaltwasser, J. Zittoun, and E. Papiernik. 1982. "Maternal Folate Status, Birthweight and Gestational Age." *Dev. Pharmacol. Ther.* 4 (supplement 1):58–65.

Tétreault, Martin. 1983. "Les maladies de la misère: Aspects de la santé publique à Montréal 1880–1914." *Revue d'histoire de l'Amérique française* 36, no. 4:507–26.

Teuteberg, Hans J. 1975. "The General Relationship between Diet and Industrialization." *European Diet from Pre-Industrial to Modern Times,* ed. Elborg Forster and Robert Forster, 61–109. New York: Harper and Row.

Teuteberg, Hans J. 1976. "Die Nahrung der sozialen Unterschichten im späten 19. Jahrhundert." *Ernährung und Ernährungslehre im 19. Jahrhundert,* ed. Edith Heischkel-Artelt, 205–87. Göttingen: Vandenhoeck und Ruprecht.

Teuteberg, Hans J. 1979. "Der Verzehr von Nahrungsmitteln in Deutschland pro Kopf und Jahr seit Beginn der Industrialisierung (1850–1975): Versuch einer quantitativen Langzeitanalyse." *Arch. Sozial.* 19:331–88.

Theis, W. 1868. *Über die Gewichtsveränderung der Neugeborenen.* M.D. diss., medizinischen Facultät, Friedrichs-Universität, Halle-Wittenberg.

Thernstrom, Stephan. 1973. *The Other Bostonians: Poverty and Progress in the American Metropolis, 1880–1970.* Cambridge, Mass.: Harvard University Press.

Thompson, W. H. 1916. *War and the Food of the Dublin Labourer.* Dublin.

Thomson, A. M. 1971. "Physiological Determinants of Birth Weight." In *Proceedings of the 2nd European Congress of Perinatal Medicine.* 174–80. Basel: Karger.

Thomson, A. M., and W. Z. Billewicz. 1976. "The Concept of the 'Light for Dates' Infant." In *The Biology of Human Fetal Growth,* ed. D. F. Roberts and A. M. Thomson. Vol. 15, 69–79. Symposia of the Society for the Study of Human Growth. London: Taylor and Francis.

Thomson, A. M., W. Z. Billewicz, and F. E. Hytten. 1968. "The Assessment of Fetal Growth." *J. Ob. Gyn. Br. Emp./Comm.* 75:903–16.

Thornton, Patricia, Sherry Olson, and Quoc Thuy Thach. 1988. "Dimensions sociales de la mortalité infantile à Montréal au milieu du XIXe siècle." *Ann. demog. hist.* 1988: 299–325.

Tomes, Nancy J. 1989. "The White Plague Revisited." *Bull. Hist. Med.* 63:467–80.

Transactions of the Edinburgh Obstetrical Society. 1868–69 to 1921–22.

Trebilcock, Clive. 1981. *The Industrialization of the Continental Powers, 1780–1914.* London and New York: Longman.

Tuberculosis in Ireland. 1908. Dublin: His Majesty's Stationery Office.

Underhill, Charles D. 1962. "Public Health." In *The Zone of Emergence: Observations of the Lower Middle and Upper Working Class Communities of Boston, 1895–1914,* ed. Robert A. Woods and Albert J. Kenny. Cambridge, Mass.: Joint Center for Urban Studies of MIT and Harvard.

United Nations. 1988. *1986 Demographic Yearbook.* New York: United Nations.

United States. *Census,* 1860–1900.

Van Heddeghem, A. 1983. *De oude Bijlokematerniteit, 1828–1978.* Ghent.

Van Wieringen, J. C. 1986. "Secular Growth Changes." *Human Growth: A Comprehensive Treatise.* 2d ed., vol. 3, *Methodology: Ecological, Genetic and Nutritional*

Effects on Growth, ed. Frank Falkner and J. M. Tanner, 307–31. New York and London: Plenum Press.

Vaughan, W. E., and A. J. Fitzpatrick, eds. 1978. *Irish Historical Statistics: Population, 1821–1971.* Dublin: Royal Irish Academy.

Veit, G. 1855. "Beiträge zur geburtshülflichen Statistik." *Monat. Geburt. Frauen.* 5:344–81.

Veit, G. 1856. "Beiträge zur geburtshülflichen Statistik." *Monat. Geburt. Frauen.* 6:101–32.

Verdenhalven, Fritz. 1968. *Alte Masse, Münzen und Gewichte aus dem deutschen Sprachgebiet.* Neustadt an der Aisch: Degener.

Vienna. *Statistisches Jahrbuch der Stadt Wien.* 1883–1937.

Villar, J., L. Altobelli, E. Kestler, and J. Belizán. 1986. "A Health Priority for Developing Countries: The Prevention of Chronic Fetal Malnutrition." *Bull. WHO.* 64, no. 6:847–51.

Villar, J., and J. M. Belizán. 1982. "The Relative Contribution of Prematurity and Fetal Growth Retardation to Low Birth Weight in Developing and Developed Societies." *Am. J. Obstet. Gynecol.* 143, no. 7:793–98.

Villar, J., and T. González-Cossío. 1986. "Nutritional Factors Associated with Low Birth Weight and Short Gestational Age." *Clin. Nutrit.* 5, no. 2:78–85.

Villar, J., M. de Onis, E. Kestler, F. Bolaños, R. Cerezo, and H. Bernedes. 1990. "The Differential Neonatal Morbidity of the Intrauterine Growth Retardation Syndrome." *Am. J. Obstet. Gynecol.* 163, no. 1:151–57.

Villar, J., and J. T. Repke. 1990. "Calcium Supplementation during Pregnancy May Reduce Preterm Delivery in High-Risk Populations." *Am. J. Obstet. Gynecol.* 163, no. 4:1124–31.

Villar, J., and J. Rivera. 1988. "Nutritional Supplementation during Two Consecutive Pregnancies and the Interim Lactation Period: Effect on Birth Weight." *Pediatrics* 81, no. 1:51–57.

Villar, J., V. Smeriglio, R. Martorell, C. H. Brown, and R. E. Klein. 1984. "Heterogeneous Growth and Mental Development of Intrauterine Growth-Retarded Infants during the First 3 Years of Life." *Pediatrics* 74, no. 5:783–91.

Vogel, Morris, J. 1980. *The Invention of the Modern Hospital: Boston, 1870–1930.* Chicago: University of Chicago Press.

Walré de Bordes, J. van. 1924. *The Austrian Crown, Its Depreciation and Stabilization.* London: P. S. King and Son.

Ward, David. 1963. "Nineteenth Century Boston: A Study in the Role of Antecedent and Adjacent Conditions in the Spatial Aspects of Urban Growth." Ph.D. thesis, University of Wisconsin.

Ward, W. Peter. 1988. "Birth Weight, Hospitalization and Nutrition in Montreal and Vienna, 1850–1930." In *Society, Health and Population during the Demographic Transition,* ed. Anders Brändström and Lars-Göran Tedebrand, 385–94. Stockholm: Almqvist and Wiksell.

Ward, W. Peter. 1988. "Birth Weight and Standards of Living in Vienna, 1865–1930." *J. Interdisc. Hist.* 19, no. 2:203–29.

Ward, W. Peter. 1984. Introduction to *The Mysteries of Montreal: Memoirs of a Midwife,* by Charlotte Führer. 2d ed., 1–33. Vancouver: University of British Columbia Press.

Ward, W. Peter. 1981. "Unwed Motherhood in Nineteenth Century English Canada." Canadian Historical Association, *Historical Papers*, 34–56.

Ward, W. Peter. 1987. "Weight at Birth in Vienna Austria, 1865 to 1930." *Ann. Hum. Biol.* 14, no. 6:495–506.

Ward, W. Peter, and Patricia C. Ward. 1984. "Infant Birth Weight and Nutrition in Industrializing Montreal." *Am. Hist. Rev.* 89, no. 2:324–45.

Warner, Sam Bass. 1969. *Streetcar Suburbs: The Process of Growth in Boston, 1870–1900*. New York: Atheneum.

Wegs, J. Robert. 1982. "Working Class Respectability: The Viennese Experience." *J. Soc. Hist.* 15, no. 4:621–36.

Wells, Robert V. 1982. *Revolutions in American Lives: A Demographic Perspective on the History of Americans, Their Families, and Their Society.* Westport, Conn.: Greenwood Press.

Wilcox, A. J., and I. T. Russell. 1983. "Birthweight and Perinatal Mortality: I. On the Frequency Distribution of Birthweight." *Int. J. Epidemiol.* 12, no. 3:314–18.

Wilcox, A. J., and I. T. Russell. 1983. "Birthweight and Perinatal Mortality: II. On Weight-Specific Mortality." *Int. J. Epidemiol.* 12, no. 3:319–325.

Williamson, Jeffrey G. 1985. *Did British Capitalism Breed Inequality?* Boston: Allen & Unwin.

Williamson, Jeffrey G., and Peter H. Lindert. 1980. *American Inequality: A Macroeconomic History.* New York: Academic Press.

Wilson, Leonard J. 1990. "The Historical Decline of Tuberculosis in Europe and America: Its Causes and Significance." *J. Hist. Med.* 45:366–96.

Winckel. 1862. "Untersuchungen über die Gewichtsverhältnisse bei hundert Neugeborenen in den ersten zehn Tagen nach der Geburt." *Monat. Geburt. Frauen.* 19:416–42.

Winckel, F. 1890. *A Text-book of Obstetrics.* Edinburgh and London: Pentland.

Winter, J. M. 1985. *The Great War and the British People.* London: Macmillan.

Wohl, Anthony S. 1983. *Endangered Lives: Public Health in Victorian Britain.* Cambridge, Mass.: Harvard University Press.

Woods, Robert A., ed. 1903. *Americans in Process: A Settlement Study.* Boston: Houghton Mifflin.

Woods, Robert A., ed. 1898. *The City Wilderness: A Settlement Study by Residents and Associates of the South End House, South End, Boston.* Boston: Houghton Mifflin.

World Health Organization. 1978. "Birth Weight and Duration of Gestation." In *Social and Biological Effects on Perinatal Mortality: A WHO Report.* Vol. 1. Reprinted in *Saudi Medical Journal*, 4, 1983, supplement no. 1.

World Health Organization. 1980. "The Incidence of Low Birth Weight: A Critical Review of Available Information." *World Health Stat. Q.* 33:197–224.

World Health Organization Working Group. 1986. "Use and Interpretation of Anthropometric Indicators of Nutritional Status." *Bull. WHO.* 64, no. 6:929–41.

Worthington-Roberts, Bonnie S. 1984. "Nutrition during Pregnancy and Lactation." In *Food, Nutrition, and Diet Therapy: A Textbook of Nutritional Care,* ed. Marie V. Krause and L. Kathleen Mahan. 7th ed., 238–72. Philadelphia: W. B. Saunders.

Wright, Carroll D. 1885. *An Analysis of the Population of the City of Boston as Shown in the State Census of May, 1885.* Boston: Wright and Potter.

Wright, Carroll D. 1882. *The Social, Commercial and Manufacturing Statistics of the City of Boston*. Boston: Wright and Potter.

Wright, Carroll D. [1889] 1969. *The Working Girls of Boston*. Reprint. New York: Arno.

Wright, J. T., I. G. Barrison, I. G. Lewis, K. D. MacRae, E. J. Waterson, P. J. Toplis, M. G. Gordon, N. F. Morris, and I. M. Murray-Lyon. 1983. "Alcohol Consumption, Pregnancy and Low Birthweight." *Lancet* no. 8326:663–65.

Yudkin, P. L., M. Aboualfa, J. A. Eyre, C. W. G. Redman, and A. R. Wilkinson. 1987. "New Birthweight and Head Circumference Centiles for Gestational Ages 24 to 42 Weeks." *Early Hum. Dev.* 15, no. 1:45–52.

INDEX